寄贈

この聖典を手にされたあなたへ

人間の生き方や価値観が根本的に問い直されている現代。いま、アジアの代表的な思想 "仏教" が、全世界から見直され、人々の心に新しい光を放っています。

この聖典は、仏教の根元であるお釈迦さまとその教えについて、わかりやすく書かれたものです。きっと、あなた自身の明日に、生きる希望をもたらしてくれるでしょう。

仏教と仲良しになるために……
〈この聖典の上手な読み方〉

• 仏教の心にちょっぴりふれてみたい、という方は……
　　569頁以降の生活索引の中から、関心のあるテーマを拾ってお読み下さい。

• 仏教の流れについて知りたい、という方は……
　　まず539頁からの仏教通史をお読み下さい。

• "仏教とは何か" を、じっくり味わいたい、という方は……
　　第1頁から最後まで通してお読み下さい。

この仏教聖典などを座右に置きたいと思われる方は、全国の書店どこでも入手できます。当協会コード番号〔7484〕と書名・価格を明記のうえ、書店にご注文ください。確実に早くお手許に届きます。

なお、ご不明な点は、財団法人仏教伝道協会（〒108東京都港区芝4－3－14、電話03－455－5851）にお問い合わせ下さい。

この聖典があなたと出会うためには、あなたがいまお泊まりの当ホテルの大きな協力がありましたことを深く感謝したいと思います。

• この聖典があなたと出会うためには、あなたがいまお泊まりの当ホテルの大きな協力がありましたことを深く感謝したいと思います。

• この聖典は日本全国の主なホテルに置かれ（のべ100万冊）、また世界の主要国語に翻訳されて、のべ数十万冊が諸外国で読まれています。（1982年現在）

• この聖典はこの部屋の備品です。
　明日手にされる人のために、大切にお取扱い下さい。

Dear friends who have opened this little book:
Present is the day when man's way of living and his values are fundamentally being searched for again. Thus, Buddhism, one of the representative Asian thoughts, has gradually become appreciated among the people of the world, giving new light unto their minds. This book contains the life of Gautama Buddha, the founder of Buddhism, and His teachings. We believe that it will give you a new light for your everyday life.

★Those who wish to know what Buddhism is in a short period of time:
Please, open to page 568 and look up any topic which interests them.
★Those who wish to know the historical development of Buddhism:
Please, read A Brief History of Buddhism on page 538
★Those who wish to master Buddhism:
Please, read all through this book, starting from the very first page.
★If you wish to have more information as well as to purchase this book, please contact either of the following:
  ●Buddhist Promoting Foundation (BUKKYO DEN DOKYOKAI) 3-14 Shiba 4-Chome, Minato-ku, Tokyo 108, JAPAN
  ●Our branch or agent nearest you, as listed on the map on the reverse side of this page.

●We express our hearty thankfulness to this Hotel where you are staying for giving this copy a chance to meet you.
●This one is for all those who wish peace, happiness, and friendship of mankind and the world. We wish you will spend a tranquil night with this copy.
●This copy is the property of this hotel; we ask you to handle it carefully for the sake of those who may open it tomorrow.
                              Thank you,
                  Buddhist Promoting Foundation

THE TEACHING

OF

BUDDHA

和英対照

仏 教 聖 典

財団法人　仏教伝道協会

BUKKYO DENDO KYOKAI
(Buddhist Promoting Foundation)
3-14, 4-chome, Shiba
Minato-ku, Tokyo, Japan, 108
Phone: (03) 455-5851

Two hundred & fifty seventh revised edition, 1982

Printed by
Kosaido Printing Co., Ltd.
Tokyo, Japan

Buddha's Wisdom is broad as the ocean and His Spirit is full of great Compassion.

Buddha has no form but manifests Himself in Exquisiteness and leads us with His whole heart of Compassion.

This book is valuable because it contains the essence of the Buddha's teachings as recorded in over five thousand volumes. These teachings have been preserved and handed down for more than twenty five hundred years extending beyond borders and racial barriers of the world.

The words of Buddha contained in this book touch on all aspects of human life and bring meaning to it.

仏の智慧は海のごとく広大にして、仏の心は大慈悲なり。仏は姿なくして妙なる姿を示し、身をもって教えを説かれた。

　この本は二千五百余年の間、国を超え民族を超えて保ち続けられてきた五千余巻の仏の教えの精髄である。

　ここには仏の言葉が凝縮されており、人びとの生活と心の実際の場面に触れて、生きた解答を与えている。

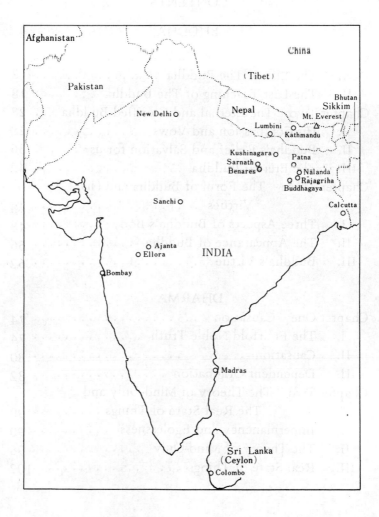

CONTENTS

BUDDHA

目　次

　本聖典中で＊印をつけてあるものは、用語解説に含まれているものである。

CHAPTER ONE

SHAKYAMUNI BUDDHA

I

THE LIFE OF THE BUDDHA

1. The Shakya clansmen dwelt along the Rohini River which flows among the southern foothills of the Himalayas. Their king, Shuddhodana Gautama, established his capital at Kapilavastu and there had a great castle built and ruled wisely, winning the acclaim of his people.

The Queen's name was Maya. She was the daughter of the King's uncle who was also the king of a neighboring district of the same Shakya clan.

For twenty years they had no children. But on night Queen Maya had a strange dream, in which s' a white elephant entering into her womb ·' right side of her chest, and she becar King and the people looked forwa· the birth of a royal child. Ac' Queen returned to her paren on her way, in the beautiful sp rest in the Lumbini Garden.

BUDDHA

ほ と け

第1章　史上の仏

第1節　偉大な生涯

1.　ヒマラヤ山の南のふもとを流れるローヒニー河のほとりに、釈迦族の都カピラヴァスツがあった。その王シユッドーダナ（浄飯）は、世々純正な血統を伝え、城を築き、善政をしき、民衆は喜び従っていた。王の姓はゴータマであった。

妃、マーヤー（摩耶）夫人は同じ釈迦族の一族でコーリヤ族とよばれるデーヴァダハ城の姫で、王の従妹にあたっていた。

結婚の後、ながく子に恵まれず、二十幾年の歳月の後、ある夜、白象が右わきから胎内に入る夢を見て懐妊した。王の一族をはじめ国民ひとしく指折り数えて王子の出生を待ちわびたが、臨月近く、妃は国の習慣に従って生家に帰ろうとし、その途中ルンビニー園に休息した。

All about her were Ashoka blossoms. In delight she reached her right arm out to pluck a branch and as she did so a prince was born. All expressed their heart-felt delight with the glory of the Queen and her princely child; Heaven and Earth rejoiced. This memorable day was the eighth day of April.

The joy of the King was extreme and he named the child, Siddhartha, which means "Every wish fulfilled."

2.   In the palace of the King, however, delight was followed quickly by sorrow, for after several days the lovely Queen Maya suddenly died. Her younger sister, Mahaprajapati, became the child's foster mother and brought him up with loving care.

A hermit, called Asita, who lived in the mountains not far away, noticed a radiance about the castle. Interpreting it as a good omen he came down to the palace and was shown the child. He predicted: "This Prince, if he remains in the palace, when grown up will become a great king and subjugate the whole world. But if he forsakes the court life to embrace a religious life, he will become a Buddha, the Savior of the world."

At first the King was pleased to hear this prophecy, but later he started to worry about the possibility of his only son leaving the palace to become a homeless recluse.

　折りから春の陽はうららかに、アショーカの花はうるわしく咲きにおっていた。妃は右手をあげてその枝を手折ろうとし、そのせつなに王子を生んだ。天地は喜びの声をあげて母と子を祝福した。ときに四月八日であった。

　シュッドーダナ王の喜びはたとえようがなく、一切の願いが成就したという意味のシッダールタ（悉達多）という名を王子に与えた。

　2．しかし、喜びの裏には悲しみもあった。マーヤー夫人は間もなくこの世を去り、太子は以後、夫人の妹マハープラジャーパティーによって養育された。

　そのころ、アシタという仙人が山で修行していたが、城のあたりに漂う吉相を見て、城に来たり、太子を見て「このお子が長じて家にいられたら世界を統一する偉大な王となり、もしまた、*出家して道を修めれば世を救う*仏になられるであろう。」と予言した。

　はじめ王はこの予言を聞いて喜んだが、次第に、もしや出家されてはという憂いを持つようになった。

At the age of seven the Prince began his lessons in the civil and military arts, but his thoughts more naturally tended to other things. One spring day he went out of the castle with his father. Together they were watching a farmer at his plowing when he noticed a bird descended to the ground and carried off a small worm which had been turned up by the farmer's plough. He sat down in the shade of a tree and thought about it, whispering to himself:

"Alas! Do all living creatures kill each other?"

The Prince, who had lost his mother so soon after his birth, was deeply affected by the tragedy of these little creatures.

This spiritual wound deepened day by day as he grew up; like a little scar on a young tree, the suffering of human life became more and more deeply engrained in his mind.

The King was increasingly worried as he recalled the hermit's prophecy and tried in every possible way to cheer the Prince and to turn his thoughts in other directions. The King arranged the marriage of the Prince at the age of nineteen to the Princess Yashodhara. She was the daughter of Suprabuddha, the Lord of Devadaha Castle and a brother of the late Queen Maya.

　太子は七歳の時から文武の道を学んだ。春祭に、父王に従って田園に出、農夫の耕すさまを見ているうち、すきの先に掘り出された小虫を小鳥がついばみ去るのを見て、「あわれ、生きものは互いに殺しあう。」とつぶやき、ひとり木陰に坐って静思した。

　生まれて間もなく母に別れ、今また生きもののかみあう有様を見て、太子の心には早くも人生の苦悩が刻まれた。それはちょうど、若木につけられた傷のように、日とともに成長し、太子をますます暗い思いに沈ませた。

　父王はこの有様を見て大いに憂い、かねての仙人の予言を思いあわせ、太子の心を引き立てようといろいろ企てた。ついに太子十九歳のとき、太子の母の兄デーヴァダハ城王スプラブッダの娘ヤショーダラーを迎えて妃と定めた。

3. For ten years, in the different Pavilions of Spring, Autumn and the Rainy Season, the Prince was immersed in rounds of music, dancing and pleasure, but always his thoughts returned to the problem of suffering as he pensively tried to understand the true meaning of human life.

"The luxuries of the palace, this healthy body, this rejoicing youth! What do they mean to me?" he thought. "Some day we may be sick, we shall become aged; from death there is no escape. Pride of youth, pride of health, pride of existence — all thoughtful people should cast them aside.

"A man struggling for existence will naturally look for something of value. There are two ways of looking — a right way and a wrong way. If he looks in the wrong way he recognizes that sickness, old age and death are unavoidable, but he searches among the same class of empty, transitory things.

"If he looks in the right way he recognizes the true nature of sickness, old age and death, and he searches for meaning in that which transcends all human sufferings. In my life of pleasures I seem to be looking in the wrong way."

4. Thus the spiritual struggle went on in the mind of

3．この後十年の間、太子は、春季・秋季・雨季それぞれの宮殿にあって歌舞管弦の生活を楽しんだが、その間もしきりに沈思瞑想して人生を見きわめようと苦心した。

「宮廷の栄華も、すこやかなこの肉体も、人から喜ばれるこの若さも、結局このわたしにとって何であるのか。人は病む。いつかは老いる。死を免れることはできない。若さも、健康も、生きていることも、どんな意味があるというのか。

人間が生きていることは、結局何かを求めていることにほかならない。しかし、この求めることについては、誤ったものを求めることと、正しいものを求めることの二つがある。誤ったものを求めることというのは、自分が老いと病と死とを免れることを得ない者でありながら、それらと反対のことを求めていることである。

正しいものを求めることというのは、この誤りをさとって、老いと病と死とを超えた、人間の苦悩のすべてを離れた境地を求めることである。今のわたしは、この誤ったものを求めている者にすぎない。」

4．このように心を悩ます日々が続いて、月日は流れ、太

the Prince until his only child, Rahula, was born when he was 29. This seemed to bring things to a climax, for he then decided to leave the palace and look for the solution of his spiritual unrest in the homeless life of a mendicant. He left the castle one night with only his charioteer, Chandaka, and his favorite horse, the snow-white Kanthaka.

His anguish did not end and many devils tempted him saying: "You would do better to return to the castle for the whole world would soon be yours." But he told the devil that he did not want the whole world. So he shaved his head and turned his steps toward the south, carrying a begging bowl in his hand.

The Prince first visited the hermit Bhagava and watched his ascetic practices. He then went to Arada Kalama and Udraka Ramaputra to learn their methods of attaining nirvana through meditation; but after practising them for a time he became convinced that they would not lead him to Enlightenment. Finally he went to the land of Magadha and practised asceticism in the forest of Uruvilva on the banks of the Nairanjana River, which flows by the Gaya Castle.

子二十九歳の年、一子ラーフラ(羅睺羅)が生まれたときに、太子はついに出家の決心をした。太子は御者のチャンダカを伴い、白馬カンタカにまたがって、住みなれた宮殿を出て行った。そして、この俗世界とのつながりを断ち切って出家の身となった。

このとき、悪魔は早くも太子につきまとった。「宮殿に帰るがいい。時を待つがいい。この世界はすべておまえのものになるのだ。」太子は叱咤した。「悪魔よ、去れ。すべて地上のものは、わたしの求めるところではないのだ。」太子は悪魔を追い払い、髪をそり、食を乞いつつ南方に下った。

太子ははじめバガバ仙人を訪れてその苦行の実際を見、次にアーラーダ・カーラーマと、ウドラカ・ラーマプトラを訪ねてその修行を見、また自らそれを実行した。しかし、それらは結局さとりの道でないと知った太子は、マガダ国に行き、ガヤーの町のかたわらを流れるナイランジャナ河（尼連禅河）のほとり、ウルビルバーの林の中において、激しい苦行をしたのである。

5. The methods of his practice were unbelievably rigorous. He spurred himself on with the thought that "no ascetic in the past, none in the present, and none in the future, ever has practised or ever will practise more earnestly than I do."

Still the Prince could not realize his goal. After six years in the forest he gave up the practice of asceticism. He went bathing in the river and accepted a bowl of milk from the hand of Sujata, a maiden, who lived in the neighboring village. The five companions who had lived with the Prince during the six years of his ascetic practice were shocked that he should receive milk from the hand of a maiden; they thought him degraded and left him.

Thus the Prince was left alone. He was still weak, but at the risk of losing his life he attempted yet another period of meditation, saying to himself, "Blood may become exhausted, flesh may decay, bones may fall apart, but I will never leave this place until I find the way to Enlightenment."

It was an intense and incomparable struggle for him. He was desperate and filled with confusing thoughts, dark shadows overhung his spirit, and he was beleaguered by

5. それはまことに激しい苦行であった。釈尊自ら「過去のどのような修行者も、現在のどのような苦行者も、また未来のどのような出家者も、これ以上の苦行をした者はなく、また、これからもないであろう。」と後に言われたほど、世にもまれな苦行であった。

しかし、この苦行も太子の求めるものを与えなかった。そこで太子は、六年の長きにわたったこの苦行を未練なく投げ捨てた。ナイランジャナ河に沐浴して身の汚れを洗い流し、スジャーターという娘の手から乳糜を受けて健康を回復した。

このとき、それまで太子と一緒に同じ林の中で苦行していた5人の出家者たちは、太子が堕落したと考え、太子を見捨てて他の地へ去って行った。

いまや天地の間に太子はただひとりとなった。太子は静かに木の下に坐って、命をかけて最後の瞑想に入った。「血も涸れよ、肉も爛れよ、骨も窩れよ。さとりを得るまでは、わたしはこの座を立たないであろう。」 これがそのときの太子の決心であった。

その日の太子の心はまことにたとえるものがないほどの悪戦苦闘であった。乱れ散る心、騒ぎ立つ思い、黒い心の影、

all the lures of the devils. Carefully and patiently he examined them one by one and rejected them all. It was a hard struggle indeed, making his blood run thin, his flesh fall away, and his bones crack.

But when the morning star appeared in the eastern sky, the struggle was over and the Prince's mind was as clear and bright as the breaking day. He had, at last, found the path to Enlightenment. It was December eighth, when the Prince became a Buddha at thirty-five years of age.

6. From this time on the Prince was known by different names: some spoke of him as Buddha, the Perfectly Enlightened One, Tathagata; some spoke of him as Shakyamuni, the Sage of the Shakya clan; others called him the World-honored One.

He went first to Mrigadava in Varanasi where the five mendicants who had lived with him during the six years of his ascetic life were staying. At first they shunned him, but after they had talked with him, they believed in him and became his first followers. He then went to the Rajagriha Castle and won over King Bimbisara who had always been his friend. From there he went about the country living on alms and teaching men to accept his way of life.

Men responded to him as the thirsty seek water and

醜い想いの姿、すべてそれは悪魔の襲来というべきものであった。太子は心のすみずみまでそれらを追求して散々に裂き破った。まことに、血は流れ、肉は飛び、骨は砕けるほどの苦闘であった。

しかし、その戦いも終わり、夜明けを迎えて明けの明星を仰いだとき、太子の心は光り輝き、さとりは開け、仏と成った。それは太子三十五歳の年の十二月八日の朝のことであった。

6. これより太子は仏陀、無上覚者、如来、釈迦牟尼、釈尊、世尊などの種々の名で知られるようになった。

釈尊はまず、六年にわたる苦行の間ともに修行してくれた恩義のある五人の出家者に道を説こうとして、彼らの住むバーラーナシーのムリガダーバ（鹿野苑）に赴き、彼らを教化した。彼らは最初釈尊を避けようとしたが、教えを聞いてから釈尊を信じ最初の弟子となった。また、ラージャグリハ（王舎城）に入ってビンビサーラ王を教化し、ここを教えを説く根拠地として、さかんに教えを広めた。

人びとは、ちょうど渇いた者が水を求めるように、飢えた者が食を求めるように、釈尊のもとに寄り集まった。シャー

the hungry food. Two great disciples, Sariputra and Maudgalyayana, and their two thousand followers, came to him.

At first the Buddha's father, King Shuddhodana, still inwardly suffering because of his son's decision to leave the palace, remained aloof, but then became his faithful disciple. Mahaprajapati, the Buddha's step-mother, and Princess Yashodhara, his wife, and all the members of the Shakya clan began to follow him. Multitudes of others also became his devoted and faithful followers.

7. For forty-five years the Buddha went about the country preaching and persuading men to follow his way of life. But when he was eighty, at Vaisali and on his way from Rajagriha to Shravasti, he became ill and predicted that after three months he would enter Nirvana. Still he journeyed on until he reached Pava where he fell seriously ill from some food offered by Chunda, a blacksmith. Eventually, in spite of great pain and weakness, he reached the forest that bordered Kusina-gara.

Lying between two large sala trees, he continued teaching his disciples until his last moment. Thus he entered into perfect tranquility after he had completed his work as the world's greatest teacher.

リプトラ（舎利弗）、マウドガルヤーヤナ（目連）の二大弟
子をはじめとする、二千余人の弟子たちは、釈尊を仰ぎ、そ
の弟子となった。

　釈尊の出家を憂えてこれを止めようとし、また釈尊の出家
によって深い苦しみを味わった父のシュッドーダナ王、養母
のマハープラジャーパティー、妃のヤショーダラーをはじめ
とする釈迦族の人たちも、みな釈尊に帰依して弟子となった。
その他非常に多くの人びとが彼の信奉者になった。

　7．このようにして伝道の旅を続けること四十五年、釈尊
'は八十歳を迎えた。ラージャグリハ（王舎城）からシュラー
　スティー（舎衛城）に赴く途中、ヴァイシャーリーにお
　　　　「三月の後に涅槃に入るであろう。」と予言され
　　　　　パーバーに至り、鍛冶屋のチュンダの供養
　　　　　　悪化し、痛みを押してクシナガラに

last

urself: do
things your
n any other

npurity. Know-

　　　　　　　　　　　に行き、シャーラの
　　　　　　　　　　　。釈尊は懇ろに弟
　　　　　　　　　　　を説いて世間の大導師
　　　　　　　　　　　静かに涅槃に入った。

—

8.   Under the guidance of Ananda, the Buddha's favorite disciple, the body was cremated by his friends in Kusinagara.

Seven neighboring rulers as well as King Ajatasatru demanded that the ashes be divided among them. The King of Kusinagara at first refused and the dispute even threatened to end in war; but under the advice of a wise man named Drona, the crisis passed and the ashes were divided among the eight great countries. The ashes, of the funeral pyre as well as the earthen jar that contained the remains were also given to two other rulers to be likewise honored. Great towers commemorating the Buddha were built to enshrine his remains and ashes.

II
THE LAST TEACHING OF THE BUDDHA

1.   Beneath the sala trees at Kusinagara, in his words to his disciples, the Buddha said:

"Make of yourself a light. Rely upon yo not depend upon anyone else. Make my tea light. Rely upon them: do not depend up teaching.

Consider your body: Think of its i

　8．クシナガラの人びとは、釈尊が涅槃に入られたのを悲しみ嘆き、アーナンダ（阿難）の指示に従って、定められたとおりに釈尊の遺骸を火葬した。

　このとき、マガダ国の王アジャータシャトルをはじめとするインドの八つの国々の王は、みな釈尊の遺骨の分配を乞うたが、クシナガラの人びとはこれを拒否し、争いが起こった。しかし、賢者ドローナの計(はか)らいにより、遺骨は八大国に分配された。その他、遺骸の瓶(かめ)と火葬の灰を受けた者があり、それぞれの国に奉安されて、この世に仏の十の大塔が建立(こんりゅう)されるに至った。

第2節　最後の教え

　1．釈尊はクシナガラの郊外、シャーラ（沙羅）樹の林の中で最後の教えを説かれた。

　弟子たちよ、おまえたちは、おのおの、自らを灯火(ともしび)とし、自らをよりどころとせよ、他を頼りとしてはならない。この法を灯火とし、よりどころとせよ、他の教えをよりどころとしてはならない。

　わが身を見ては、その汚れを思って貪(むさぼ)らず、苦しみも楽し

ing that both its pain and its delight are alike causes of suffering, how can you indulge in its desires? Consider your 'self'; think of its transiency; how can you fall into delusion about it and cherish pride and selfishness, knowing that they must all end in inevitable suffering? Consider all substances; can you find among them any enduring 'self'? Are they not all aggregates that sooner or later will break apart and be scattered? Do not be confused by the universality of suffering, but follow my teaching, even after my death, and you will be rid of pain. Do this and you will indeed be my disciples."

2.   "My disciples, the teachings that I have given you are never to be forgotten or abandoned. They are always to be treasured, they are to be thought about, they are to be practised. If you follow these teachings you will always be happy.

"The point of the teachings is to control your own mind. Keep your mind from greed, and you will keep your behaviour right, your mind pure and your words faithful. By always thinking about the transiency of your life, you will be able to resist greed and anger, and will be able to avoid all evils.

"If you find your mind tempted and so entangled in greed, you must suppress and control the temptation; be the master of your own mind.

みもともに苦しみの因であると思ってふけらず、わが心を観ては、その中に「我」はないと思い、それらに迷ってはならない。そうすれば、すべての苦しみを断つことができる。わたしがこの世を去った後も、このように教えを守るならば、これこそわたしのまことの弟子である。

2. 弟子たちよ、これまでおまえたちのために説いたわたしの教えは、常に聞き、常に考え、常に修めて捨ててはならない。もし教えのとおりに行うなら常に幸いに満たされるであろう。

教えのかなめは心を修めることにある。だから、欲をおさえておのれに克つことに努めなければならない。身を正し、心を正し、ことばをまことあるものにしなければならない。貪ることをやめ、怒りをなくし、悪を遠ざけ、常に無常を忘れてはならない。

もし心が邪悪に引かれ、欲にとらわれようとするなら、これをおさえなければならない。心に従わず、心の主となれ。

"A man's mind may make him a Buddha, or it may make him a beast. Misled by error, one becomes a demon; enlightened, one becomes a Buddha. Therefore, control your mind and do not let it deviate from the right path."

3.   "You should respect each other, follow my teachings, and refrain from disputes; you should not, like water and oil, repel each other, but should, like milk and water, mingle together.

"Study together, learn together, practise my teachings together. Do not waste your mind and time in idleness and quarreling. Enjoy the blossoms of Enlightenment in their season and harvest the fruit of the right path.

"The teachings which I have given you, I gained by following the path myself. You should follow these teachings and conform to their spirit on every occasion.

"If you neglect them, it means that you have never really met me. It means that you are far from me, even if you are actually with me; but if you accept and practise my teachings, then you are very near to me, even though you are far away."

4.   "My disciples, my end is approaching, our parting is

心は人を仏にし、また、畜生にする。迷って鬼となり、さとって仏と成るのもみな、この心のしわざである。だから、よく心を正しくし、道に外れないよう努めるがよい。

3．弟子たちよ、おまえたちはこの教えのもとに、相和し、相敬い、争いを起こしてはならない。水と乳とのように和合せよ。水と油のようにはじきあってはならない。

ともにわたしの教えを守り、ともに学び、ともに修め、励ましあって、道の楽しみをともにせよ。つまらないことに心をつかい、むだなことに時をついやさず、さとりの花を摘み、道の果実を取るがよい。

弟子たちよ、わたしは自らこの教えをさとり、おまえたちのためにこの教えを説いた。おまえたちはよくこれを守って、ことごとにこの教えに従って行わなければならない。

だから、この教えのとおりに行わない者は、わたしに会っていながらわたしに会わず、わたしと一緒にいながらわたしから遠く離れている。また、この教えのとおりに行う者は、たとえわたしから遠く離れていてもわたしと一緒にいる。

4．弟子たちよ、わたしの終わりはすでに近い。別離も遠

near, but do not lament. Life is ever changing; none can escape the dissolution of the body. This I am now to show by my own death, my body falling apart like a delapidated cart.

"Do not vainly lament, but realize that nothing is permanent and learn from it the emptiness of human life. Do not cherish the unworthy desire that the changeable might become unchanging.

"The demon of worldly desires is always seeking chances to deceive the mind. If a viper lives in your room and you wish to have a peaceful sleep, you must first chase it out.

"You must break the bonds of worldly passions and drive them away as you would a viper. You must positively protect your own mind."

5.   "My disciples, my last moment has come, but do not forget that death is only the end of the physical body. The body was born from parents and was nourished by food; just as inevitable are sickness and death.

"But the true Buddha is not a human body: — it is Enlightenment. A human body must die, but the Wisdom of Enlightenment will exist forever in the truth

いことではない。しかし、いたずらに悲しんではならない。世は無常であり、生まれて死なない者はない。今わたしの身が朽ちた車のようにこわれるのも、この無常の道理を身をもって示すのである。

　いたずらに悲しむことをやめて、この無常の道理に気がつき、人の世の真実のすがたに眼を覚まさなければならない。変わるものを変わらせまいとするのは無理な願いである。

　煩悩[ぼんのう]の賊は常におまえたちのすきをうかがって倒そうとしている。もしおまえたちの部屋に毒蛇[じゃ]が住んでいるのなら、その毒蛇を追い出さない限り、落ちついてその部屋で眠ることはできないであろう。

　煩悩の賊は追わなければならない。煩悩の蛇は出さなければならない。おまえたちは慎んでその心を守るがよい。

　5．弟子たちよ、今はわたしの最期の時である。しかし、この死は肉体の死であることを忘れてはならない。肉体は父母より生まれ、食によって保たれるものであるから、病み、傷つき、こわれることはやむを得ない。

　仏の本質は肉体ではない。さとりである。肉体はここに滅びても、さとりは永遠に法と道とに生きている。だから、わ

of the Dharma, and in the practice of the Dharma. He who sees merely my body does not truly see me. Only he who accepts my teaching truly sees me.

"After my death, the Dharma shall be your teacher. Follow the Dharma and you will be true to me.

"During the last forty-five years of my life, I have withheld nothing from my teachings. There is no secret teaching, no hidden meaning; everything has been taught openly and clearly. My dear disciples, this is the end. In a moment, I shall be passing into Nirvana. This is my instruction."

たしの肉体を見る者がわたしを見るのではなく、わたしの教えを知る者こそわたしを見る。

　わたしの亡き後は、わたしの説き遺した法がおまえたちの師である。この法を保ち続けてわたしに仕えるようにするがよい。

　弟子たちよ、わたしはこの人生の後半四十五年間において、説くべきものはすべて説き終わり、なすべきことはすべてなし終わった。わたしにはもはや秘密はない。内もなく、外もなく、すべてみな完全に説きあかし終わった。

　弟子たちよ、今やわたしの最期である。わたしは今より涅槃に入るであろう。これがわたしの最後の教誡である。

THE ETERNAL AND GLORIFIED BUDDHA

I
HIS COMPASSION AND VOWS

1.   The Spirit of Buddha is that of great loving kindness and compassion. The great loving kindness is the spirit to save all people by any and all means. The great compassion is the spirit that prompts it to be ill with the illness of people, to suffer with their suffering.

"Your suffering is my suffering and your happiness is my happiness," said Buddha, and, just as a mother always loves her child, He does not forget that spirit even for a single moment, for it is the nature of Buddhahood to be compassionate.

The Buddha's spirit of compassion is stimulated according to the needs of men; man's faith is the reaction to this spirit, and it leads him to Enlightenment, just as a mother realizes her motherhood by loving her child; then the child, reacting to that love, feels safe and at ease.

第2章　永遠の仏

第1節　いつくしみと願い

1. *仏の心とは大慈悲である。あらゆる手だてによって、すべての人びとを救う大慈の心、人とともに病み、人とともに悩む大悲の心である。

ちょうど子を思う母のように、しばらくの間も捨て去ることなく、守り、育て、救い取るのが仏の心である。「おまえの悩みはわたしの悩み、おまえの楽しみはわたしの楽しみ。」と、かたときも捨てることがない。

仏の大悲は人によって起こり、この大悲に触れて信ずる心が生まれ、信ずる心によってさとりが得られる。それは、子を愛することによって母であることを自覚し、母の心に触れて子の心が安らかとなるようなものである。

Yet people do not understand this spirit of Buddha and go on suffering from the illusions and desires that arise from their ignorance; they suffer from their own deeds accumulated through worldly passions, and wander about among the mountains of delusion with the heavy burden of their evil deeds.

2. Do not think that the compassion of the Buddha is only for the present life; it is a manifestation of the timeless compassion of the eternal Buddha that has been operative since unknown time, when mankind went astray due to ignorance.

The eternal Buddha always appears before people in the most friendly forms and brings to them the wisest methods of relief.

Shakyamuni Buddha, born a Prince among his Shakya kinsmen, left the comforts of his home to live a life of asceticism. Through the practice of silent meditation, he realized Enlightenment. He preached the Dharma (the teaching) among his fellow men and finally manifested it by his earthly death.

The working of Buddhahood is as everlasting as human ignorance is endless; and as the depth of ignorance is bottomless, so Buddha's compassion is boundless.

ところが、人びとはこの仏の心を知らず、その無知からとらわれを起こして苦しみ、煩悩のままにふるまって悩む。罪業の重荷を負って、あえぎつつ、迷いの山から山を駆けめぐる。

2．仏の慈悲をただこの世一生だけのことと思ってはならない。それは久しい間のことである。人びとが生まれ変わり、死に変わりして迷いを重ねてきたその初めから今日まで続いている。

仏は常に人びとの前に、その人びとにもっとも親しみのある姿を示し、救いの手段を尽くす。

釈迦族の太子と生まれ、出家し、苦行をし、道をさとり、教えを説き、死を示した。

人びとの迷いに限りがないから、仏のはたらきにも限りがなく、人びとの罪の深さに底がないから仏の慈悲にも底がない。

When Buddha decided to break from the worldly life, he made four great vows: 1) To save all people; 2) To renounce all worldly desires; 3) To learn all the teachings; and to attain perfect Enlightenment. These vows were manifastations of the love and compassion that are fundamental to the nature of Buddhahood.

3. Buddha first taught himself to avoid the sin of killing any living creature, he wished that all people might know the blessedness of a long life.

Buddha trained himself to avoid the sin of stealing, he wished that all people might have everything they needed.

Buddha trained himself to avoid ever committing adultery, he wished that all people might know the blessedness of a pure spirit and not suffer from insatiable desires.

Buddha, aiming at his ideal, trained himself to remain free from all deception, he wished that all people might know the tranquillity of mind that would follow in speaking the truth.

He trained himself to avoid double-talk, he wished that all people might know the joy of fellowship.

　だから、仏はその修行の初めに四つの大誓願を起こした。一つには誓ってすべての人びとを救おう。二つには誓ってすべての煩悩を断とう。三つには誓ってすべての教えを学ぼう。四つには誓ってこの上ないさとりを得よう。この四つの誓願をもととして仏は修行した。仏の修行のもとがこの誓願であることは、そのまま仏の心が人びとを救う大慈悲であることを示している。

　3. 仏は、仏に成ろうとして殺生の罪を離れることを修め、そしてその功徳によって人びとの長寿を願った。

　仏は盗みの罪を離れることを修め、その功徳によって人びとが求めるものを得られるようにと願った。

　仏はみだらな行いを離れることを修め、その功徳によって人びとの心に害心がなく、また身に飢えや渇きがないようにと願った。

　仏は、仏に成ろうとして、偽りの言葉を離れる行を修め、その功徳によって人びとが真実を語る心の静けさを知るようにと願った。

　二枚舌を離れる行を修めては、人びとが常に仲良くして互いに道を語るようにと願った。

He trained himself to avoid abusing others, and then he wished that all might have the serene mind that would follow by living in peace with others.

He kept himself free from idle talk, and then wished that all might know the blessedness of sympathetic understanding.

Buddha, aiming at his ideal, trained himself to keep free from greed, and by this virtuous deed he wished that all people might know the peacefulness that would go with this freedom.

He trained himself to avoid anger, and he wished that all people might love one another.

He trained himself to avoid ignorance, and he wished that all people might understand and not disregard the law of causation.

Thus Buddha's compassion embraces all people, and his constant consideration is for their happiness. He loves people as parents love their children and he wishes the highest blessedness for them, namely, that they will be able to pass beyond this ocean of life and death.

　また悪口を離れる行を修めては、人びとの心が安らいでうろたえ騒ぐことがないようにと願った。

　むだ口を離れる行を修めては、人びとに思いやりの心をつちかうようにと願った。

　また仏は、仏に成ろうとして、貪りを離れる行を修め、その功徳によって人びとの心に貪りがないようにと願った。

　憎しみを離れる行を修めて、人びとの心に慈しみの思いがあふれるようにと願った。

　愚かさを離れる行を修めて、人びとの心に因果の道理を無視する誤った考えがないようにと願った。

　このように、仏の慈悲はすべての人びとに向かうものであり、その本領はすべての人びとの幸福のため以外の何ものでもない。仏はあたかも父母のように人びとをあわれみ、人びとに迷いの海を渡らせようと願ったのである。

II

BUDDHA'S RELIEF AND
SALVATION FOR US

1. It is very difficult for the words spoken by Buddha from the far bank of Enlightenment to reach the people still struggling in the world of delusion; therefore Buddha returns to this world Himself and uses His methods of salvation.

"Now I will tell you a parable," Buddha said. "Once there lived a wealthy man whose house caught on fire. The man was away from home and when he came back, he found that his children were so absorbed in play, had not noticed the fire and were still inside the house. The father screamed, 'Get out, children! Come out of the house! Hurry!' But the children did not heed him.

"The anxious father shouted again. 'Children, I have some wonderful toys here; come out of the house and get them!' Heeding his cry this time, the children ran out of the burning house."

This world is a burning house. The people, unaware that the house is on fire, are in danger of being burned to death so Buddha in compassion devises ways of saving them.

第2節　救いとその手だて

1. さとりの岸に立って、迷いの海に沈んでいる人びとに呼びかける仏のことばは、人びとの耳には容易に聞こえない。だから、仏は、自ら迷いの海に分け入って、救いの手段を講じた。

さて、それでは一つの比喩を説こう。ある町に長者があって、その家が火事になった。たまたま外にあった長者は帰宅して驚き、子供たちを呼んだが、彼らは遊びにふけって火に気づかず、家の中にとどまっていた。

父は子供たちに向かって――「子供たちよ、逃げなさい、出なさい。」と叫んだが、子供たちは父の呼び声に気がつかなかった。

子供たちの安否を気遣う父はこう叫んだ――「子供たちよ、ここに珍しいおもちゃがある。早く出て来て取るがよい。」子供たちはおもちゃと聞いて勇み立ち、火の家から飛び出して災いから免れることができた。

この世はまことに火の家である。ところが人びとは、家の燃えていることを知らず、焼け死ぬかも知れない恐れの中にある。だから、仏は大悲の心から限りなくさまざまに手段をめぐらして人びとを救う。

2. Buddha said: "I will tell you another parable. Once upon a time the only son of a wealthy man left his home and fell into extreme poverty.

"When the father travelled far from home in search of his son, he lost track of him. He did everything he could to find his son, but in vain.

"Several decades later, his son, now reduced to wretchedness, wandered near where his father was living.

"The father quickly recognized his son and sent his servants to bring the wanderer home; who was overcome by the majestic appearance of the mansion. He feared that they were deceiving him and would not go with them. He did not realize it was his own father.

"The father again sent his servants to offer him some money to become a servant in their rich master's household. The son accepted the offer and returned with them to his father's house and became a servant.

"The father gradually advanced him until he was put in charge of all the property and treasures, but still the son did not recognize his own father.

"The father was pleased with his son's faithfulness,

2．さらに別の比喩を説こう。昔、長者のひとり子が、親のもとを離れてさすらいの身となって、貧困のどん底に落ちぶれた。

父は故郷を離れて息子の行方を求め、あらゆる努力をしたにもかかわらず、どうしてもその行方を求めることができなかった。

それから何十年か経って、今はみじめな境遇に成り果てた息子が、たまたま父の住んでいる町の方へさすらってきた。

めざとくもわが子を認めた父は喜びに躍り上がり、召使いを遣って放浪の息子を連れもどそうとした。しかし、息子は疑い、だまされるのを恐れて、行こうとしなかった。

そこで父はもう一度召使いを息子に近よらせ、よい賃金の仕事を長者の家で与えようと言わせた。息子はその手段に引き寄せられて仕事を引き受け、召使いのひとりとなった。

父の長者は、わが家とも知らずに働いているわが子をおいおいに引き立て、ついには金銀財宝の蔵を管理させるに至ったが、それでも息子はなお父とは知らないでいた。

父はわが子が素直になったのを喜び、またわが命のやがて尽きようとするのを知って、ある日、親族・友人・知己を呼び集めてこう語った――「人びとよ、これはわが子である。

and as the end of his life drew near, he called together his relatives and friends and told them: 'Friends, this is my only son, the son I sought for many years. From now on, all my property and treasures belong to him.'

"The son was surprised at his father's confession and said: 'Not only have I found my father but all this property and treasure is now mine.' "

The wealthy man in this parable represents Buddha, and the wandering son, all people. Buddha's compassion embraces all people with the love of a father for his only son. In that love he conceives the wisest methods to lead, teach and enrich them with the treasure of Enlightenment.

3. Just as rain falls on all vegetation, so Buddha's compassion extends equally to all people. Just as different plants receive particular benefits from the same rain, so people of different natures and circumstances are blessed in different ways.

4. Parents love all their children, but their love is expressed with special tenderness toward a sick child.

Buddha's compassion is equal toward all people, but it is expressed with special care toward those who, because of their ignorance, have heavier burdens of evil

永年探し求めていた息子である。今より後、わたしのすべて
の財宝はみなこの子のものである。」

　息子は父の告白に驚いてこう言った——「今、わたしは父
親を見いだしたばかりでなく、思いがけずこれらすべての財
宝までもわたしのものとなった。」

　ここにいう長者とは仏のことである。迷える息子とはすべ
ての人びとのことである。仏の慈悲は、ひとり子に向かう父
の愛のようにすべての人びとに向かう。仏はすべての人びと
を子として教え導き、さとりの宝をもって彼らを富める者と
する。

　３．すべての人びとを子のようにひとしく慈しむ仏の大悲
は平等であるが、人びとの性質の異なるのに応じてその救い
の手段には相違がある。ちょうど、降る雨は同じであっても、
受ける草木によって、異なった恵みを得るようなものである。

　４．親はどれほど多くの子供があっても、そのかわいさに
変わりがないが、その中に病める子があれば、親の心はとり
わけその子にひかれてゆく。

　仏の大悲もまた、すべての人びとに平等に向かうけれども、
ことに罪の重い者、愚かさゆえに悩める者に慈しみとあわれ

and suffering to bear.

The sun rises in the eastern sky and clears away the darkness of the world without prejudice or favoritism toward any particular region. So Buddha's compassion encompasses all people, encouraging them to do right and guides them against evil. Thus, He clears away the darkness of ignorance and leads people to Enlightenment.

Buddha is a father in His compassion and a mother in His loving-kindness. In their ignorance and bondage to worldly desire, people often act with excessive zeal. Buddha is also zealous, but out of compassion for all people. They are helpless without Buddha's compassion and must receive His methods of salvation as His children.

III
THE ETERNAL BUDDHA

1. Common people believe that Buddha was born a prince and learned the way to Enlightenment as a mendicant; actually, Buddha has always existed in the world which is without beginning or end.

As the Eternal Buddha, He has known all people and

みとをかける。

　また、例えば、太陽が東の空に昇って、闇を滅ぼし、すべてのものを育てるように、仏は人びとの間に出て、悪を滅ぼし、善を育て、智慧の光を恵んで、無知の闇を除き、さとりに至らせる。

　仏は慈しみの父であり、悲みの母である。仏は、世間の人びとに対する慈悲の心から、ひたすら人びとのために尽くす。人びとは仏の慈悲なくしては救われない。人びとはみな仏の子として仏の救いの手段を受けなければならない。

第3節　仏はとわに

　1．人びとはみな、仏は王子として生まれ、出家してさとりを得たのだと信じているけれども、実は仏と成ってよりこの方、限りのない時を経ている。

　限りない時の間、仏は常にこの世にあり、永遠の仏として、すべての人びとの性質を知り尽くし、あらゆる手段を尽くして救ってきた。

applied all methods of relief.

There is no falsity in the Eternal Dharma which Buddha taught, for He knows all things in the world as they are, and He teaches them to all people.

Indeed, it is very difficult to understand the world as it is, for, although it seems true, it is not, and, although it seems false, it is not. Ignorant people can not know the truth concerning the world.

Buddha alone truly and fully knows the world as it is and He never says that it is true or false, or good or evil. He simply portrays the world as it is.

What Buddha does teach is this: "That all people should cultivate roots of virtue according to their natures, their deeds, and their beliefs." This teaching transcends all affirmation and negation of this world.

2.   Buddha teaches not only through words, but also through His life. Although His life is endless, in order to awaken greedy people, He uses the expedient of death.

"While a certain physician was away from home, his children accidentally took some poison. When the physician returned, he noticed their sickness and prepared an

仏の説いた永遠の法の中には偽りがない。なぜなら、仏は、世の中のことをあるがままに知り、すべての人びとに教えるからである。

まことに、世の中のことをあるがままに知ることはむつかしい。なぜなら、世の中のことは、まことかと見ればまことではなく、偽りかと見れば偽りでもない。愚かな者たちはこの世の中のことを知ることはできない。

ひとり仏のみはそれをあるがままに知っている。だから、仏はこの世の中のことがまことであるとも言わず、偽りであるとも言わず、善いとも言わず、悪いとも言わず、ただありのままに示す。

仏が教えようとしていることはこうである——「すべての人びとは、その性質、行い、信仰心に応じて善の根を植えるべきである。」

2. 仏はただことばで教えるだけではなく、身をもって教える。仏は、その寿命に限りはないが、欲を貪って飽くことのない人びとを目覚ますために、手段として死を示す。

例えば多くの子を持つ医師が、他国へ旅をした留守に子供らが毒を飲んで悶え苦しんだとしよう。医師は帰ってこの有様を見、驚いてよい薬を与えた。

antidote. Some of the children who were not seriously poisoned accepted the medicine and were cured, but others were so seriously affected that they refused to take the medicine.

The physician, prompted by his paternal love for his children, decided on an extreme method to press the cure upon them. He said to the children: "I must go off on a long journey. I am old and may pass away any day. If I am with you I can care for you, but if I should pass away, you will become worse and worse. If you hear of my death, I implore you to take the antidote and be cured of this subtle poisoning." Then he went on the long journey. After a time, he sent a messenger to his children to inform them of his death.

The children, receiving the message, were deeply affected by the thought of their father's death and by the realization that they would no longer have the benefit of his benevolent care. Recalling his parting request, in a feeling of sorrow and helplessness, they took the medicine and recovered.

People must not condemn the deception of this father-physician. Buddha is like that father. He, too, employs the fiction of life and death to save people who are entangled in the bondage of desires.

　子供たちのうち、正常な心を失っていない者はその薬を飲んで病を除くことができたけれども、すでに正常な心を失ってしまった者はその薬を飲もうとしなかった。

　父である医師は、彼らの病をいやすために思いきった手段をとろうと決心した。彼は子供たちに言った――「わたしは長い旅に出かけなければならない。わたしは老いて、いつ死ぬかもわからない。もしわたしの死を聞いたなら、ここに残しておく薬を飲んで、おのおの元気になるがよい。」こうして彼はふたたび長い旅に出た。そして使いを遣わしてその死を告げさせた。

子供たちはこれを聞いて深く悲しみ、「父は死んだ。もはやわれわれにはたよる者がなくなった。」と嘆いた。悲しみと絶望の中で、彼らは父の遺言を思い出し、その薬を飲み、そして回復した。

　世の人はこの父である医師のうそを責めるであろうか。仏もまたこの父のようなものである。仏は、欲望に追いまわされている人びとを救うために、仮にこの世に生と死を示したのである。

THE FORM OF BUDDHA AND HIS VIRTUES

I
THREE ASPECTS OF BUDDHA'S BODY

1.   Do not seek to know Buddha by His form or attributes; for neither the form nor the attributes are the real Buddha. The true Buddha is Enlightenment itself. The true way to know Buddha is to realize Enlightenment.

   If someone sees some excellent features of Buddha and then thinks he knows Buddha, his is the mistake of an ignorant eye, for the true Buddha can not be embodied in a form or seen by human eyes. Neither can one know Buddha by a faultless description of his attributes. It is not possible to describe His attributes in human words.

   Though we speak of His form, the Eternal Buddha has no set form, but can manifest Himself in any form. Though we describe His attributes, yet the Eternal Buddha has no set attributes, but can manifest Himself in any and all excellent attributes.

第3章　仏の姿と仏の徳

第1節　3つのすがた

1. 姿や形だけで仏[*]を求めてはならない。姿、形はまことの仏ではない。まことの仏はさとりそのものである。だから、さとりを見る者がまことに仏を見る。

世に優れた仏の相(すがた)を見て、仏を見たというならば、それは無知の眼の過ちである。仏のまことの相は、世の人には見ることもできない。どんなにすぐれた描写によっても仏を知ることはできないし、どんな言葉によっても仏の相は言い尽くすことはできない。

まことの相とはいっても、実は、相あるものは仏ではない。仏には相がない。しかも、また、思いのままにすばらしい相を示す。

So, if one sees distinctly the form of Buddha, or perceives His attributes clearly, and yet does not become attached to His form or to His attributes, he has the capacity to see and know Buddha.

2.   Buddha's body is Enlightenment itself. Being formless and without substance, it always has been and always will be. It is not a physical body that must be nourished by food. It is an eternal body whose substance is Wisdom. Buddha, therefore, has neither fear nor disease; He is eternally changeless.

Therefore, Buddha will never disappear as long as Enlightenment exists. Enlightenment appears as the light of Wisdom that awakens people into a newness of life and causes them to be born into the world of Buddha.

Those who realize this become the children of Buddha; they keep His Dharma, honor His teachings and pass them on to posterity. Nothing can be more miraculous than the power of Buddha.

3.   Buddha has a three-fold body. There is an aspect of Essence or Dharma-kaya; there is an aspect of Potentiality or Sambhoga-kaya; and there is an aspect of Manifestation or Nirmana-kaya.

　だから、明らかに見て、しかもその相にとらわれないなら、この人は自在の力を得て仏を見たのである。

　２．仏の身はさとりであるから、永遠の存在であってこわれることがない。食物によって保たれる肉体ではなく、智慧^{＊ち　え}より成る堅固な身であるから、恐れもなく、病もなく、永遠不変である。

　だから、仏は永遠に滅びない。さとりが滅びない限り、滅びることはない。このさとりが智慧の光となって現われ、この光が人をさとらせ、仏の国に生まれさせる。

　この道理をさとった者は仏の子となり、仏の教えを受持し、仏の教えを守って後の世に伝える。まことに、仏の力ほど不思議なものはない。

　３．仏には三つの身^{からだ}がそなわっている。一つには法身^{ほっしん}、二つには報身^{ほうじん}、三つには応身^{おうじん}である。

Dharma-kaya is the substance of the Dharma; that is, it is the substance of Truth itself. In the aspect of Essence, Buddha has no shape or color, and since Buddha has no shape or color, He comes from nowhere and there is nowhere for Him to go. Like the blue sky, He arches over everything, and since He is all things, He lacks nothing.

He does not exist because people think He exists; neither does He disappear because people forget Him. He is under no particular compulsion to appear when people are happy and comfortable, neither is it necessary for Him to disappear when people are inattentive and idle. Buddha transcends every conceivable direction of human thought.

Buddha's body in this aspect fills every corner of the universe; it reaches everywhere, it exists forever, regardless of whether people believe in Him or doubt His existence.

4.　　Sambhoga-kaya signifies that the nature of Buddha, the merging of both Compassion and Wisdom, which is imageless spirit, manifests itself through the symbols of birth and death, through the symbols of vow-making, training and revealing His sacred name, in order to lead all people to salvation.

法身とは、法そのものを身とするものである。この世のあ
りのままの道理と、それをさとる智慧とが一つになった法そ
のものである。

法そのものが仏であるから、この仏には色もなく形もない。
色も形もないから、来るところもなく、去るところもない。
来るところも去るところもないから充満しないところがなく
大空のようにすべてのものの上にあまねくゆきわたっている。

人が思うから有るのではなく、人が忘れるから無いのでも
なく、人の喜ぶときに来るのでもなく、人の怠るときに去る
のでもない。仏そのものは、人の心のさまざまな動きを超え
て存在する。

仏の身は、あらゆる世界に満ち、すべてのところにゆきわ
たり、人びとがふつう持っている仏に関する考えにかかわら
ず永遠に住する。

4. 報身というのは、形のない法身の仏が、人びとの苦し
みを救うために形を現わし、願を起こし、行を積み、名を示
して、導き救う仏である。

Compassion is the Essence of this body and in its spirit Buddha uses all devices to emancipate all those who are ready for emancipation. Like a fire that, once kindled, never dies until the fuel is exhausted, so the Compassion of Buddha will never falter until all worldly passions are exhausted. Just as the wind blows away the dust, so the Compassion of Buddha in this body blows away the dust of human suffering.

Nirmana-kaya signifies that, in order to complete the relief of Buddha of Potentiality, Buddha appeared in the world in bodily form and showed the people, according to their natures and capacities, the aspects of the birth, renunciation of this world and attainment of Enlightenment. In order to lead the people, Buddha in this body uses every means such as illness and death.

The form of Buddha is originally one Dharma-kaya, but as the nature of people varies, Buddha's form appears differently. Although the form of Buddha varies according to the different desires, deeds and abilities of people, Buddha is concerned only with the truth of the Dharma.

Though Buddha has a three-fold body, His spirit and purpose are one — to save all people.

In all circumstances Buddha is manifest in His

この仏は大悲をもととし、いろいろな手段によって限りなき人びとを救い、すべてのものを焼き払う火のように、人びとの煩悩の薪を焼き、また、ちりを吹き払う風のように、人びとの悩みのちりを払う。

応身の仏は、仏の救いを全うするために、人びとの性質に応じてこの世に姿を現わし、誕生し、出家し、成道し、さまざまの手段をめぐらして人びとを導き、病と死を示して人びとを警める仏である。

仏の身は、もともと一つの法身であるけれども、人びとの性質が異なっているから、仏の身はいろいろに現われる。しかし、人びとの求める心や、行為や、その能力によって、人の見る仏の相は違っていても、仏は一つの真実を見せるのみである。

仏の身は三つに分かれるが、それはただ一つのことをなしとげるためである。一つのこととは、いうまでもなく人びとを助け救うことである。

限りのないすぐれた身をもって、あらゆる境界に現われても、その身は仏ではない。

purity, yet this manifestation is not Buddha because Buddha is not a form. Buddhahood fills everything; it makes Enlightenment its body and, as Enlightenment, it appears before all those capable of realizing the Truth.

II
THE APPEARANCE OF BUDDHA

1.   It is seldom that a Buddha appears in this world. When a Buddha does appear, He attains Enlightenment, introduces the Dharma, severs the net of suspicion, removes the lure of desire at its root, plugs the fountain of evil. Completely unhindered He walks at will over the world. There is nothing greater than to revere the Buddha.

Buddha appears in the world of suffering because He can not desert suffering people. His only purpose is to spread the Dharma and to bless all people with its Truth.

It is very difficult to introduce the Dharma into a world filled with injustice and false standards, a world that is vainly struggling with insatiable desires and discomforts. Buddha faces these difficulties because of His great love and compassion.

2.   Buddha is a good friend to all people. If Buddha

仏は肉体ではないからである。たださとりを身としてすべてのものに満ちみち、真実を見る人の前に仏は常に現われる。

第2節　仏との出会い

1. 仏がこの世に現われるのは、はなはだまれである。仏は今この世界においてさとりを開き、法を説き、疑いの網を断ち、愛欲の根を抜き、悪の源をふさぎ、妨げられることなく、自由自在にこの世を歩く。世に仏を敬うより以上の善はない。

仏がこの世に現われるのは、法を説いて、人びとにまことの福利を恵むためである。苦しみ悩む人びとを捨てることができないから、仏はこの苦難の世界に現われる。

世に道理なく、不正はびこり、欲に飽くことなく、心身ともに堕落し、命短きこの世に、法をとくことは、はなはだむつかしい。ただ大悲のゆえに、仏はこの困難に打ち勝つ。

2. 仏はこの世におけるすべての人びとの善い友である。

finds a man suffering from the heavy burden of worldly passions, He feels compassion and shares the burden with him. If He meets a man suffering from delusion, He will clear away the delusion by the pure light of His wisdom.

Like a calf which enjoys its life with its mother, those who have heard the Buddha's teachings are afterward unwilling to leave Him because His teachings bring them happiness.

3.   When the moon sets, people say that the moon has disappeared; and when the moon rises, they say that the moon has appeared. In fact, the moon neither goes nor comes, but shines continually in the sky. Buddha is exactly like the moon: He neither appears nor disappears; He only seems to do so out of love for the people that He may teach them.

People call one phase of the moon a full moon, they call another phase a crescent moon; in reality, the moon is always perfectly round, neither waxing nor waning. Buddha is precisely like the moon. In the eyes of men, Buddha may seem to change in appearance, but, in truth, Buddha does not change.

The moon appears everywhere, over a crowded city, a sleepy village, a mountain, a river. It is seen in the

*_{ぼんのう}
煩悩の重荷に悩む者が仏に会えば、仏はそのために代わって
その重荷をになう。

　仏はこの世におりるまことの師である。愚かな迷いに苦し
む者が仏に会えば、仏は*智慧の光によってその闇を払う。

　子牛がいつまでも母牛のそばを離れないように、ひとたび
仏の教えを聞いた者は仏を離れない。教えを聞くことは常に
楽しいからである。

　3．月が隠れると、人びとは月が沈んだといい、月が現わ
れると、人びとは月が出たという。けれども月は常に住して
出没することがない。仏もそのように、常に住して生滅しな
いのであるが、ただ人びとを教えるために生滅を示す。

　人びとは月が満ちるとか、月が欠けるとかいうけれども、
月は常に満ちており、増すこともなく減ることもない。仏も
またそのように、常に住して生滅しないのであるが、ただ人
びとの見るところに従って生滅があるだけである。

　月はまたすべての上に現われる。町にも、村にも、山にも、
川にも、池の中にも、かめの中にも、葉末の露にも現われる。

depths of a pond, in a jug of water, in a drop of dew hanging on a leaf. If a man walks hundreds of miles the moon goes with him. To men the moon seems to change, but the moon does not change. Buddha is like the moon in following the people of this world in all their changing circumstances, manifesting various appearances; but in His Essence He does not change.

4.　　The fact that Buddha appears and disappears can be explained by causality: namely, when the cause and conditions are propitious, Buddha appears; when causes and conditions are not propitious, Buddha seems to disappear from the world.

Whether Buddha appears or disappears, Buddhahood always remains the same. Knowing this principle, one must keep to the path of Enlightenment and attain Perfect Wisdom, undisturbed by the apparent changes in the image of Buddha, in the condition of the world, or in the fluctuations of human thought.

It has been explained that Buddha is not a physical body but is Enlightenment. A body may be thought of as a receptacle; then, if this receptacle is filled with Enlightenment, it may be called Buddha. Therefore, if anyone is attached to the physical body of Buddha and laments His disappearance, he will be unable to see the true Buddha.

人が行くこと百里千里であっても、月は常にその人に従う。月そのものに変わりはないが、月を見る人によって月は異なる。仏もまたそのように、世の人びとに従って、限りない姿を示すが、仏は永遠に存在して変わることがない。

4. 仏がこの世に現われたことも、また隠れたことも、因縁を離れてあるのではない。人びとを救うのによい時が来ればこの世にも現われ、その因縁が尽きればこの世から隠れる。

仏に生滅の相はあっても、まことに生滅することはない。この道理を知って、仏の示す生滅と、すべてのもののうつり変わりに驚かず、悲しまず、まことのさとりを開いて、この上ない智慧を得なければならない。

仏は肉体ではなくさとりであることはすでに説いた。肉体はまことに容器であり、その中にさとりを盛ればこそ仏といわれる。だから、肉体にとらわれて、仏のなくなることを悲しむ者は、まことの仏を見ることはできない。

In reality, the true nature of all things transcends the discrimination of appearance and disappearance, of coming and going, of good and evil. All things are substanceless and perfectly homogeneous.

Such discriminations are caused by an erroneous judgement by those who see these phenomena. The true form of Buddha neither appears nor disappears.

III
BUDDHA'S VIRTUE

1.   Buddha receives the respect of the world because of five virtues: superior conduct; superior point of view; perfect wisdom; superior preaching ability; and the power to lead people to the practice of His teaching.

In addition, eight other virtues enable Buddha to bestow blessings and happiness upon the people: the ability to bring immediate benefits in the world through the practice of His teaching, the ability to judge correctly between good and bad, right and wrong, the ability to lead people to Enlightenment by teaching the right way, the ability to lead all people by an equal way, the ability to avoid pride and boasting, the ability to do what He has spoken, the ability to say what He has done, and, thus doing, to fulfill the vows of His compassionate heart.

Through meditation, Buddha preserves a calm and

もともと、あらゆるもののまことの相は、生滅・去来・善悪の差別を離れた空にして平等なものである。

それらの差別は、見る者の偏見から起こるもので、仏のまことの相も、実は現われることもなく隠れることもない。

第3節　すぐれた徳

1．仏は五つのすぐれた徳をそなえて、尊敬を受ける。すぐれた行い、すぐれた見方、すぐれた智慧、さとりの道を明らかに説くこと、人びとをしてよく教えのとおりに修めさせることである。

また仏には八つのすぐれた能力がある。一つには、仏は人びとに利益と幸福とを与える。二つには、仏の教えはこの世においてただちに利益がある。三つには、世の善悪正邪を正しく教える。四つには、正しい道を教えてさとりに入らせる。五つには、どんな人をも一つの道に導く。六つには、仏にはおごる心がない。七つには、言ったとおり実行し、実行するとおりに語る。八つには、惑いなく、願いを満たし、完全に行をなしとげる。

また仏は、冥想に入って静けさと平和を得、あらゆる人びと

peaceful spirit, radiant with mercy, compassion, happiness and even equanimity. He deals equitably with all people, cleansing their minds of defilement and bestowing happiness in a perfect singleness of spirit.

2.   Buddha is both father and mother to the people of the world. For sixteen months after a child is born the father and mother have to speak to him in babyish words; then gradually they teach him to speak as an adult. Like earthly parents, Buddha first takes care of the people and then leaves them to care for themselves. He first brings things to pass according to their desires and then He brings them to a peaceful and safe shelter.

What Buddha preaches in His language, people receive and assimilate in their own language as if it were intended exclusively for them.

Buddha's state of mind surpasses human thought; it can not be made clear by words; it can only be hinted at in parables.

A river is stirred up by the tramping of horses and elephants and disturbed by the movements of fish and turtles; but the river flows on, pure and undisturbed by such trifles. Buddha is like the great river. The fish and

に対して慈しみの心、悲みの心、とらわれのない心を持ち、心のあらゆる汚れを去って、清らかな者だけが持つ喜びを持つ。

2. この仏はすべての人びとの父母である。子が生まれて十六か月の間、父母は子の声に合わせて赤子のように語り、それからおもむろにことばを教えるように、仏もまた、人びとのことばに従って教えを説き、その見るところに従って相を現わし、人びとをして安らかな揺らぎのない境地に住まわせる。

また仏は、一つのことばをもって教えを説くが、人びとはみなその性質に応じてそれを聞き、仏は今、わたしのために教えを説かれたと喜ぶ。

仏の境地は、迷える人びとの考えを超えており、ことばでは説き尽くすことはできないが、強いてその境地を示そうとすれば、たとえによるほかはない。

ガンジス河は常に亀や魚、馬や象などに汚されているが、いつも清らかである。仏もこの河のように、異教の魚や亀な

turtles of other teachings swim about in its depths and push against its current, but in vain. Buddha's Dharma flows on, pure and undisturbed.

3.   Buddha's Wisdom, being perfect, keeps away from extremes of prejudice and preserves a moderation that is beyond all words to describe. Being all-wise He knows the thoughts and feelings of all men and realizes everything in this world in a moment.

As the stars of heaven are reflected in the calm sea, so people's thoughts, feelings and circumstances are reflected in the depths of Buddha's Wisdom. This is why Buddha is called the Perfectly Enlightened One, the Omniscience.

Buddha's Wisdom refreshes the arid minds of people, enlightens them and teaches them the significance of this world, its causes and its effects, appearings and disappearings. Indeed, without the aid of Buddha's Wisdom, what aspect of the world is at all comprehensible for people?

4.   Buddha does not always appear as a Buddha. Sometimes He appears as an incarnation of evil, sometimes as a woman, a god, a king, or a statesman; sometimes He appears in a brothel or in a gambling house.

どが競い来って乱しても、少しも思いを乱されることなく清らかである。

3．仏の智慧*はすべての道理を知り、かたよった両極端を離れて中道*に立ち、また、すべての文字やことばを超え、すべての人びとの考えを知り、一瞬のうちにこの世のすべてのことを知っている。

静かな大海に、大空の星がすべてその形を映し出すように、仏の智慧の海には、すべての人びとの心や思いや、その他あらゆるものがそのままに現われる。だから仏を一切知者という。

この仏の智慧はあらゆる人びとの心をうるおし、光を与え、人びとにこの世の意味、盛衰、因果の道理を明らかに知らせる。まことに仏の智慧によってのみ人びとはよくこの世のことを知る。

4．仏はただ仏として現われるだけでなく、あるときは悪魔となり、あるときは女の姿となり、神々の像となり、国王、大臣となり、あるいは娼婦の家、賭博者の家にも現われる。

In an epidemic He appears as a healing physician and in war He preaches forbearance and mercy for the suffering people; for those who believe that things are everlasting, He preaches transiency and uncertainty; for those who are proud and egoistic, He preaches humility and self-sacrifice; for those who are entangled in the web of worldly pleasures, He reveals the misery of the world.

The work of Buddha is to manifest in all affairs and on all occasions the pure essence of Dharma-kaya (the absolute nature of Buddha); so Buddha's mercy and compassion flow out from this Dharma-kaya in endless life and boundless light, bringing salvation to mankind.

5. The world is like a burning house that is forever being destroyed and rebuilt. People, being confused by the darkness of their ignorance, lose their minds in anger, displeasure, jealousy, prejudice and worldly passion. They are like babies in need of a mother; everyone must be dependent upon Buddha's mercy.

Buddha is a father to all the world; all human beings are the children of Buddha. Buddha is the most saintly of saints. The world is afire with decrepitude and death; there is suffering everywhere. But people, engrossed in the vain search for worldly pleasure, are not wise enough to fully realize this.

　病のあるときには医師となって薬を施して教えを説き、戦いが起これば正しい教えを説いて災いを離れさせ、固定的な考えにとらわれている者には無常の道理を説き、自我と誇りにこだわっている者には無我を説き、世俗的悦楽の網にとらわれているものには世のいたましい有様を明らかにする。

　仏のはたらきは、このようにこの世の事物の上に現われるが、それはすべてみな法身の源から流れ出るもので、限りない命、限りない光の救いも、その源は法身の仏にある。

　5．この世は火の宅のように安らかでない。人びとは愚かさの闇につつまれて、怒り、ねたみ、そねみ、あらゆる煩悩に狂わされている。赤子に母が必要であるように、人びとはみなこの仏の慈悲に頼らなければならない。

　仏は実に聖者の中の尊い聖者であり、この世の父である。だから、あらゆる人びとはみな仏の子である。彼らはひたすらこの世の楽しみにのみかかわり、その災いを見通す智慧を持たない。この世は苦しみに満ちた恐るべきところ、老いと病と死の炎は燃えてやまない。

Buddha saw that this world of delusion was really a burning house, so He turned from it and found refuge and peace in the quiet forest. There, out of His great compassion, he calls to us: "This world of change and suffering belongs to me; all these ignorant, heedless people are my children; I am the only one who can save them from their delusion and misery."

As Buddha is the great king of the Dharma, He can preach to all people as He wishes. Buddha appears in the world to bless the people. To save them from suffering He preaches the Dharma, but the ears of people are dulled by greed and they are inattentive.

But those who listen to His teachings are free from the delusions and the miseries of life. "People can not be saved by relying on their own wisdom," He said, "and through faith they must enter into my teaching." Therefore, one should listen to the Buddha's teaching and put it into practice.

　ところが、仏は迷いの世界という火の宅を離れ、静寂な林にあって、

「いまこの世界はわがものであり、その中の生けるものたちはみなわが子である。限りない悩みを救うのはわれひとりである。」と言う。

　仏は実に、大いなる*法の王であるから、思いのままに教えを説く。仏はただ、人びとを安らかにし、恵みをもたらすためにこの世に現われた。人びとを苦しみから救い出すために、仏は法を説いた。ところが、人びとは欲に引かれて聞く耳を持たず気にもしていない。

　しかし、この教えを聞いて喜ぶ人は、もはや決して迷いの世界に退くことのない境地におかれるであろう。「わが教えは、ただ信によってのみ入ることができる。すなわち、仏のことばを信ずることによって教えにかなうので、自分の知恵によるのではない。」と仏は言った。したがって仏の教えに耳を傾け、それを実践すべきである。

DHARMA
おしえ

CAUSATION

I
THE FOURFOLD NOBLE TRUTH

1.   The world is full of suffering. Birth is suffering, old age is suffering, sickness and death are sufferings. To meet a man whom one hates is suffering, to be separated from a beloved one is suffering, to be vainly struggling to satisfy one's needs is suffering. In fact, life that is not free from desire and passion is always involved with distress. This is called the Truth of Suffering.

The cause of human suffering is undoubtedly found in the thirsts of the physical body and in the illusions of worldly passion. If these thirsts and illusions are traced to their source, they are found to be rooted in the intense desires of physical instincts. Thus, desire, having a strong will-to-live as its basis, seeks that which it feels desirable, even if it is sometimes death. This is called the Truth of the Cause of Suffering.

If desire, which lies at the root of all human passion, can be removed, then passion will die out and all human

第1章　因　　縁

第1節　四つの真理

1．この人間世界は苦しみに満ちている。生も苦しみであり、老いも病も死もみな苦しみである。怨みあるものと会わなければならないことも、愛するものと別れなければならないことも、また求めて得られないことも苦しみである。まことに、執着を離れない人生はすべて苦しみである。これを苦しみの真理（苦諦）という。

　この人生の苦しみが、どうして起こるかというと、それは人間の心につきまとう*煩悩から起こることは疑いない。その煩悩をつきつめていけば、生まれつきそなわっている激しい欲望に根ざしていることがわかる。このような欲望は、生に対する激しい執着をもととしていて、見るもの聞くものを欲しがる欲望となる。また転じて、死をさえ願うようにもなる。これを苦しみの原因（集諦）という。

　この煩悩の根本を残りなく滅ぼし尽くし、すべての執着を離れれば人間の苦しみもなくなる。これを苦しみを滅ぼす

suffering will be ended. This is called the Truth of the Cessation of Suffering.

In order to enter into a state where there is no desire and no suffering, one must follow a certain Path. The stages of this Noble Eightfold Path are: Right View, Right Thought, Right Speech, Right Behavior, Right Livelihood, Right Effort, Right Mindfulness and Right Concentration. This is called the Truth of the Noble Path to the Cessation of the Cause of Suffering.

People should keep these Truths clearly in mind, for the world is filled with suffering and if anyone wishes to escape from suffering, he must sever the ties of worldly passion which is the sole cause of suffering. The way of life which is free from all worldly passion and suffering can only be known through Enlightenment, and Enlightenment can only be attained through the discipline of the Noble Eightfold Path.

2. All those who are seeking Enlightenment must understand the Fourfold Noble Truth. Without understanding this, they will wander about interminably in the bewildering maze of life's illusions. Those who understand this Fourfold Noble Truth are called "the people who have acquired the eyes of Enlightenment."

Therefore, those who wish to follow the Buddha's

真理（滅諦）という。

　この苦しみを滅ぼし尽くした境地に入るには、八つの正しい道（八正道）を修めなければならない。八つの正しい道というのは、正しい見解、正しい思い、正しい言葉、正しい行い、正しい生活、正しい努力、正しい記憶、正しい心の統一である。これらの八つは欲望を滅ぼすための正しい道の真理（道諦）といわれる。

　これらの真理を人はしっかり身につけなければならない。というのは、この世は苦しみに満ちていて、この苦しみから逃れようとする者はだれでも煩悩を断ち切らなければならないからである。煩悩と苦しみのなくなった境地は、さとりによってのみ到達し得る。さとりはこの八つの正しい道によってのみ達し得られる。

　２．道に志す人も、この四つの聖い真理を知らなければならない。これらを知らないために、長い間、迷いの道にさまよってやむときがない。この四つの聖い真理を知る人をさとりの眼を得た人という。

　だから、よく心を一つにして仏の教えを受け、この四つの

teachings should concentrate their minds on this Four-fold Noble Truth and seek to make their understanding of its meaning clear. In all ages, a saint, if he is a true saint, is one who understands it and teaches it to others.

When a man clearly understands the Fourfold Noble Truth, then the Noble Eightfold Path will lead him away from greed; and if he is free from greed, he will nor quarrel with the world, he will not kill, nor steal, nor commit adultery, nor cheat, nor abuse, nor flatter, nor envy, nor lose his temper, nor forget the transiency of life nor will he be unjust.

3.   Following the Noble Path is like entering a dark room with a light in the hand: the darkness will all be cleared away and the room will be filled with light.

People who understand the meaning of the Noble Truths and have learned to follow the Noble Path are in possession of the light of wisdom that will clear away the darkness of ignorance.

Buddha leads people, merely by indicating to them the Fourfold Noble Truth. Those who understand it properly will attain Enlightenment; they will be able to guide and support others in this bewildering world, and they will be worthy of trust. When the Fourfold Noble

聖い真理の道理を明らかに知らなければならない。

いつの世のどのような聖者も、正しい聖者であるならば、みなこの四つの聖い真理をさとった人であり、四つの聖い真理を教える人である。

　この四つの聖い真理が明らかになったとき、人は初めて、欲から遠ざかり、世間と争わず、殺さず、盗まず、よこしまな愛欲を犯さず、欺かず、そしらず、へつらわず、ねたまず、瞋らず、人生の無常を忘れず、道にはずれることがない。

　3．道を行うものは、例えば、燈火をかかげて、暗黒の部屋に入るようなものである。闇はたちまち去り、明るさに満たされる。

　道を学んで、明らかにこの四つの聖い真理を知れば、智慧の燈火を得て、無知の闇は滅びる。

　仏は単にこの四つの真理を示すことによって人びとを導くのである。教えを正しく身に受けるものは、この四つの聖い真理によって、はかないこの世において、まことのさとりを開き、この世の人びとの守りとなり、頼りとなる。

Truth is clearly understood, all the sources of worldly passion are dried up.

Advancing from this Fourfold Noble Truth, the disciples of Buddha will attain all other precious truths; they will gain the wisdom and insight to understand all meanings, and will become capable of preaching the Dharma to all the peoples of the world.

II
CAUSATION

1.   There are causes for all human suffering, and there is a way by which they may be ended, because everything in the world is the result of a vast concurrence of causes and conditions, and everything disappears as these causes and conditions change and pass away.

Rain falls, winds blow, plants bloom, leaves mature and are blown away. These phenomena are all inter-related with causes and conditions, and are brought about by them, and disappear as the causes and conditions change.

One is born through the conditions of parentage. His body is nourished by food: his spirit is nurtured by teaching and experience.

Therefore, both flesh and spirit are related to

それは、この四つの聖い真理が明らかになれば、あらゆる煩悩のもとである*無明が滅びるからである。

　仏の弟子たちはこの四つの聖い真理によって、あらゆる教えに達し、すべての道理を知る智慧と功徳とをそなえ、どんな人びとに向かっても、自在に教えを説くことができる。

第2節　不思議なつながり

1．人びとの苦しみには原因があり、人びとのさとりには道があるように、すべてのものは、みな縁（条件）によって生まれ、縁によって滅びる。

　雨の降るのも、風の吹くのも、花の咲くのも、葉の散るのも、すべて縁によって生じ、縁によって滅びるのである。

　この身は父母を縁として生まれ、食物によって維持され、またこの心も経験と知識とによって育ったものである。

　だから、この身も、この心も、縁によって成り立ち、縁によって変わるといわなければならない。

conditions and are changed as conditions change.

As a net is made up by a series of knots, so everything in this world is connected by a series of knots. If anyone thinks that the mesh of a net is an independent, isolated thing, he is mistaken.

It is called a net because it is made up of a series of connected meshes, and each mesh has its place and responsibilities in relation to other meshes.

2. Blossoms come about because of a series of conditions that lead up to their blooming. Leaves are blown away because a series of conditions lead up to it. Blossoms do not appear independently, nor does a leaf fall of itself, out of its season. So everything has its coming forth and passing away; nothing can be independent without any change.

It is the everlasting and unchanging rule of this world that everything is created by a series of causes and conditions and everything disappears by the same rule; everything changes, nothing remains constant.

III
THE DEPENDENT ORIGINATION

1. Where is the source of human grief, lamentation, pain and agony? Is it not to be found in the fact that

　網の目が、互いにつながりあって網を作っているように、すべてのものは、つながりあってできている。

　　一つの網の目が、それだけで網の目であると考えるならば、大きな誤りである。

　網の目は、ほかの網の目とかかわりあって、一つの網の目といわれる。網の目は、それぞれ、ほかの網が成り立つために、役立っている。

　2．花は咲く縁が集まって咲き、葉は散る縁が集まって散る。ひとり咲き、ひとり散るのではない。

　縁によって咲き、縁によって散るのであるから、どんなものも、みなうつり変わる。ひとりで存在するものも、常にとどまるものもない。

　すべてのものが、縁によって生じ、縁によって滅びるのは永遠不変の道理である。だから、うつり変わり、常にとどまらないということは、天地の間に動くことのないまことの道理であり、これだけは永久に変わらない。

第3節　ささえあって

　1．それでは、人びとの憂い、悲しみ、苦しみ、もだえは、どうして起こるのか。つまりそれは、人に執着があるからで

people are generally desirous.

They cling obstinately to lives of wealth and honor, comfort and pleasure, excitement and self indulgence, ignorant of the fact that the desire for these very things is the source of human suffering.

From its beginning, the world has been filled with a succession of calamities, over and above the unavoidable facts of illness, old age and death.

But if one carefully considers all the facts, one must be convinced that at the basis of all suffering lies the principle of craving desire. If avarice can be removed, human suffering will come to an end.

Ignorance is manifested in greed that fills the human mind.

It comes from the fact that men are unaware of the true reason for the succession of things.

From ignorance and greed there spring impure desires for things that are, in fact, unobtainable, but for which men restlessly and blindly search.

Because of ignorance and greed, people imagine

ある。

　富に執着し、名誉利欲に執着し、恍楽に執着し、自分自身
に執着する。この執着から苦しみ悩みが生まれる。

　初めから、この世界にはいろいろの災いがあり、そのうえ、
老いと病と死とを避けることができないから、悲しみや苦し
みがある。

　しかし、それらもつきつめてみれば、執着があるから、悲
しみや苦しみとなるのであり、執着を離れさえすれば、すべ
ての悩み苦しみはあとかたもなく消えうせる。

　さらにこの執着を押しつめてみると、人びとの心のうちに、
*無明と貪愛とが見いだされる。

　無明はうつり変わるもののすがたに眼が開けず、因果の道
理に暗いことである。貪愛とは、得ることのできないものを
貪って、執着し愛着することである。

　もともと、ものに差別はないのに、差別を認めるのは、こ

discriminations where, in reality, there are no discriminations. Inherently, there is no discrimination of right and wrong in human behavior; but people, because of ignorance, imagine such distinctions and judge them as right or wrong.

Because of their ignorance, all people are always thinking wrong thoughts and always losing the right viewpoint and, clinging to their egos, they take wrong actions. As a result, they become attached to a delusive existence.

Making their deeds the field for their egos, using the working of discrimination of the mind as seed, beclouding the mind by ignorance, fertilizing it with the rain of craving desires, irrigating it by the willfulness of egotism, they add the conception of evil, and carry this incarnation of delusion about with them.

2.   In reality, therefore, it is their own mind that causes the delusions of grief, lamentation, pain and agony.

This whole world of delusion is nothing but a shadow caused by the mind. And yet, it is also from this same mind that the world of Enlightenment appears.

3.   In this world there are three wrong viewpoints.

の*無明と*貪愛とのはたらきである。もともと、ものに良否は
ないのに、良否を見るのは、この無明と貪愛とのはたらきで
ある。

　すべての人びとは、常によこしまな思いを起こして、愚か
さのために正しく見ることができなくなり、自我にとらわれ
て間違った行いをし、その結果、迷いの身を生ずることにな
る。

　*業を田とし心を種とし、無明の土に覆われ、貪愛の雨でう
るおい、自我の水をそそぎ、よこしまな見方を増して、この
迷いを生み出している。

　2．だから、結局のところ、憂いと悲しみと苦しみと悩み
のある迷いの世界を生み出すものは、この心である。

　迷いのこの世は、ただこの心から現われた心の影にほかな
らず、さとりの世界もまた、この心から現われる。

　3．この世の中には、三つの誤った見方がある。

If one clings to these viewpoints, then all things in this world are but to be denied.

First, some say that all human experience is based on destiny; second, some hold that everything is created by God and controlled by His will; third, some say that everything happens by chance without having any cause or condition.

If all has been decided by destiny, both good deeds and evil deeds are predetermined, weal and woe are predestined; nothing would exist that has not been fore-ordained. Then all human plans and efforts for improvement and progress would be in vain and humanity would be without hope.

The same is true of the other viewpoints, for, if everything in the last resort is in the hands of an unknowable God, or of blind chance, what hope has humanity except in submission? It is no wonder that people holding these conceptions lose hope and neglect efforts to act wisely and to avoid evil.

In fact, these three conceptions or viewpoints are all wrong: everything is a succession of appearances whose source is the accumulation of causes and conditions.

もしこれらの見方に従ってゆくと、この世のすべてのことが否定されることになる。

　一つには、ある人は、人間がこの世で経験するどのようなことも、すべて運命であると主張する。二つには、ある人は、それはすべて神のみ業であるという。三つには、またある人は、すべて因も縁もないものであるという。

　もしも、すべてが運命によって定まっているならば、この世においては、善いことをするのも、悪いことをするのも、みな運命であり、幸・不幸もすべて運命となって、運命のほかには何ものも存在しないことになる。

　したがって、人びとに、これはしなければならない、これはしてはならないという希望も努力もなくなり、世の中の進歩も改良もないことになる。

　次に、神のみ業であるという説も、最後の因も縁もないとする説も、同じ非難があびせられ、悪を離れ、善をなそうという意志も努力も意味もすべてなくなってしまう。

　だから、この三つの見方はみな誤っている。どんなことも縁によって生じ、縁によって滅びるものである。

THE THEORY OF MIND-ONLY AND THE REAL STATE OF THINGS

I
IMPERMANENCY AND EGOLESSNESS

1. Though both body and mind appear because of cooperating causes, it does not follow that there is an ego-personality. As the body of flesh is an aggregate of elements, it is, therefore, impermanent.

If the body were an ego-personality, it could do this and that as it would determine.

A king has the power to praise or punish as he wishes, but he becomes ill despite his intent or desire, he comes to old age unwillingly, and his fortune and his wishes often have little to do with each other.

Neither is the mind the ego-personality. The human mind is an aggregate of causes and conditions. It is in constant change.

If the mind were an ego-personality, it could do this and that as it would determine; but the mind often flies

第2章　人の心とありのままの姿

第1節　変わりゆくものには実体がない

1. 身も心も、*因縁によってできているものであるから、この身には実体はない。この身は因縁の集まりであり、だから、*無常なものである。

もしも、この身に実体があるならば、わが身は、かくあれ、かくあることなかれ、と思って、その思いのままになし得るはずである。

王はその国において、罰すべきを罰し、賞すべきを賞し、自分の思うとおりにすることができる。それなのに、願わないのに病み、望まないのに老い、一つとしてわが身については思うようになるものはない。

それと同じく、この心にもまた実体はない。心もまた因縁の集まりであり、常にうつり変わるものである。

もしも、心に実体があるならば、かくあれ、かくあることなかれ、と思って、そのとおりにできるはずであるのに、

from what it knows is right and chases after evil reluctantly. Still, nothing seems to happen exactly as its ego desires.

2.   If one is asked whether the body is constant or impermanent, he will be obliged to answer "impermanent."

If one is asked whether impermanent existence is happiness or suffering, he will generally have to answer "suffering."

If a man believes that such an impermanent thing, so changeable and filled with suffering, is the ego-personality, it is a serious mistake.

The human mind is also impermanent and suffering; it has nothing that can be called an ego-personality.

Our true body and mind, which make up an individual life, and the external world surrounding it, are far apart from both the conceptions of "me" and "mine".

It is simply the mind clouded over by impure desires, and impervious to wisdom, that obstinately persists in thinking of "me" and "mine".

Since both the body and its surroundings are origi-

心は欲しないのに悪を思い、願わないのに善から遠ざかり、一つとして自分の思うようにはならない。

2. この身は永遠に変わらないものなのか、それとも無常であるのかと問うならば、だれも無常であると答えるに違いない。

無常なものは苦しみであるのか、楽しみであるのかと問うならば、生まれた者はだれでもやがて老い、病み、死ぬと気づいたとき、だれでも、苦しみであると答えるに違いない。

このように無常であってうつり変わり、苦しみであるものを、実体である、わがものである、と思うのは間違っている。

心もまた、そのように、無常であり、苦しみであり、実体ではない。

だから、この自分を組み立てている身と心や、それをとりまくものは、我とかわがものとかという観念を離れたものである。

＊智慧のない心が、我である、わがものであると執着するにすぎない。

身もそれをとりまくものも、縁によって生じたものであるから、変わりに変わって、しばらくもとどまることがない。

nated by cooperating causes and conditions, they are continually changing and never can come to an end.

The human mind, in its never-ending changes, is like the flowing water of river or the burning flame of a candle; like an ape, it is forever jumping about, not ceasing for even a moment.

A wise man, seeing and hearing such, should break away from any attachment to body or mind, if he is ever to attain Enlightenment.

3. There are five things which no one is able to accomplish in this world: first, to cease growing old when he is growing old; second, to cease being sick; third, to cease dying; fourth, to deny extinction when there is extinction; fifth, to deny exhaustion.

All the ordinary people in the world sooner or later run into these facts, and most people suffer consequently, but those who have heard the Buddha's teaching do not suffer because they understand that these are unavoidable.

There are four truths in this world: first, all living beings rise from ignorance; second, all objects of desire are impermanent, uncertain and suffering; third, all existing things are also impermanent, uncertain and

流れる水のように、また燈火のようにうつり変わっている。また、心の騒ぎ動くこと猿のように、しばらくの間も、静かにとどまることがない。

智慧あるものは、このように見、このように聞いて、身と心とに対する執着を去らなければならない。心身ともに執着を離れたとき、さとりが得られる。

3．この世において、どんな人にもなしとげられないことが五つある。一つには、老いゆく身でありながら、老いないということ。二つには、病む身でありながら、病まないということ。三つには、死すべき身でありながら、死なないということ。四つには、滅ぶべきものでありながら、滅びないということ。五つには、尽きるべきものでありながら、尽きないということである。

世の常の人びとは、この避け難いことにつき当たり、いたずらに苦しみ悩むのであるが、仏の教えを受けた人は、避け難いことを避け難いと知るから、このような愚かな悩みをいだくことはない。

また、この世に四つの真実がある。第一に、すべて生きとし生けるものはみな無明から生まれること。第二に、すべて

suffering; fourth, there is nothing that can be called an "ego," and there is no such thing as "mine" in all the world.

These truths that everything is impermanent and passing and egoless, have no connection with the fact of Buddha's appearing or not appearing in this world. These truths are certain; Buddha knows this and, therefore, preaches the Dharma to all people.

II
THE THEORY OF MIND-ONLY

1.   Both delusion and Enlightenment originate within the mind, and every existence or phenomenon arises from the functions of the mind, just as different things appear from the sleeve of a magician.

The activities of the mind have no limit, they form the surroundings of life. An impure mind surrounds itself with impure things and a pure mind surrounds itself with pure things; hence, surroundings have no more limits than the activities of the mind.

Just as a picture is drawn by an artist, surroundings are created by the activities of the mind. While the surroundings created by Buddha are pure and free from defilement, those created by ordinary men are not so.

欲望の対象となるものは、無常であり、苦しみであり、うつり変わるものであること。第三に、すべて存在するものは、無常であり、苦しみであり、うつり変わるものであること。第四に、我も、わがものもないということである。

すべてのものは、みな無常であって、うつり変わるものであること、どのようなものにも我がないということは、仏がこの世に出現するとしないとにかかわらず、いつも定まっているまことの道理である。仏はこれを知り、このことをさとって、人びとを教え導く。

第2節　心の構造

1.　迷いもさとりも心から現われ、すべてのものは心によって作られる。ちょうど手品師が、いろいろなものを自由に現わすようなものである。

人の心の変化には限りがなく、そのはたらきにも限りがない。汚れた心からは汚れた世界が現われ、清らかな心からは清らかな世界が現われるから、外界の変化にも限りがない。

絵は絵師によって描かれ、外界は心によって作られる。仏の作る世界は、煩悩を離れて清らかであり、人の作る世界は煩悩によって汚れている。

A single picture is capable of an infinite variety of details. So the human mind fills in the surroundings of its life. There is nothing in the world that is not mind-created.

Buddha has a right understanding of all things as fashioned by the mortal mind. Therefore, those who know this are able to see the real Buddha.

2.   But the mind that creates its surroundings is never free from memories, fears or laments, not only in the past but in the present and the future, because they have arisen from ignorance and greed.

It is from ignorance and greed that the world of delusion is born, and all the vast complexity of co-ordinating causes and conditions exists within the mind and nowhere else.

Both life and death arise from the mind and exist within the mind. Hence, when the mind that concerns itself with life and death passes on, the world of life and death passes with it.

　心はたくみな絵師のように、さまざまな世界を描き出す。
この世の中で心のはたらきによって作り出されないものは何
一つない。心のように仏もそうであり、仏のように人びとも
そうである。だから、すべてのものを描き出すということに
おいて、心と仏と人びとと、この三つのものに差別はない。

　すべてのものは、心から起こると、仏は正しく知っている。
だから、このように知る人は、真実の仏を見ることになる。

　2．ところが、この心は常に恐れ悲しみ悩んでいる。すで
に起こったことを恐れ、まだ起こらないことをも恐れている。
なぜなら、この心の中に無明と病的な愛着とがあるからであ
る。
　　　　　　　　　＊じみょう

　この貪りの心から迷いの世界が生まれ、迷いの世界のさま
　　　　＊
ざまな因縁も、要約すれば、みな心そのものの中にある。
　しさば

　生も死も、ただ心から起こるのであるから、迷いの生死に
かかわる心が滅びると、迷いの生死は尽きる。
　　　　　　　　　　　　　　　　　　　しょうじ

An unenlightened life rises from a mind that is bewildered by its own world of delusion. If we learn that there is no world of delusion outside the mind, the bewildered mind becomes clear; and because we cease to create impure surroundings, we attain Enlightenment.

In this way the world of life and death is created by the mind, is in bondage to the mind, is ruled by the mind; the mind is the master of every situation. The world of suffering is brought about by the deluded mortal mind.

3. Therefore, all things are primarily controlled and ruled by the mind, and are created up by the mind. As the wheels follow the ox that draws the cart, so does suffering follow the person who speaks and acts with an impure mind.

But if a man speaks and acts with a good mind, happiness follows him like his shadow. Those who act in evil are followed by the thought, "I have done wrong," and the memory of the act is stored to work out its inevitable retribution in the lives to follow. But those who act from good motives are made happy by the thought, "I have done good," and are made happier by the thought that the good act will bring continuing happiness in the lives to follow.

　迷いの世界はこの心から起こり、迷いの心で見るので、迷いの世界となる。心を離れて迷いの世界がないと知れば、汚れを離れてさとりも得んであろう。

　このように、この世界は心に導かれ、心に引きずられ、心の支配を受けている。迷いの心によって、悩みに満ちた世間が現われる。

　3．すべてのものは、みな心を先とし、心を主とし、心から成っている。汚れた心でものを言い、また身で行うと、苦しみがその人に従うのは、ちょうど牽く牛に車が従うようなものである。

　しかし、もし善い心でものを言い、または身で行うと、楽しみがその人に従うのは、ちょうど影が形に添うようなものである。悪い行いをする人は、この世では、悪いことをしたと苦しみ、後の世では、その悪い報いを受けてますます苦しむ。
　善い行いをする人は、この世において、善いことをしたと楽しみ、後の世では、その善い報いを受けてますます楽しむ。

If the mind is impure, it will cause the feet to stumble along a rough and difficult road; there will be many a fall and much pain. But if the mind is pure, the path will be smooth and the journey peaceful.

One who is to enjoy the purity of both body and mind walks the path to Buddhahood, breaking the net of selfish, impure thoughts and evil desires. He who is calm in mind acquires peacefulness and thus is able to cultivate his mind day and night with more diligence.

III
REAL STATE OF THINGS

1. Since everything in this world is brought about by causes and conditions, there can be no fundamental distinctions among things. The apparent distinctions exist because of people's absurd and discriminating thoughts.

In the sky there is no distinction of east and west; people create the distinctions out of their own minds and then believe them to be true.

Mathematical numbers from one to infinity are each complete numbers, and each in itself carries no distinction of quantity; but people make the discrimination for their own convenience, so as to be able to indicate vary-

この心が濁ると、その道は平らでなくなり、そのために倒れなければならない。また、心が清らかであるならば、その道は平らになり、安らかになる。

身と心との清らかさを楽しむものは、悪魔の網を破って仏の大地を歩むものである。心の静かな人は安らかさを得て、ますます努めて夜も昼も心を修めるであろう。

第3節　真実のすがた

1. この世のすべてのものは、みな縁によって現われたものであるから、もともと差別はない。差別を見るのは、人びとの偏見である。

大空に東西の差別がないのに、人びとは東西の差別をつけ、東だ西だと執着する。

数はもともと、一から無限の数まで、それぞれ完全な数であって、量には多少の差別はないのであるけれども、人びとは欲の心からはからって、多少の差別をつける。

ing amounts.

Inherently there are no distinctions between the process of life and the process of destruction; people make a discrimination and call one birth and the other death. In action there is no discrimination between right and wrong, but people make a distinction for their own convenience.

Buddha keeps away from these discriminations and looks upon the world as upon a passing cloud. To Buddha every definitive thing is illusion; He knows that whatever the mind grasps and throws away is insubstantial; thus He transcends the pitfalls of images and discriminative thought.

2. People grasp at things for their own imagined convenience and comfort; they grasp at wealth and treasure and honors; they cling desperately to mortal life.

They make arbitrary distinctions between existence and non-existence, good and bad, right and wrong. For people, life is a succession of graspings and attachments, and then, because of this, they must assume the illusions of pain and suffering.

Once there was a man on a long journey who came

もともと生もなければ滅もないのに、生死の差別を見、ま
た、人間の行為それ自体には善もなければ悪もないのに、善
悪の差別を見るのが、人びとの偏見である。

*仏はこの差別を離れて、世の中は空に浮かぶ雲のような、
また幻のようなもので、捨てるも取るもみなむなしいことで
あると見、心のはからいを離れている。

2．人ははからいから、すべてのものに執着する。富に執
着し、財に執着し、名に執着し、命に執着する。

有無、善悪、正邪、すべてのものにとらわれて迷いを重ね
苦しみと悩みとを招く。

ここに、ひとりの人がいて、長い旅を続け、とあるところ
で大きな河を見て、こう思った。この河のこちらの岸は危い
が、向こう岸は安らかに見える。そこで筏を作り、その筏に

to a river. He said to himself: "This side of the river is very difficult and dangerous to walk on, and the other side seems easier and safer, but how shall I get across?" So he built a raft out of branches and reeds and safely crossed the river. Then he thought to himself: "This raft has been very useful to me in crossing the river; I will not abandon it to rot on the bank, but will carry it along with me." And thus he voluntarily assumed an unnecessary burden. Can this man be called a wise man?

This parable teaches that even a good thing, when it becomes an unnecessary burden, should be thrown away; much more so if it is a bad thing. Buddha made it the rule of his life to avoid useless and unnecessary discussions.

3. Things do not come and go; neither do they appear and disappear; therefore, one does not get things or lose things.

Buddha teaches that things neither appear nor disappear since they transcend both the affirmation of existence and the denial of existence. That is, everything being a concordance and succession of causes and conditions, a thing in itself does not exist, so it can be said that it is non-existent. At the same time, because it has a relative connection with causes and conditions, it

よって、向こうの岸に安らかに着くことができた。そこで「こ
の筏は、わたしを安らかにこちらの岸へ渡してくれた。大変
役に立った筏である。だから、この筏を捨てることなく、肩
に担いで、行く先へ持って行こう。」と思ったのである。

　このとき、この人は筏に対して、しなければならないこと
をしたといわれるであろうか。そうではない。

　この比喩は、「正しいことさえ執着すべきではなく、捨て
離れなければならない。まして、正しくないことは、なおさ
ら捨てなければならない。」ということを示している。

　3．すべてのものは、来ることもなく、去ることもなく、
生ずることもなく、滅することもなく、したがって得ること
もなければ、失うこともない。

　仏は、「すべてのものは有無の範疇を離れているから、有
にあらず、無にあらず、生ずることもなく、滅することもな
い。」と説く。すなわち、すべてのものは因縁から成っていて、
ものそれ自体の本性は実在性がないから、有にあらずといい、
また因縁から成っているので無でもないから、無にあらずと

can be said that it is not non-existent.

To adhere to a thing because of its form is the source of delusion. If the form is not grasped and adhered to, this false imagination and absurd delusion will not occur. Enlightenment is seeing this truth and being free from such a foolish delusion.

The world, indeed, is like a dream and the treasures of the world are an alluring mirage. Like the apparent distances in a picture, things have no reality in themselves but are like heat haze.

4. To believe that things created by an incalculable series of causes can last forever is a serious mistake and is called the theory of permanency; but it is just as great a mistake to believe that things completely disappear; this is called the theory of non-existence.

These categories of everlasting life and death, and existence and non-existence, do not apply to the essential nature of things, but only to their appearances as they are observed by defiled human eyes. Because of human desire, people become related and attached to these appearances; but in the essential nature of things, they are free from all such discriminations and attachments.

いうのである。

　ものの姿を見て、これに執着するのは、迷いの心を招く原因となる。もしも、ものの姿を見ても執着しないならば、はからいは起こらない。さとりは、このまことの道理を見て、はからいの心を離れることである。

　まことに世は夢のようであり、財宝もまた幻のようなものである。絵に見える高低と同じく、見えるけれども、あるのではない。すべては陽炎（かげろう）のようなものである。

　4．無量の因縁によって現われたものが、永久にそのまま存在すると信ずるのは、常見（じょうけん）という誤った見方である。また、まったくなくなると信ずるのは、断見（だんけん）という誤った見方である。

　この断（だん）・常（じょう）・有（う）・無（む）は、ものそのものの姿ではなく、人の執着から見た姿である。すべてのものは、もともとこの執着の姿を離れている。

The Theory of Mind-only and the Real State of Things

Since everything is created by a series of causes and conditions, the appearances of things are constantly changing; that is, there is no consistency about it as there should be about authentic substances. It is because of this constant changing of appearances that we liken things to a mirage and a dream. But, in spite of this constant changing in appearances, things, in their essential spiritual nature, are constant and changeless.

To a man a river seems like a river, but to a hungry demon which sees fire in water, it may seem to be like fire. Therefore, to speak to a man about a river existing would have some sense, but to the demon it would have no meaning.

In like manner, it can be said that things are like illusions; they can be said neither to be existent nor non-existent.

Further, it is a mistake to identify this passing life for the changeless life of truth. Yet it can not be said that, apart from this world of change and appearance, there is another world of permanence and truth. It is a mistake to regard this world as either a temporal world or as a real one.

But ignorant people of this world assume that this is a real world and proceed to act upon that absurd

　ものはすべて縁によって起こったものであるから、みなう
つり変わる。実体を持っているもののように永遠不変ではな
い。うつり変わるので、幻のようじあり、陽炎のようではあ
るが、しかも、また、同時に、そのままで真実である。うつ
り変わるままに永遠不変なのである。

　川は人にとっては川と見えるけれども、水を火と見る餓鬼
にとっては、川とは見えない。だから、川は餓鬼にとっては
「ある」とはいえず、人にとっては「ない」とはいえない。

　これと同じように、すべてのものは、みな「ある」ともい
えず、「ない」ともいえない、幻のようなものである。

　しかも、この幻のような世界を離れて、真実の世も永遠不
変の世もないのであるから、この世を、仮のものと見るのも
誤り、実の世と見るのも誤りである。

　ところが、世の人びとは、この誤りのもとは、この世の上に
あると見ているが、この世がすでに幻とすれば、幻にはからう

assumption. But as this world is only an illusion, their acts, being based upon error, only lead them into harm and suffering.

A wise man, recognizing that the world is but an illusion, does not act as if it were real, so he escapes the suffering.

IV
THE MIDDLE WAY

1. To those who choose the path that leads to Enlightenment, there are two extremes that should be carefully avoided. First, there is the extreme of indulgence in the desires of the body. Second, there is the opposite extreme that comes to one who wants to renounce this life and to go to an extreme of ascetic discipline, torturing one's body and mind unreasonably.

The Noble Path, that transcends these two extremes and leads to Enlightenment and wisdom and peace of mind, may be called the Middle Way. What is the Middle Way? It consists of the Eightfold Noble Path: right view, right thought, right speech, right behavior, right livelihood, right effort, right mindfulness, and right concentration.

心があって、人に誤りを生じさせるはずはない。誤りは、この道理を知らず、仮の世と考え、実の世と考える愚かな人の心に起こる。

＊智慧ある人は、この道理をさとって、幻を幻と見るから、ついにこの誤りを犯すことはない。

第4節　かたよらない道

1. 道を修めるものとして、避けなければならない二つの＊偏った生活がある。その一は、欲に負けて、欲にふける卑しい生活であり、その二は、いたずらに自分の心身を責めさいなむ苦行の生活である。

　この二つの偏った生活を離れて、心眼を開き、＊智慧を進め、さとりに導く＊中道の生活がある。

　この中道の生活とは何であるか。正しい見方、正しい思い、正しいことば、正しい行い、正しい生活、正しい努力、正しい記憶、正しい心の統一、この八つの正しい道である。

As has been said, all things appear or disappear by reason of an endless series of causes. Ignorant people see life as either existence or non-existence, but wise men see beyond both existence and non-existence to something that transcends them both; this is an observation of the Middle Way.

2. Suppose a log is floating in a river. If the log does not become grounded, or sink, or is not taken out by a man, or does not decay, ultimately it will reach the sea. Life is like this log caught in the current of a great river. If a person does not become attached to a life of self-indulgence, or, by renouncing life, does not become attached to a life of self-torture; if a person does not become proud of his virtues or does not become attached to his evil acts; if in his search for Enlightenment he does not become contemptuous of delusion, nor fear it, such a person is following the Middle Way.

The important thing in following the path to Enlightenment is to avoid being caught and entangled in any extreme, that is, always to follow the Middle Way.

Knowing that things neither exist nor do not exist, remembering the dream-like nature of everything, one should avoid being caught by pride of personality or praise for good deeds; or caught and entangled by anything else.

　すべてのものは縁によって生滅するものであるから、有と
無とを離れている。愚かな者は、あるいは有と見、あるいは
無と見るが、正しい智慧の見るところは、有と無とを離れて
いる。これが中道の正しい見方である。

　２．一本の材木が、大きな河を流れているとする。その材
木が、右左の岸に近づかず、中流にも沈まず、陸にも上らず、
人にも取られず、渦にも巻き込まれず、内から腐ることもな
ければ、その材木はついに海に流れ入るであろう。

　この材木のたとえのように、内にも外にもとらわれず、有
にも無にもとらわれず、正にも邪にもとらわれず、迷いを離
れ、さとりにこだわらず、中流に身をまかせるのが、道を修
めるものの中道の見方、中道の生活である。

　道を修める生活にとって大事なことは、両極端にとらわれ
ず、常に中道を歩むことである。

　すべてのものは、生ずることもなく、滅することもなく、
きまった性質のないものと知ってとらわれず、自分の行って
いる善にもとらわれず、すべてのものに縛られてはならない。

If a person is to avoid being caught in the current of his desires, he must learn at the very beginning not to grasp at things lest he should become accustomed to them and attached to them. He must not become attached to existence nor to non-existence, to anything inside or outside, neither to good things nor to bad things, neither to right nor to wrong.

If he becomes attached to things, just at that moment, all at once, the life of delusion begins. The one who follows the Noble Path to Enlightenment will not maintain regrets, neither will he cherish anticipations, but, with an equitable and peaceful mind, will meet what comes.

3. Enlightenment has no definite form or nature by which it can manifest itself; so in Enlightenment itself, there is nothing to be enlightened.

Enlightenment exists solely because of delusion and ignorance; if they disappear, so will Enlightenment. And the opposite is true also: delusion and ignorance exist because of Enlightenment; when Enlightenment ceases, ignorance and delusion will cease also.

Therefore, be on guard against thinking of Enlightenment as a "thing" to be grasped at, lest it, too, should become an obstruction. When the mind that was in

　とらわれないとは握りしめないこと、執着しないことである。道を修める者は、死を恐れず、また、生をも願わない。この見方、あの見方と、どのような見方のあとをも追わないのである。

　人が執着の心を起こすとき、たちまち、迷いの生活が始まる。だから、さとりへの道を歩むものは、握りしめず、取らず、とどまらないのが、とらわれのない生活である。

　３．さとりにはきまった形やものがないから、さとることはあるがさとられるものはない。

　迷いがあるからさとりというのであって、迷いがなくなればさとりもなくなる。迷いを離れてさとりはなく、さとりを離れて迷いはない。

　だから、さとりのあるのはなお障げとなる。闇があるから照らすということがあり、闇がなくなれば照らすということ

darkness becomes enlightened, it passes away, and with its passing, the thing which we call Enlightenment passes also.

As long as people desire Enlightenment and grasp at it, it means that delusion is still with them; therefore, those who are following the way to Enlightenment must not grasp at it, and if they reach Enlightenment they must not linger in it.

When people attain Enlightenment in this sense, it means that everything is Enlightenment itself as it is; therefore, people should follow the path to Enlightenment until in their thoughts, worldly passions and Enlightenment become identical as they are.

4.   This concept of universal oneness — that things in their essential nature have no distinguishing marks — is called "Śūnyatā " Śūnyatā means non-substantiality, the un-born, having no self-nature, no duality. It is because things in themselves have no form or characteristics that we can speak of them as neither being born nor being destroyed. There is nothing about the essential nature of things that can be described in terms of discrimination; that is why things are called non-substantial.

As has been pointed out, all things appear and

もなくなる。照らすことと照らされるものと、ともになくなってしまうのである。

まことに、道を修めるものは、さとってさとりにとどまらない。さとりのあるのはなお迷いだからである。

この境地に至れば、すべては、迷いのままにさとりであり、闇のままに光である。すべての煩悩*がそのままさとりであるところまで、さとりきらなければならない。

4．ものが平等であって差別のないことを空*という。ものそれ自体の本質は、実体がなく、生ずることも、滅することもなく、それはことばでいい表わすことができないから、空というのである。

すべてのものは互いに関係して成り立ち、互いによりあっ

disappear because of causes and conditions. Nothing ever exists entirely alone; everything is in relation to everything else.

Wherever there is light, there is shadow; wherever there is length, there is shortness; wherever there is white, there is black. Just like these, as the self-nature of things can not exist alone, they are called non-substantial.

By the same reasoning, Enlightenment can not exist apart from ignorance, nor ignorance apart from Enlightenment. Since things do not differ in their essential nature, there can be no duality.

5. People habitually think of themselves as being connected with birth and death, but in reality there are no such conceptions.

When people are able to realize this truth, they have realized the truth of the non-duality of birth and death.

It is because people cherish the idea of an ego-personality that they cling to the idea of possession; but since there is no such thing as an "ego," there can be no such things as possessions. When people are able to realize this truth, they will be able to realize the truth of "non-duality."

て存在するものであり、ひとりで成り立つものではない。

　ちょうど、光と影、長さと短かさ、白と黒のようなもので、ものそれ自体の本質が、ただひとりであり得るものではないから無自性(むじしょう)という。

　また、迷いのほかにさとりがなく、さとりのほかに迷いがない。これら二つは、互いに相違するものではないから、ものには二つの相反した姿があるのではない。

　5. 人はいつも、ものの生ずることと、滅することとを見るのであるが、ものにはもともと生ずることがないのであるから、滅することもない。

　このものの真実の姿を見る眼を得て、ものに生滅の二つのないことを知り別のものではないという真理をさとるのである。

　人は我(が)があると思うから、わがものに執着する。しかし、もともと、我がないのであるから、わがもののあるはずがない。我とわがもののないことを知って、別のものではないという真理をさとるのである。

People cherish the distinction of purity and impurity; but in the nature of things, there is no such distinction, except as it rises from false and absurd images in their mind.

In a like manner people make a distinction between good and evil, but good and evil do not exist separately. Those who are following the path to Enlightenment recognize no such duality, and it leads them to neither praise the good and condemn the evil, nor despise the good and condone the evil.

People naturally fear misfortune and long for good fortune; but if the distinction is carefully studied, misfortune often turns out to be good fortune and good fortune to be misfortune. The wise man learns to meet the changing circumstances of life with an equitable spirit, being neither elated by success nor depressed by failure. Thus one realizes the truth of non-duality.

Therefore, all the words that express relations of duality — such as existence and non-existence, worldly-passions and true-knowledge, purity and impurity, good and evil — none of these terms of contrast in one's thinking are expressed or recognized in their true nature. When people keep free from such terms and from the emotions engendered by them, they realize Śūnyatā's universal truth.

　人は清らかさと汚れとがあると思って、この二つにこだわる。しかし、ものにはもともと、清らかさもなければ汚れもなく、清らかさも汚れも、ともに人が心のはからいの上に作ったものにすぎない。

　人は善と悪とを、もともと別なものと思い、善悪にこだわっている。しかし、単なる善もなく、単なる悪もない。さとりの道に入った人はこの善悪はもともと別ではないと知って、その真理をさとるのである。

　人は不幸を恐れて幸福を望む。しかし、真実の智慧をもってこの二つをながめると、不幸の状態がそのままに、幸福となることがわかる。それだから、不幸がそのままに幸福であるとさとって、心身にまとわりついて自由を束縛する迷いも真実の自由も特別にはないと知って、こうして、人はその真理をさとるのである。

　だから、有と無といい、迷いとさとりといい、実と不実といい、正と邪といっても、実は相反した二つのものがあるのではなく、まことの姿においては、言うことも示すことも、識ることもできない。このことばやはからいを離れることが必要である。人がこのようなことばやはからいを離れたとき、真実の空をさとることができる。

6. Just as the pure and fragrant lotus flower grows out of the mud of a swamp rather than out of the clean loam of an upland field, so from the muck of worldly passions springs the pure Enlightenment of Buddhahood. Even the mistaken views of heretics and the delusions of worldly passions may be the seeds for Buddhahood.

If a diver is to secure pearls he must descend to the bottom of the sea, braving all dangers of jagged coral and vicious sharks. So man must face the perils of worldly passion if he is to secure the precious pearl of Enlightenment. He must first be lost among the mountainous crags of egoism and selfishness, before there will awaken in him the desire to find a path that will lead him to Enlightenment.

There is a legend of a hermit who had such a great desire to find the true path that he climbed a mountain of swords and threw himself into fire, enduring them because of his hope. He who is willing to risk the perils of the path will find a cool breeze blowing on the sword-bristling mountains of selfishness and among the fires of hatred and, in the end, will come to realize that the selfishness and worldly passions against which he has struggled and suffered are Enlightenment itself.

7. Buddha's teaching leads us to non-duality, from the

6. 例えば、蓮華が清らかな高原や陸地に生えず、かえって汚い泥の中に咲くように、迷いを離れてさとりがあるのではなく、誤った見方や迷いから仏の種が生まれる。

あらゆる危険をおかして海の底に降りなければ、価も知れないほどにすばらしい宝は得られないように、迷いの泥海の中に入らなければ、さとりの宝を得ることはできない。山のように大きな、我への執着を持つ者であって、はじめて道を求める心も起こし、さとりもついに生ずるであろう。

だから、昔、仙人が刃の山に登っても傷つかず、自分の身を大火の中に投げ入れても焼け死なず、すがすがしさを覚えたというように、道を求める心があれば、名誉利欲の刃の山や、憎しみの大火の中にも、さとりの涼しい風が吹き渡ることであろう。

7. 仏の教えは、相反する二つを離れて、それらが別のも

discriminating concept of two conflicting points of view. It is a mistake for people to seek a thing supposed to be good and right, and to flee from another supposed to be bad and evil.

If people insist that all things are empty and transitory, it is just as great a mistake to insist that all things are real and do not change. If a person becomes attached to his ego-personality, it is a mistake because it cannot save him from dissatisfaction or suffering. If he believes there is no ego, it is also a mistake and it would be useless for him to practise the Way of Truth. If people assert that everything is suffering, it is also a mistake; if they assert that everything is happiness, that is a mistake, too. Buddha teaches the Middle Way transcending these prejudiced concepts, where duality merges into oneness.

のではないという真理をさとるのである。もしも、相反する
二つの中の一つを取って執着すれば、たとえ、それが善であ
っても、正であっても、誤ったものゆになる。

　もしも、人がすべてのものはうつり変わるという考えにと
らわれるならば、これも間違った考えにおちいるものであり、
また、もしも、すべてのものは変わらないという考えにとら
われるならば、これももとより間違った考えなのである。も
しまた人が我があると執着すれば、それは誤った考えで、常
に苦しみを離れることができない。もしも我がないと執着す
るならば、それも間違った考えで、道を修めても効果がない。
　また、すべてのものはただ苦しみであるととらわれれば、
これも間違った考えであり、また、すべてのものはただ楽し
みだけであるといえば、これも間違った考えである。仏の教
えは中道であって、これらの二つの偏(かたよ)りから離れている。

CHAPTER THREE

BUDDHA-NATURE

I

THE MIND OF PURITY

1.   Among humans there are many kinds and degrees of mentality: some are wise, some are foolish, some are good-natured, some are bad-tempered, some are easily led, some are difficult to lead, some possess pure minds and some have minds that are defiled; but these differences are negligible when it comes to the attainment of Enlightenment. The world is like a lotus pond filled with many varieties of the plant; there are blossoms of many different tints. Some are white, some pink, some blue, some yellow; some grow under water, some spread their leaves on the water, and some raise their leaves above the water. Mankind has many more differences. There is the difference of sex, but it is not an essential difference, for, with proper training, both men and women may attain Enlightenment.

To be a trainer of elephants, one must possess five qualifications: good health, confidence, diligence, sincerity of purpose, and wisdom. To follow the Buddha's Noble Path to Enlightenment, one must have the same

第3章　さとりの種

第1節　清らかな心

1. 人にはいろいろの種類がある。心の曇りの少ないもの
もあれば、曇りの多いものもあり、賢いものもあれば、愚か
なものもある。

善い性質のものもあれば、悪い性質のものもあり、教えや
すいものもあれば、教えにくいものもある。

例えていうと、青・赤・黄・白・色さまざまな蓮の池があ
って、水中に生え、水中に育って、水の表面にでない蓮もあ
れば、水面にとどまる蓮もあり、水面を離れて、水にもぬれ
ない蓮もあるようなものである。

この差別の上に、さらにまた、男・女の区別があるが、し
かし、人の本性として差別があるのではない。男が道を修め
てさとりを得るように、女もまた道を修めれば、しかるべき
心の道すじを経て、さとりに至るであろう。

象を扱う術を学ぶのには、信念と健康をもち、勤勉であっ
て、偽りがなく、その上に智慧がなければならない。仏に従

five good qualities. If one has these qualities, then regardless of gender, it is possible to attain Enlightenment. It need not take long to learn Buddha's teaching, for all humans possess a nature that has an affinity for Enlightenment.

2.   In the practice of the way to Enlightenment, people see the Buddha with their own eyes and believe in Buddha with their own minds. The eyes that see Buddha and the mind that believes in Buddha are the same eyes and the same mind that, until that day, had wandered about in the world of birth and death.

If a king is plagued by bandits, he must find out where their camp is before he can attack them. So, when a man is beset by worldly passions, he should first ascertain their origins.

When a man is in a house and opens his eyes he will first notice the interior of the room and only later will he see the view outside the windows. In like manner we can not have the eye notice external things before there is recognition by the eye of the things in the house.

If there is a mind within the body, it ought first to know the things inside the body; but generally people are interested in external things and seem to know or care

ってさとりを得るにも、やはりこの五つがなければならない。この五つがあれば、男でも女でも、仏の教えを学ぶのに長い年月を要しない。これは、人にはみな、さとるべき性質がそなわっているからである。

2. さとりの道において、人はおのれの眼をもって仏を見、心をもって仏を信ずる。それと同じく、人をして生死の巷に今日まで流転させたのも、また、この眼と心である。

国王が、侵入した賊を討とうとするとき、何よりも先に、その賊のありかを知ることが必要であるように、いま迷いをなくそうとするのにも、まずその眼と心のありかを確かめなければならない。

人が室内にいて目を開けば、まず、部屋の中のものを見、やがて窓を通して、外の景色を見る。部屋の内のものを見ないで、外のものばかりを見る目はない。

ところが、もしもこの身の内に心があるならば、何よりも先に、身の内のことを詳しく知らなければならないはずであるのに、人びとは、身の外のことだけをよく知っていて、

little for the things within the body.

If the mind is located outside the body, it should keep in contact with the needs of the body. But, in fact, the body feels what the mind knows, and the mind knows what the body feels. Therefore, it can not be said that the human mind is outside of the body. Where, then, does the substance of the mind exist?

3. From the unknown past, being conditioned by their own deeds and deluded by two fundamental misconceptions, people have wandered about in ignorance.

First, they believed that the discriminating mind, which lies at the root of this life of birth and death, was their real nature; and, second, they did not know that, hidden behind the discriminating mind, they possessed a pure mind of Enlightenment which is their true nature.

When a man closes his fist and raises his arm, the eyes see it and the mind discriminates it, but the mind that discriminates it is not the true mind.

The discriminating mind is only a mind for the discrimination of imagined differences that greed and other moods relating to the self have created. The discriminating mind is subject to causes and conditions, it

身の内のことについては、ほとんど何ごとも知ることができない。

　また、もしも心が身の外にあるとするならば、身と心とが互いに離れて、心の知るところを身は知らず、身の知るところを心は知らないはずである。ところが、事実は、心の知るところを身が感じ、身に感ずるところを心はよく知っているから、心は身の外にあるということもできない。いったい、心の本体はどこにあるのであろうか。

　3．もともと、すべての人びとが、始めも知れない昔から、業のきずなに縛られて、迷いを重ねているのは、二つのもとを知らないからである。

　一つには生死のもとである迷いの心を、自己の本性と思っていること。二つには、さとりの本性である清浄な心が、迷いの心の裏側に隠されたまま自己の上にそなわっていることを知らないことである。

拳をかためて臂をあげると、目はこれを見て心はこのことを知る。しかし、その知る心は、真実の心ではない。

　はからいの心は欲から起こり、自分の都合をはからう心で

is empty of any self-substance, and it is constantly changing. But, since people believe that this mind is their real mind, the delusion enters into the causes and conditions that produce suffering.

A man opens his hand and the mind perceives it; but what is it that moves? Is it the mind, or is it the hand? Or is it neither of them? If the hand moves, then the mind moves accordingly, and vice versa; but the moving mind is only a superficial appearance of mind: it is not the true and fundamental mind.

4. Fundamentally, everyone has a pure clean mind, but it is usually covered by the defilement and dust of worldly desires which have arisen from one's circumstances. This defiled mind is not of the essence of one's nature: something has been added, like an intruder or even a guest in a home, but not its host.

The moon is often hidden by clouds, but it is not moved by them and its purity remains untarnished. Therefore, people must not be deluded into thinking that this defiled mind is that of their own true mind.

They must continually remind themselves of this fact by striving to awaken within themselves the pure and unchanging fundamental mind of Enlightenment. Being caught by a changing, defiled mind and being deluded by

あり、縁に触れて起こる心であって、真実の本体のない、うつり変わる心である。この心を、実体のある心と思うところに、迷いが起こる。

次に、その拳を開くと、心は拳の開いたことを知る。動くものは手であろうか、心であろうか、それとも、そのいずれでもないのか。

手が動けば心も動き、また、心の動きにつれて手も動く。しかし、動く心は、心の表面であって根本の心ではない。

4．すべての人びとには、清浄の本心がある。それが外の
*因縁によって起こる迷いのちりのために覆われている。しかし、あくまでも迷いの心は従であって主ではない。

月は、しばらく雲に覆われても、雲に汚されることもなく、また動かされることもない。

だから、人は浮動するちりのような迷いの心を自分の本性と思ってはならない。

また、人は、動かず、汚されないさとりの本心に目覚めて、真実の自己に帰らなければならない。浮動する迷いの心にと

their own perverted ideas, they wander about in a world of delusion.

The disturbances and defilements of the human mind are aroused by greed as well as by its reactions to the changing circumstances.

The mind that is not disturbed by things as they occur, that remains pure and tranquil under all circumstances, is the true mind and should be the master.

We cannot say that an inn disappears just because the guest is out of sight; neither can we say that the true self has disappeared when the defiled mind which has been aroused by the changing circumstances of life has disappeared. That which changes with changing conditions is not the true nature of mind.

5.   Let us think of a lecture hall that is light while the sun is shining but is dark after the sun goes down.

We can think of the light departing with the sun and the dark coming with the night, but we cannot so think of the mind that perceives lightness and darkness. The mind that is susceptible to lightness and darkness can not be given back to anybody; it can only revert to a truer nature which is its fundamental nature.

らわれ、さかさまの見方に追われているので、人は迷いの巷（ちまた）
をさまようのである。

　人の心の迷いや汚れは、欲とその変化する外界の縁に触れ
て起こるものである。

　この縁の来ること去ることに関係なく、永久に動かず滅びな
い心、これが人の心の本体であって、また主（あるじ）でもある。

　客が去ったからといって、宿屋がなくなったとはいえない
ように、縁によって生じたり滅したりするはからいの心がな
くなったからといって、自分がなくなったとはいえない。外
の縁によってうつり変わるはからいは、心の本体ではない。

　5．ここに講堂があって、太陽が出て明るくなり、太陽が
隠れて暗くなるとする。

　明るさは太陽に返し、暗さは夜に返すこともできよう。し
かし、その明るさや暗さを知る力は、どこにも返すことはで
きない。それは心の本性、本体に返すよりほかに道はない。

It is only a "temporary" mind that momentarily notes changes of lightness and darkness as the sun rises and sets.

It is only a "temporary" mind that has different feelings from moment to moment with the changing circumstances of life; it is not the real and true mind. The fundamental and true mind which realizes the lightness and the darkness is the true nature of man.

The temporary feelings of good and evil, love and hatred, that have been aroused by surroundings and changing external conditions, are only momentary reactions that have their cause in the defilement accumulated by the human mind.

Behind the desires and worldly passions which the mind entertains, there abides, clear and undefiled, the fundamental and true essence of mind.

Water is round in a round receptacle and square in a square one, but water itself has no particular shape. People often forget this fact, if they ever even realize it.

People see this good and that bad, they like this and dislike that, and they discriminate existence from non-existence; and then, being caught in these entanglements and becoming attached to them, they suffer.

太陽が現われて、明るいと見るのもひとときの心であり、太陽が隠れて、暗いと見るのもひとときの心である。

このように、明暗という外の縁に引かれて、明暗を知る心が起こるが、明暗を知る心は、ひとときの心であって、心の本体ではなく、その明暗を知る力の根本は、心の本体である。

外の因縁に引かれて生じたり滅したりする善悪・愛憎の念は、人の心に積まれた汚れによって起こるひとときの心なのである。

*煩悩のちりに包まれて、しかも染まることも、汚れることもない、本来清浄な心がある。

まるい器に水を入れるとまるくなり、四角な器に水を入れると四角になる。しかし、本来、水にまるや四角の形があるのではない。ところが、すべての人びとはこのことを忘れて、水の形にとらわれている。

善し悪しと見、好む好まぬと考え、有り無しと思い、その考えに使われ、その見方に縛られて、外のものを追って苦しんでいる。

If people would only give up their attachments to these imaginary and false discriminations, and restore the purity of their original minds, then both their mind and their body would be free from defilement and suffering; they would know the peacefulness that comes with that freedom.

II
BUDDHA-NATURE

1.   We have spoken of the pure and true mind as being fundamental; it is the Buddha-nature, that is, the seed of Buddhahood.

One can get fire if one holds a lens between the sun and moxa, but where does the fire come from? The lens is at an enormous distance from the sun, but the fire certainly appears upon the moxa by means of the lens. But if the moxa would not have the nature to kindle, there would be no fire.

In a like manner, if the light of Buddha's Wisdom is concentrated upon the human mind, its true nature, which is Buddhahood, will be enkindled, and its light will illuminate the minds of the people with its brightness, and will awaken faith in Buddha. He holds the lens of Wisdom before all human minds and thus their faith may be quickened.

　縛られた見方を外の縁に返し、縛られることのない自己の本性にたち帰ると、身も心も、何ものにもさえぎられることのない、自由な境地が得られるであろう。

第2節　かくれた宝

　1. 清浄の本心とは、言葉を変えていえば仏性＊である。仏性とは、すなわち仏の種である。

　レンズを取って太陽に向かい、もぐさを当てて火を求めるときに、火はどこから来るのであろうか。太陽とレンズとはあいへだたること遠く、合することはできないけれども、太陽の火がレンズを縁とし、もぐさの上に現われたことは疑いを入れない。また、もしも太陽があっても、もぐさに燃える性質がなければ、もぐさに火は起こらない。

　いま、仏を生む根本である仏性のもぐさに、仏の智慧＊のレンズを当てれば、仏の火は、仏性の開ける信の火として、人びというもぐさの上に燃えあがる。

　仏はその智慧のレンズを取って世界に当てられるから、世をあげて信の火が燃えあがるのである。

2. Often people disregard the affinity of their true minds for Buddha's enlightened wisdom, and, because of it, are caught by the entanglement of worldly passions, becoming attached to the discrimination of good and evil, and then lament over their bondage and suffering.

Why is it that people, possessing this fundamental and pure mind, should still cling to illusions and doom themselves to wander about in a world of delusion and suffering, covering their own Buddha-nature while all about them is the light of Buddha's Wisdom?

Once upon a time a man looked into the reverse side of a mirror and, not seeing his face and head, he became insane. How unnecessary it is for a man to become insane merely because he carelessly looks into the reverse side of a mirror!

It is just as foolish and unnecessary for a person to go on suffering because he does not attain Enlightenment where he expects to find it. There is no failure in Enlightenment; the failure lies in those people who, for a long time, have sought Enlightenment in their discriminating minds, not realizing that theirs are not true minds but are imaginary minds that have been caused by the accumulation of greed and illusion covering and hiding their true mind.

2. 人びとは、この本来そなわっているさとりの仏性にそむいて、*煩悩のちりにとらわれ、ものの善し悪しの姿に心を縛られて、不自由に嘆いている。

なぜ、人びとは、本来さとりの心をそなえていながら、このように偽りを生み、仏性の光を隠し、迷いの世界にさまよっているのであろうか。

昔ある男が、ある朝鏡に向かって、自分の顔も頭もないのにあわて驚いた。しかし、顔も頭もなくなったのではなく、それは鏡を裏返しに見ていて、なくなったと思っていたのであった。

さとりに達しようとして達せられないからといって苦しむのは愚かであり、また、必要のないことである。さとりの中に迷いはないのであるが、限りない長い時間に、外のちりに動かされて、妄想を描き、その妄想によって迷いの世界を作り出していたのである。

If the accumulation of false beliefs is cleared away, Enlightenment will appear. But, strange enough, when people attain Enlightenment, they will realize that without false beliefs there could be no Enlightenment.

3.   Buddha-nature is not something that comes to an end. Though wicked men should be born beasts or hungry demons, or fall into hell, they never lose their Buddha-nature.

However buried in the defilement of flesh or concealed at the root of worldly desires and forgotten it may be, the human affinity for Buddhahood is never completely extinguished.

4.   There is an old story told of a man who fell into a drunken sleep. His friend stayed by him as long as he could but, being compelled to go and fearing that he might be in want, the friend hid a jewel in the drunken man's garment. When the drunken man recovered, not knowing that his friend had hid a jewel in his garment, he wandered about in poverty and hunger. A long time afterwards the two men met again and the friend told the poor man about the jewel and advised him to look for it.

Like the drunken man of the story, people wander

　だから、妄想がやめば、さとりはおのずと返ってきて、さとりのほかに妄想があるのではないとわかるようになる。しかも、不思議なことに、ひとたびさとった者には妄想はなく、さとられるものもなかったことに気づくのである。

　3．この仏性は尽きることがない。たとえ畜生に生まれ、餓鬼となって苦しみ、地獄に落ちても、この仏性は絶えることはない。

　汚い体の中にも、汚れた煩悩の底にも、仏性はその光を包み覆われている。

　4．昔、ある人が友の家に行き、酒に酔って眠っているうちに、急用で友は旅立った。友はその人の将来を気づかい、価の高い宝石をその人の着物のえりに縫いこんでおいた。

　そうとは知らず、その人は酔いからさめて他国へとさすらい、衣食に苦しんだ。その後、ふたたびその旧友にめぐり会い、「おまえの着物のえりに縫いこまれている宝石を用いよ。」と教えられた。

　このたとえのように、仏性の宝石は、貪りや瞋りという煩

about suffering in this life of birth and death, unconscious of what is hidden away in their inner nature, pure and untarnished, the priceless treasure of Buddha-nature.

However unconscious people may be of the fact that everyone has within his possession this supreme nature, and however degraded and ignorant they may be, Buddha never loses faith in them because He knows that even in the least of them there are, potentially, all the virtues of Buddhahood.

So Buddha awakens faith in them who are deceived by ignorance and cannot see their own Buddha-nature, leads them away from their illusions and teaches them that originally there is no difference between themselves and Buddhahood.

5.　Buddha is one who has attained Buddhahood and people are those who are capable of attaining Buddhahood; that is all the difference that lies between them.

But if a man thinks that he has attained Enlightenment, he is deceiving himself, for, although he may be moving in that direction, he has not yet reached Buddhahood.

Buddha-nature does not appear without diligent and faithful effort, nor is the task finished until Buddhahood

悩の着物のえりに包まれて、汚されずにいるのである。

　このように、どんな人でも仏の智慧のそなわらないものは
ないから、仏は人びとを見通して、「すばらしいことだ、人
びとはみな仏の智慧と功徳とをそなえている。」とほめたた
える。

　しかも、人びとは愚かさに覆われて、ものごとをさかさま
に見、おのれの仏性を見ることができないから、仏は人びと
に教えて、その妄想を離れさせ、本来、仏と違わないもので
あることを知らせる。

　5．ここでいう仏とはすでに成ってしまった仏であり、人
びとは将来まさに成るべき仏であって、それ以外の相違はな
い。

　しかし、成るべき仏ではあるけれども、仏と成ったのでは
ないから、すでに道を成しとげたかのように考えるなら、そ
れは大きな過ちを犯しているのである。

　仏性はあっても、修めなければ現われず、現われなければ
道を成しとげたのではない。

is attained.

6.   Once upon a time a king gathered some blind men about an elephant and asked them to tell him what an elephant was like. The first man felt a tusk and said an elephant was like a giant carrot; another happened to touch an ear and said it was like a big fan; another touched its trunk and said it was like a pestle; still another, who happened to feel its leg, said it was like a mortar; and another, who grasped its tail said it was like a rope. Not one of them was able to tell the king the elephant's real form.

In a like manner, one might partially describe the nature of man but would not be able to describe the true nature of a human being, the Buddha-nature.

There is only one possible way by which the everlasting nature of man, his Buddha-nature, that can not be disturbed by worldly desires or destroyed by death, can be realized, and that is by the Buddha and the Buddha's noble teaching.

III
BUDDHA-NATURE AND EGOLESSNESS

1.   We have been speaking of Buddha-nature as though

6. 昔、ひとりの王があって、多くの盲人を集め、象に触れさせて、象とはどんなものであるかを、めいめいに言わせたことがある。象の牙に触れた者は、象は大きな人参のようなものであるといい、耳に触れた者は、扇のようなものであるといい、鼻に触れた者は、杵のようなものであるといい、足に触れた者は、臼のようなものであるといい、尾に触れた者は、縄のようなものであると答えた。ひとりとして象そのものをとらえ得た者はなかった。

人を見るのもこれと同じで、人の一部分に触れることができても、その本性である仏性を言い当てることは容易ではない。

死によっても失われず、煩悩の中にあっても汚れず、しかも永遠に滅びることのない仏性を見つけることは、仏と法によるもののほかは、でき得ないのである。

第3節　とらわれを離れて

1. このように、人には仏性があるというと、それは他の

—149—

it were something that could be described, as though it were similar to the "soul" of other teachings, but it is not.

The concept of an "ego-personality" is something that has been imagined by a discriminating mind which first grasped it and then become attached to it, but which must abandon it. On the contrary, Buddha-nature is something indescribable that must first be discovered. In one sense, it resembles an "ego-personality" but it is not the "ego" in the sense of "I am" or "mine."

To believe in the existence of an ego is an erroneous belief that supposes non-existence; to deny Buddha-nature is wrong, for it supposes that existence is non-existence.

This can be explained in a parable. A mother took her sick child to a doctor. The doctor gave the child medicine and instructed the mother not to nurse the child until the medicine was digested.

The mother anointed her breast with something bitter so that the child would keep away from her of his own volition. After the medicine had time enough to be digested, the mother cleansed her breast and let the child suck her. The mother took this method of saving her child out of kindness because she loved the child.

教えでいう我と同じであると思うかも知れないが、それは誤りである。

　我の考えは執着心によって考えられるけれども、さとった人にとっては、我は否定されなければならない執着であり、仏性は開き現わさなければならない宝である。仏性は我に似ているけれども、「われあり」とか「わがもの」とかいう場合の我ではない。

　我があると考えるのは、ないものをあると考える、さかさまの見方であり、仏性を認めないことも、あるものをないと考える、さかさまの見方である。

　例えば、幼子が病にかかって医師にかかるとすると、医師は薬を与えて、この薬のこなれるまでは乳を与えてはならないと言いつける。

　母は乳房ににがいものを塗り、子に乳をいやがらせる。後に、薬のこなれたときに、乳房を洗って、子の口にふくませる。母のこのふるまいは、わが子をいとおしむやさしい心からくるものである。

Like the mother in the parable, Buddha, in order to remove misunderstanding and to break up attachments to an ego-personality, denies the existence of an ego; and when the misunderstanding and attachments are done away with, then He explains the reality of the true mind that is the Buddha-nature.

Attachment to an ego-personality leads people into delusions, but faith in their Buddha-nature leads them to Enlightenment.

It is like the woman in a story to whom a chest was bequeathed. Not knowing that the chest contained gold, she continued to live in poverty until another person opened it and showed her the gold. Buddha opens the minds of people and shows them the purity of their Buddha-nature.

2. If everyone has this Buddha-nature, why is there so much suffering from people cheating one another or killing one another? And why are there so many distinctions of rank and wealth, rich and poor?

There is a story of a wrestler who used to wear an ornament on his forehead of a precious stone. One time when he was wrestling the stone was crushed into the

　ちょうどこのように、世の中の誤った考えを取り去り、我の執着を取り去るために、我はないと説いたが、その誤った見方を取り去ったのち、あらためて仏性があると説いたのである。

　我は迷いに導くものであり、仏性はさとりに至らせるものである。

　家に黄金の箱を持ちながら、それを知らないために、貧しい生活をする女をあわれんで、その黄金の箱を掘り出して与えるように、仏は人びとの仏性を開いて、彼らに見せる。

　2．それなら、人びとは、みなこの仏性をそなえているのに、どうして貴賤・貧富という差別があり、殺したり、欺かれたりするようないとわしいことが起こるのであろうか。

　例えば、宮廷に仕える一力士が、眉間に小さな金剛の珠玉を飾ったまま相撲をとって、その額を打ち、玉が膚の中に隠

flesh of his forehead. He thought he had lost the gem and went to a surgeon to have the wound dressed. When the surgeon came to dress the wound he found the gem embedded in the flesh and covered over with blood and dirt. He held up a mirror and showed the stone to the wrestler.

Buddha-nature is like the precious stone of this story: it becomes covered over by the dirt and dust of other interests and people think that they have lost it, but a good teacher recovers it again for them.

Buddha-nature exists in everyone no matter how deeply it may be covered over by greed, anger and foolishness, or buried by his own deeds and retribution. Buddha-nature can not be lost or destroyed; and when all defilements are removed, sooner or later it will reappear.

Like the wrestler in the story who was shown the gem buried in his flesh and blood by means of a mirror, so people are shown their Buddha-nature, buried beneath their worldly desires and passions, by means of the light of Buddha.

3. Buddha-nature is always pure and tranquil no matter how varied the conditions and surroundings of people may be. Just as milk is always white regardless of the

れてできものを生じた。力士は、玉をなくしたと思い、ただ
そのできものを治すために医師に頼む。医師は一目見て、そ
のできものが膚の中に隠れた玉のせいであると知り、それを
取り出して力士に見せた。

人びとの仏性も煩悩の塵の中に隠れ、見失われているが、
善き師によってふたたび見いだされるものである。

このように、仏性はあっても貪りと瞋りと愚かさのために
覆われ、業と報いとに縛られて、それぞれ迷いの境遇を受け
るのである。しかし、仏性は実際には失われても破壊されて
もおらず、迷いを取り除けばふたたび見いだされるものであ
る。

たとえの中の力士が、医師によって取り出されたその玉を
見たように、人びとも、仏の光によって仏性を見ることであ
ろう。

3. 赤・白・黒と、さまざまに毛色の違った牝牛でも、
乳をしぼると、みな同じ白い色の乳を得るように、境遇が異

color of the cow's hide, either red, white, or black, so it does not matter how differently their deeds may condition people's life or what different effects may follow their acts and thoughts.

There is a fable told in India of a mysterious medical herb that was hidden under the tall grasses of the Himalayas. For a long time men sought for it in vain, but at last a wise man located it by its sweetness. As long as the wise man lived he collected this medical herb in a tub, but after his death, the sweet elixir remained hidden in some far-off spring in the mountains, and the water in the tub turned sour and harmful and of a different taste.

In a like manner Buddha-nature is hidden away beneath the wild growth of worldly passions and can rarely be discovered, but Buddha found it and revealed it to the people, and as they receive it by their varying faculties it tastes differently to each person.

4.   The diamond, the hardest of known substances, cannot be crushed. Sand and stones can be ground to powder but diamonds remain unscatched. Buddha-nature is like the diamond, and thus cannot be broken.

Human nature, both its body and mind, will wear away, but the nature of Buddhahood can not be

なり、生活が異なる、さまざまの人びとも、その業の報いの異なるにもかかわらず、同じ仏性《ぶっしょう》をそなえている。

　例えば、ヒマラヤ山に貴い薬があるが、それは深い草むらの下にあって、人びとはこれを見つけることができない。昔、ひとりの賢人がいて、その香りを尋ねてありかを知り、樋《とい》を作って、その中に薬を集めた。しかし、その人の死後、薬は山にうもれ、樋の中の薬は窩り、流れるところによって、その味を異にした。

　仏性も、このたとえのように、深く煩悩の草むらに覆われているから、人びとはこれを容易に見つけることができない。いまや仏はその草むらを開いて、彼らに示した。仏性の味は一つの甘さであるが、煩悩のためにさまざまの味を出し、人びとはさまざまな生き方をする。

　4．この仏性は金剛石のように堅いから、破壊することはできない。砂や小石に穴をあけることはできても、金剛石に穴をあけることはできない。

　身と心は破られることがあっても、仏性を破ることはできない。

destroyed.

Buddha-nature is, indeed, the most excellent characteristic of human nature. Buddha teaches that, although in human nature there may be endless varieties such as men and women, there is no discrimination with regard to Buddha-nature.

Pure gold is procured by melting ore and removing all impure substances. If people would melt the ore of their minds and remove all the impurities of worldly passion and egoism, they would all recover the same pure Buddha-nature.

　仏性は、実にもっともすぐれた人間の特質である。世に、男はまさり女は劣るとするならわしもあるが、仏の教えにおいては、男女の差別を立てず、ただこの仏性を知ることを尊いとする。

　黄金の粗金を溶かして、そのかすを去り、錬りあげると貴い黄金になる。心の粗金を溶かして煩悩のかすを取り去ると、どんな人でも、みなすべて同一の仏性を開き現わすことができる。

CHAPTER FOUR

HUMAN DEFILEMENTS

I
HUMAN NATURE

1.   There are two kinds of worldly passions that defile and cover the purity of Buddha-nature.

The first is the passion for analysis and discussion by which people become confused in judgement. The second is the passion for emotional experience by which people's values become confused.

Both delusions of reasoning and delusions of practice can be thought of as a classification of all human defilements, but really there are two original worldly predicaments in their bases. The first is ignorance, and the second is desire.

The delusions of reasoning are based upon ignorance, and the delusions of practice are based upon desire, so that the two sets are really one set after all, and together they are the source of all unhappiness.

If people are ignorant they cannot reason correctly

第4章 煩悩(ぼんのう)

第1節 心のけがれ

1. 仏性(ぶっしょう)を覆いつつむ煩悩(ぼんのう)に二種類ある。

一つは知性の煩悩である。二つには感情の煩悩である。

この二つの煩悩は、あらゆる煩悩の根本的な分類であるが、このあらゆる煩悩の根本となるものを求めれば、一つには無明(みょう)、二つには愛欲となる。

この無明と愛欲とは、あらゆる煩悩を生み出す自在の力を持っている。そしてこの二つこそ、すべての煩悩の源なのである。

無明とは無知のことで、ものの道理をわきまえないことで

and safely. As they yield to a desire for existence, graspings, clingings and attachments to everything inevitably follow. It is this constant hunger for every pleasant thing seen and heard that leads people into the delusions of habit. Some people even yield to the desire for the death of the body.

From these primary sources all greed, anger, foolishness, misunderstanding, resentment, jealousy, flattery, deceit, pride, contempt, inebriety, selfishness, have their generations and appearances.

2. Greed rises from wrong ideas of satisfaction; anger rises from wrong ideas concerning the state of one's affairs and surroundings; foolishness rises from the inability to judge what correct conduct is.

These three — greed, anger and foolishness — are called the three fires of the world. The fire of greed consumes those who have lost their true minds through greed; the fire of anger consumes those who have lost their true minds through anger; the fire of foolishness consumes those who have lost their true minds through their failure to hear and to heed the teachings of Buddha.

Indeed, this world is burning up with its many and

ある。愛欲は激しい欲望で、生に対する執着が根本であり、見るもの聞くものすべてを欲しがる欲望ともなり、また転じて、死を願うような欲望ともなる。

この無明と愛欲とをもとにして、これから貪り、瞋り、愚かさ、邪見、恨み、嫉み、へつらい、たぶらかし、おごり、あなどり、ふまじめ、その他いろいろの煩悩が生まれてくる。

2. 貪りの起きるのは、気に入ったものを見て、正しくない考えを持つためである。瞋りの起きるのは、気に入らないものを見て、正しくない考えを持つためである。愚かさはその無知のために、なさなければならないことと、なしてはならないこととを知らないことである。邪見は正しくない教えを受けて、正しくない考えを持つことから起きる。

この貪りと瞋りと愚かさは、世の三つの火といわれる。貪りの火は欲にふけって、真実心を失った人を焼き、瞋りの火は、腹を立てて、生けるものの命を害なう人を焼き、愚かさの火は、心迷って仏の教えを知らない人を焼く。

まことに、この世は、さまざまの火に焼かれている。貪り

various fires. There are fires of greed, fires of anger, fires of foolishness, fires of infatuation and egoism, fires of decrepitude, sickness and death, fires of sorrow, lamentation, suffering and agony. Everywhere these fires are raging. They not only burn the self, but also cause others to suffer and lead them into wrong acts of body, speech and mind. From the wounds that are caused by these fires there issues a pus that infects and poisons those who approach it, and leads them into evil paths.

3. Greed rises in the face of satisfaction; anger rises in the face of dissatisfaction; and foolishness rises from impure thoughts. The evil of greed has little impurity but is hard to remove; the evil of anger has more impurity but is easy to remove; the evil of foolishness has much impurity and is very hard to overcome.

Therefore, people should quench these fires whenever and wherever they appear by correctly judging as to what can give true satisfaction, by strictly controlling the mind in the face of the unsatisfactory things of life, and by ever recalling Buddha's teachings of good-will and kindness. If the mind is filled with wise and pure and unselfish thoughts, there will be no place for worldly passions to take root.

.4. Greed, anger and foolishness are like a fever. If a

の火、瞋りの火、愚かさの火、生・老・病・死の火、憂い・悲しみ・苦しみ・悶えの火、さまざまの火によって炎炎と燃えあがっている。これらの煩悩の火はおのれを焼くばかりでなく、他をも苦しめ、人を身・口・意の三つの悪い行為に導くことになる。しかも、これらの火によってできた傷口のうみは触れたものを毒し、悪道に陥し入れる。

３．貪りは満足を得たい気持ちから、瞋りは満足を得られない気持ちから、愚かさは不浄な考えから生まれる。貪りは罪の汚れは少ないけれども、これを離れることは容易でなく、瞋りは罪の汚れが大きいけれども、これを離れることは早いものである。愚かさは罪の汚れも大きく、またこれを離れることも容易ではない。

したがって、人びとは気に入ったものの姿を見聞きしては正しく思い、気に入らないものの姿を見ては慈しみの心を養い、常に正しく考えて、この三つの火を消さなければならない。もしも、人びとが正しく、清く、無私の心に満ちているならば、煩悩によって惑わされることはない。

４．貪り、瞋り、愚かさは熱のようなものである。どんな

man gets this fever, even if he lies in a comfortable room, he will suffer and be tormented by sleeplessness.

Those who have no such fever have no difficulty in sleeping peacefully, even on a cold winter night, on the ground with only a thin covering of leaves, or on a hot summer's night in a small closed room.

These three — greed, anger and foolishness — are, therefore, the sources of all human woe. To get rid of these sources of woe, one must observe the precepts, must practise concentration of mind and must have wisdom. Observance of the precepts will remove the impurities of greed; right concentration of mind will remove the impurities of anger; and wisdom will remove the impurities of foolishness.

5.   Human desires are endless. It is like the thirst of a man who drinks salt water: he gets no satisfaction and his thirst is only increased.

So it is with a man who seeks to gratify his desires; he only gains increased dissatisfaction and his woes are multiplied.

The gratification of desires never satisfies; it always leaves behind unrest and irritation that can never be allayed, and then, if the gratification of his desires is

人でも、この熱の一つでも持てば、いかに美しい広びろとした部屋に身を横たえても、その熱にうなされて、寝苦しい思いをしなりればならない。

この三つの煩悩のない人は、寒い冬の夜、木の葉を敷物とした薄い寝床でも、快く眠ることができ、むし暑い夏の夜、閉じこめられた狭苦しい部屋でも、安らかに眠ることができる。

この三つは、この世の悲しみと苦しみのもとである。この悲しみと苦しみのもとを絶つものは、戒めと心の統一と智慧*である。戒めは貪(むさぼ)りの汚れを取り去り、正しい心の統一は瞋(いか)りの汚れを取り去り、智慧は愚かさの汚れを取り去る。

5．人間の欲にははてしがない。それはちょうど塩水を飲むものが、いっこうに渇きがとまらないのに似ている。彼はいつまでたっても満足することがなく、渇きはますます強くなるばかりである。

人はその欲を満足させようとするけれども、不満がつのっていらだつだけである。

人は欲を決して満足させることができない。そこには求めて得られない苦しみがあり、満足できないときには、気も狂

thwarted, it will often drive him "insane."

To satisfy their desires, people will struggle and fight with each other, king against king, vassal against vassal, parent against child, brother against brother, sister against sister, friend against friend; they will fight and even kill each other to satisfy their desires.

People often ruin their lives in the attempt to satisfy desires. They will steal and cheat and commit adultery, and then, being caught, will suffer from the disgrace of it and its punishment.

They will sin with their own bodies and words, sin with their own minds, knowing perfectly well that the gratification will ultimately bring unhappiness and suffering, so imperious is desire. And then, the various sufferings in the following world and the agonies of falling into it follow.

6.   Of all the worldly passions, lust is the most intense. All other worldly passions seem to follow in its train.

Lust seems to provide the soil in which other passions flourish. Lust is like a demon that eats up all the good deeds of the world. Lust is a viper hiding in a flower garden; it poisons those who come in search only

うばかりとなる。

　人は欲のために争い、欲のために戦う。王と王、臣と臣、親と子、兄と弟、姉と妹、友人同志、互いにこの欲のために狂わされて相争い、互いに殺しあう。

　また人は、欲のために身をもちくずし、盗み、詐欺(さぎ)し、姦淫(かんいん)する。ときには捕らえられて、さまざまな刑を受け、苦しみ悩む。

　また、欲のために、身(しん)・口(く)・意(い)の罪を重ね、この世で苦しみを受けるとともに、死んで後の世には、暗黒の世界に入って、さまざまな苦しみを受ける。

　6．愛欲は煩悩(ぼんのう)の王、さまざまの煩悩がこれにつき従う。

　愛欲は煩悩の芽をふく湿地、さまざまな煩悩を生ずる。愛欲は善を食う鬼女、あらゆる善を滅ぼす。

　愛欲は花に隠れ住む毒蛇、欲の花を貪るものに毒を刺して

of beauty. Lust is a vine that climbs a tree and spreads over the branches until the tree is strangled. Lust insinuates its tentacles into human emotions and sucks away the good sense of the mind until the mind withers. Lust is a bait cast by the evil demon that foolish people snap at and are dragged down by into the depths of the evil world.

If a dry bone is smeared with blood a dog will gnaw at it until he is tired and frustrated. Lust to a man is precisely like this bone to a dog; he will covet it until he is exhausted.

If a single piece of meat is thrown to two wild beasts they will fight and claw each other to get it. A man foolish enough to carry a torch against the wind will likely burn himself. Like these two beasts and this foolish man, people hurt and burn themselves because of their worldly desires.

7. It is easy to shield the outer body from poisoned arrows, but it is impossible to shield the mind from the poisoned darts that originate within itself. Greed, anger, foolishness and the infatuations of egoism — these four poisoned darts originate within the mind and infect it with deadly poison.

If people are infected with greed, anger and foolish-

殺す。愛欲は木を枯らすつる草、人の心に巻きつき、人の心の中の善のしるを吸い尽くす。愛欲は悪魔の投げた餌、人はこれにつられて悪魔の道に沈む。

　飢えた犬に血を塗った乾いた骨を与えると、犬はその骨にしゃぶりつき、ただ疲れと悩みとを得るだけである。愛欲が人の心を養わないのは、まったくこれと同じである。

　一切れの肉を争って獣は互いに傷つく。たいまつを持って風に向かう愚かな人は、ついにおのれ自身を焼く。この獣のように、また、この愚かな人のように、人は欲のためにおのれの身を傷つけ、その身を焼く。

　7．外から飛んでくる毒矢は防ぐすべがあっても、内からくる毒矢は防ぐすべがない。貪りと瞋りと愚かさと高ぶりとは、四つの毒矢にもたとえられるさまざまな病を起こすものである。

　心に貪りと瞋りと愚かさがあるときは、口には偽りと無駄

ness, they will lie, cheat, abuse and be double-tongued, and, then will actualize their words by killing, stealing and committing adultery.

These three evil states of mind, the four evil utterances, and the three evil acts, if added together, become the ten gross evils.

If people become accustomed to lying, they will unconsciously commit every possible wrong deed. Before they can act wickedly they must lie, and once they begin to lie they will act wickedly with unconcern.

Greed, lust, fear, anger, misfortune and unhappiness all derive from foolishness. Thus, foolishness is the greatest of the poisons.

8.   From desire action follows; from action suffering follows; desire, action and suffering are like a wheel rotating endlessly.

The rolling of this wheel has no beginning and no end; people cannot escape such reincarnation. One life follows another life according to this transmigrating cycle in endless recurrence.

If one were to pile the ashes and bones of himself burnt in this everlasting transmigration, the pile would be

口悪口と二枚舌を使い、身には殺生と盗みとよこしまな愛欲
を犯すようになる。

　意の三つ、口の四つ、身の三つ、これらを十悪という。

　知りながらも偽りを言うようになれば、どんな悪事をも犯
すようになる。悪いことをするから、偽りを言わなければな
らないようになり、偽りを言うようになるから、平気で悪い
ことをするようになる。

　人の貪りも、愛欲も恐れも瞋りも、愚かさからくるし、人
の不幸も難儀も、また愚かさからくる。愚かさは実に人の世
の病毒にほかならない。

　8．人は煩悩によって業を起こし、業によって苦しみを招
く。煩悩と業と苦しみの三つの車輪はめぐりめぐってはてし
がない。

　この車輪の回転には始めもなければ終わりもない。しかも
人はこの輪廻から逃れるすべを知らない。永遠に回帰する輪
廻に従って、人はこの現在の生から、次の生へと永遠に生ま
れ変わってゆく。

　限りない輪廻の間に、ひとりの人が焼き捨てた骨を積み重

mountain high; if one were to collect the milk of mothers which he suckled during his transmigration, it would be deeper than the sea.

Although the nature of Buddhahood is possessed by all people, it is buried so deeply in the defilements of worldly passion that it long remains unknown. That is why suffering is so universal and why there is this endless recurrence of miserable lives.

But, just as by yielding to greed, anger and foolishness, evil deeds are accumulated and condition rebirth, so, by following the Buddha's teaching, the evil sources will be cleared away and rebirth in the world of suffering will be ended.

II
MAN'S NATURE

1.   Man's nature is like a dense thicket that has no entrance and is difficult to penetrate. In comparison, the nature of an animal is much easier to understand. Still, we can in a general way classify the nature of man according to four outstanding differences.

First, there are those who, because of wrong teachings, practise austerities and cause themselves to suffer. Second, there are those who, by cruelty, by

ねるならば、山よりも高くなり、また、その間に飲んだ母の
乳を集めるならば、海の水よりも多くなるであろう。

　だから、人には仏性があるとはいえ、煩悩の泥があまりに
も深いため、その芽生えは容易でない。芽生えない仏性はあ
ってもあるとはいわれないので人びとの迷いははてしない。

第2節　人の性質

　1．人の性質は、ちょうど入口のわからない薮のように、
わかりにくい。これに比べると、獣の性質はかえってわかり
やすい。このわかりにくい性質の人を区分して、次の四種類
とする。

　一つには、自ら苦しむ人で、間違った教えを受けて苦行す
る。

　二つには、他人を苦しめる人で、生きものを殺したり盗ん
だり、そのほかさまざまなむごい仕業をする。

　三つには、自ら苦しむとともに他人をも苦しめる人である。

　四つには、自らも苦しまず、また他人をも苦しめない人で、
欲を離れて安らかに生き、*仏の教えを守って、殺すことなく

stealing, by killing, or by other unkind acts, cause others to suffer. Third, there are those who cause other people to suffer along with themselves. Fourth, there are those who do not suffer themselves and save others from suffering. These people of the last category, by following the teachings of Buddha, do not give way to greed, anger or foolishness, but live peaceful lives of kindness and wisdom without killing or stealing.

2.   There are three kinds of people in the world. The first are those who are like letters carved in rock; they easily give way to anger and retain their angry thoughts for a long time. The second are those who are like letters written in sand; they give way to anger also, but their angry thoughts quickly pass away. The third is those who are like letters written in running water; they do not retain their passing thoughts; they let abuse and uncomfortable gossip pass by unnoticed; their minds are always pure and undisturbed.

There are three other kinds of people. The first are those who are proud, act rashly and are never satisfied; their natures are easy to understand. Then there are those who are courteous and always act after consideration; their natures are hard to understand. Then there are those who have overcome desire completely; it is impossible to understand their natures.

盗むことなく、清らかな行いをする人である。

　2．またこの世には三種の人がある。岩に刻んだ文字のような人と、砂に書いた文字のような人と、水に書いた文字のような人である。

　岩に刻んだ文字のような人とは、しばしば腹を立てて、その怒りを長く続け、怒りが、刻みこんだ文字のように消えることのない人をいう。

　砂に書いた文字のような人とは、しばしば腹を立てるが、その怒りが、砂に書いた文字のように、速やかに消え去る人を指す。

　水に書いた文字のような人とは、水の上に文字を書いても、流れて形にならないように、他人の悪口や不快なことばを聞いても、少しも心に跡を留めることもなく、温和な気の満ちている人のことをいう。

　また、ほかにも三種類の人がある。第一の人は、その性質がわかりやすく、心高ぶり、かるはずみであって、常に落ち着きのない人である。第二の人は、その性質がわかりにくく、静かにへりくだって、ものごとに注意深く、欲を忍ぶ人である。第三の人は、その性質がまったくわかりにくく、自分の

＊ぼんのう
煩悩を滅ぼし尽くした人のことである。

Thus people can be classified in many different ways, but nevertheless, their natures are hard to understand. Only Buddha understands them and, by His wisdom, leads them through varied teachings.

III
HUMAN LIFE

1. There is an allegory that depicts human life. Once there was a man rowing a boat down a river. Someone on the shore warned him, "Stop rowing so gaily down the swift current; there are rapids ahead and a dangerous whirlpool, and there are crocodiles and demons lying in wait in rocky caverns. You will perish if you continue."

In this allegory, "the swift current" is a life of lust; "rowing gaily" is giving rein to one's passion; "rapids ahead" means the ensuing suffering and pain; "whirlpool" means pleasure, "crocodiles and demons" refers to the decay and death that follow a life of lust and indulgence; "Someone on the shore," who calls out, is Buddha.

Here is another allegory. A man who has committed a crime is running away; some guards are following him, so he tries to hide himself by descending into a well by means of some vines growing down the sides. As he descends he sees vipers at the bottom of the well, so he

　このように、さまざまに人を区別することができるが、その実、人の性質は容易に知ることはできない。ただ、仏だけがこれらの性質を知りぬいて、さまざまに教えを示す。

第3節　現実の人生

　1．ここに人生にたとえた物語がある。ある人が、河の流れに舟を浮かべて下るとする。岸に立つ人が声をからして叫んだ。「楽しそうに流れを下ることをやめよ。下流には波が立ち、渦巻きがあり、鰐と恐ろしい夜叉との住む淵がある。そのままに下れば死ななければならない。」と。

　このたとえで「河の流れ」とは、愛欲の生活をいい、「楽しそうに下る」とは、自分の身に執着することであり、「波立つ」とは、怒りと悩みの生活を表わし、「渦巻き」とは、欲の楽しみを示し、「鰐と恐ろしい夜叉の住む淵」とは、罪によって滅びる生活を指し、「岸に立つ人」とは、＊仏をいうのである。

　ここにもう一つのたとえがある。ひとりの男が罪を犯して逃げた。追手が迫ってきたので、彼は絶体絶命になって、ふと足もとを見ると、古井戸があり、藤蔓が下がっている。彼はその藤蔓をつたって、井戸の中へ降りようとすると、下で毒蛇が口を開けて待っているのが見える。

decides to cling to the vine for safety. After a time when his arms are getting tired, he notices two mice, one white and the other black, gnawing at the vine.

If the vine breaks, he will fall to the vipers and perish. Suddenly, on looking upward, he notices just above his face a bee-hive from which occasionally falls a drop of honey. The man, forgetting all his danger, tastes the honey with delight.

"A man" means the one who is born to suffer and to die alone. "Guards" and "vipers" refer to the body with all its desires. "Vines" means the continuity of the human life. "Two mice, one white and the other black" refer to the duration of time, days and nights, and the passing years. "Honey" indicates the physical pleasures that beguiles the suffering of the passing years.

2. Here is still another allegory. A king places four vipers in a box and gives the box into the safekeeping of a servant. He commands the servant to take good care of them and warns that if he angers even one of them he will be punished with death. The servant, in fear, decides to throw away the box and escape.

The king sends five guards to capture the servant. At first they approach the servant in a friendly manner, intending to take him back safely, but the servant does

しかたなくその藤蔓を命の綱にして、宙にぶら下がっている。やがて、手が抜けそうに痛んでくる。そのうえ、白黒2匹の鼠が現われて、その藤蔓をかじり始める。

　藤蔓がかみ切られたとき、下へ落ちて餌食にならなければならない。そのとき、ふと頭をあげて上を見ると、蜂の巣から蜂蜜の甘いしずくが一滴二滴と口の中へしたたり落ちてくる。すると、男は自分の危い立場を忘れて、うっとりとなるのである。

　この比喩で、「ひとり」とは、ひとり生まれひとり死ぬ孤独の姿であり、「追手」や「毒蛇」は、この欲のもとになるおのれの身体のことであり、「古井戸の藤蔓」とは、人の命のことであり、「白黒2匹の鼠」とは、歳月を示し、「蜂蜜のしずく」とは、眼前の欲の楽しさのことである。

　2．また、さらにもう一つのたとえを説こう。王が一つの箱に四匹の毒蛇を入れ、ひとりの男にその蛇を養うことを命じて、もし一匹の蛇でも怒らせれば、命を奪うと約束させる。男は王の命令を恐れて、蛇の箱を捨てて逃げ出す。

　これを知った王は、五人の臣下に命じて、その後を追わせる。彼らは偽って彼に近づき、連れ帰ろうとする。男はこれ

not trust their friendliness and escapes to another village.

Then, in a vision, a voice tells him that in this village there is no safe shelter, and that there are six bandits who will attack him, so the servant runs away in fright until he comes to a wild river that blocks his way. Thinking of the dangers that are following him, he makes a raft and succeeds in crossing the turbulent current, beyond which he finally finds safety and peace.

"Four vipers in a box" indicate the four elements of earth, water, fire and air that make up the body of flesh. The body is given into the charge of lust and is an enemy of the mind. Therefore, he tries to run away from the body.

"Five guards who approach in friendly manner" mean the five aggregates — form, feeling, perception, volition and consciousness — which frame body and mind.

"The safe shelter" is the six senses, which are no safe shelter after all, and "the six bandits" are the six objects of the six senses. Thus, seeing the dangers within the six senses, he runs away once more and comes to the wild current of worldly desires.

Then he makes himself a raft of the Buddha's good teachings and crosses the wild current safely.

を信じないで、ふたたび逃げて、とある村に入り、隠れ家を探す。

　そのとき、空に声あって、この村は住む人もなく、そのうえ今夜、六人の賊が来て襲うであろうと告げる。彼は驚いて、ふたたびそこを逃げ出す。行く手に荒波を立てて激しく流れている河がある。渡るには容易でないが、こちら岸の危険を思って筏（いかだ）を作り、かろうじて河を渡ることを得、はじめて安らぎを得た。

「四匹の毒蛇の箱」とは地水火風（ち すい か ふう）の四大要素から成るこの身のことである。この身は、欲のもとであって、心の敵である。だから、彼はこの身を厭（いと）って逃げ出した。

「五人の男が偽って近づいた」とは、同じくこの身と心とを組み立てている五つの要素のことである。

「隠れ家」とは、人間の六つの感覚器官のことであり、「六人の賊」とは、この感覚器官に対する六つの対象のことである。このように、すべての官能の危いのを見て、さらに逃げ出し、「流れの強い河を見た」とは、煩悩の荒れ狂う生活のことである。

　この深さの測（はか）り知れない煩悩（＊ぼんのう）の河に、教えの筏を浮かべて、安らかな彼（か）の岸に達したのである。

—183—

3. There are three occasions full of perils when a son is helpless to aid his mother and a mother cannot help her son: — a fire, a flood and a burglary. Yet, even on these perilous and sad occasions, there still exists a chance for aiding each other.

But there are three occasions when it is impossible for a mother to save her son or a son to save his mother. These three occasions are the time of sickness, the period of growing old, and the moment of death.

How can a son take his mother's place when she is growing old? How can a mother take her son's place when he is sick? How can either help the other when the moment of death approaches? No matter how much they may love each other or how intimate they may have been, neither can help the other on such occasions.

4. Once Yama, the legendary King of Hell, asked a man who had fallen into hell about his evil deeds in life, whether, during his life, he had ever met the three heavenly messengers. The man replied: "No, my Lord, I never met any such persons."

Yama asked him if he had ever met an old person bent with age and walking with a cane. The man replied: "Yes, my Lord, I have met such persons frequently." Then Yama said to him: "You are suffering this present

　3．世に母も子を救い得ず、子も母を救い得ない三つの場合がある。すなわち、大火災と大水害と、大盗難のときである。しかし、この三つの場合においても、ときとしては、母と子が互いに助けあう機会がある。

　ところがここに、母は子を絶対に救い得ず、子も母を絶対に救い得ない三つの場合がある。それは、老いの恐れと、病の恐れと、死の恐れとの襲い来ったときのことである。

　母の老いゆくのを、子はどのようにしてこれに代わることができるであろうか。子の病む姿のいじらしさに泣いても、母はどうして代わって病むことができよう。子供の死、母の死、いかに母子であっても、どうしても代わりあうことはできない。いかに深く愛しあっている母子でも、こういう場合には絶対に助けあうことはできないのである。

　4．この世において悪事をなし、死んで地獄に落ちた罪人に、閻魔王が尋ねた。「おまえは人間の世界にいたとき、三人の天使に会わなかったか。」「大王よ、わたくしはそのような方には会いません。」

「それでは、おまえは年老いて腰を曲げ、杖にすがって、よぼよぼしている人を見なかったか。」「大王よ、そういう老人

punishment because you did not recognize in that old man a heavenly messenger sent to warn you that you must quickly change your ways before you, too, become an old man."

Yama asked him again if he had ever seen a poor, sick and friendless man. The man replied: "Yes, my Lord, I have seen many such men." Then, Yama said to him: "You have come into this place because you failed to recognize in these sick men the messengers from heaven sent to warn you of your own sickness."

Then, Yama asked him once more if he had ever seen a dead man. The man replied: "Yes, my Lord, I have been in the presence of death many times." Yama said to him: "It is because you did not recognize in these men the heavenly messengers sent to warn you that you are brought to this. If you had recognized these messengers and taken their warnings you would have changed your course, and would not have come to this place of suffering."

5. Once there was a young woman named Kisagotami, the wife of a wealthy man, who lost her mind because of the death of her child. She took the dead child in her arms and went from house to house begging people to heal the child.

ならば、いくらでも見ました。」「おまえはその天使に会いな
がら、自分も老いゆくものであり、急いで善をなさなければ
ならないと思わず、今日の報いを受けるようになった。」

「おまえは病にかかり、ひとりで寝起きもできず、見るも哀
れに、やつれはてた人を見なかったか。」「大王よ、そういう
病人ならいくらでも見ました。」「おまえは病人というその天
使に会いながら、自分も病まなければならない者であること
を思わず、あまりにもおろそかであったから、この地獄へく
ることになったのだ。」

「次に、おまえは、おまえの周囲で死んだ人を見なかったか。」
「大王よ、死人ならば、わたくしはいくらでも見てまいりまし
た。」「おまえは死を警め告げる天使に会いながら、死を思わ
ず善をなすことを怠って、この報いを受けることになった。
おまえ自身のしたことは、おまえ自身がその報いを受けなけ
ればならない。」

　5．裕福な家の若い嫁であったキサゴータミーは、そのひ
とり子の男の子が、幼くして死んだので、気が狂い、冷たい
骸を抱いて巷に出、子供の病を治す者はいないかと尋ね回っ
た。

Of course, they could do nothing for her, but finally a follower of Buddha advised her to see the Blessed One who was then staying at Jetavana, and so she carried the dead child to Buddha.

The Blessed One looked upon her with sympathy and said: "To heal the child I need some poppy seeds; go and beg four or five poppy seeds from some home where death has never entered."

So the demented woman went out and sought a house where death had never entered, but in vain. At last, she was obliged to return to Buddha. In his quiet presence her mind cleared and she understood the meaning of his words. She took the body away and buried it, and then returned to Buddha and became one of his disciples.

IV
REALITY OF HUMAN LIFE

1. People in this world are prone to be selfish and unsympathetic; they do not know how to love and respect one another; they argue and quarrel over trifling affairs only to their own harm and suffering, and life becomes but a dreary round of unhappinesses.

Regardless of whether they are rich or poor, they

　この狂った女をどうすることもできず、町の人びとはただ
哀れげに見送るだけであったが、釈尊の信者がこれを見かね
て、その女に祇園精舎の釈尊のもとに行くようにすすめた。
彼女は早速、釈尊のもとへ子供を抱いて行った。

　釈尊は静かにその様子を見て、「女よ、この子の病を治すに
は、芥子の実がいる。町に出て四・五粒もらってくるがよい。
しかし、その芥子の実は、まだ一度も死者の出ない家からも
らってこなければならない。」と言われた。

　狂った母は、町に出て芥子の実を求めた。芥子の実は得や
すかったけれども、死人の出ない家は、どこにも求めること
ができなかった。ついに求める芥子の実を得ることができず、
仏のもとにもどった。かの女は釈尊の静かな姿に接し、初め
て釈尊のことばの意味をさとり、夢から覚めたように気がつ
き、わが子の冷たい骸を墓所におき、釈尊のもとに帰ってき
て弟子となった。

第4節　迷いのすがた

　1．この世の人びとは、人情が薄く、親しみ愛することを
知らない。しかも、つまらないことを争いあい、激しい悪と

worry about money; they suffer from poverty and they suffer from wealth. Because their lives are controlled by greed, they are never contented, never satisfied.

A wealthy man worries about his estate if he has one; he worries about his mansion and all other possessions. He worries lest some disaster befall him, his mansion burn down, robbers break in, kidnappers carry him off. Then he worries about death and the disposition of his wealth. Indeed, his way to death is lonely, and nobody follows him to death.

A poor man always suffers from insufficiency and this serves to awaken endless desires — for land and a house. Being aflamed with covetousness he wears out both his body and mind, and comes to death in the middle of his life.

The whole world seems pitted against him and even the path to death seems lonesome as though he has a long journey to make and no friends to keep him company.

2. Now, there are five evils in the world. First, there is cruelty; every creature, even insects, strives against one another. The strong attack the weak; the weak deceive the strong; everywhere there is fighting and cruelty.

苦しみの中にあって、それぞれの仕事を勤めて、ようやく、その日を過ごしている。

　身分の高下にかかわらず、富の多少にかかわらず、すべてみな金銭のことだけに苦しむ。なければないで苦しみ、あればあるで苦しみ、ひたすらに欲のために心を使って、安らかなときがない。

　富める人は、田があれば田を憂え、家があれば家を憂え、すべて存在するものに執着して憂いを重ねる。あるいは災いにあい、困難に出会い、奪われ焼かれてなくなると、苦しみ悩んで命までも失うようになる。しかも死への道はひとりで歩み、だれもつき従う者はない。

　貧しいものは、常に足らないことに苦しみ、家を欲しがり、田を欲しがり、この欲しい欲しいの思いに焼かれて、心身ともに疲れはててしまう。このために命を全うすることができずに、中途で死ぬようなこともある。

　すべての世界が敵対するかのように見え、死出の旅路は、ただひとりだけで、はるか遠くに行かなければならない。

　２．また、この世には五つの悪がある。一つには、あらゆる人から地に這う虫に至るまで、すべてみな互いにいがみあ

Second, there is the lack of a clear demarcation between the rights of a father and a son; between an elder brother and a younger; between a husband and a wife; between a senior relative and a younger; on every occasion each one desires to be the highest and to profit off the others. They cheat each other, there is deception and a lack of sincerity.

Third, there is the lack of a clear demarcation as to the behavior between men and women. Everyone at times has impure and lascivious thoughts and desires that lead them into questionable acts and often into disputes, fighting, injustice and wickedness.

Fourth, there is the tendency for people to disrespect the rights of others, to exaggerate their own importance at the expense of others, to set bad examples of behavior and, being unjust in their speech, to deceive, slander and abuse others.

Fifth, there is the tendency for people to neglect their duties toward others. They think too much of their own comfort and their own desires; they forget the favors they have received and cause annoyance to others that often passes into great injustice.

3.   People should have more sympathy for one another; they should respect one another for their good traits and

い、強いものは弱いものを倒し、弱いものは強いものを欺き、互いに傷つけあい、いがみあっている。

二つには、親子、兄弟、夫婦、親族など、すべて、それぞれおのれの道がなく、守るところもない。ただ、おのれを中心にして欲をほしいままにし、互いに欺きあい、心と口とが別々になっていて誠がない。

三つには、だれも彼もみなよこしまな思いを抱き、みだらな思いに心をこがし、男女の間に道がなく、そのために、徒党を組んで争い戦い、常に非道を重ねている。

四つには、互いに善い行為をすることを考えず、ともに教えあって悪い行為をし、偽り、むだ口、悪口、二枚舌を使って、互いに傷つけあっている。ともに尊敬しあうことを知らないで、自分だけが尊い偉いものであるかのように考え、他人を傷つけて省みるところがない。

五つには、すべてのものは怠りなまけて、善い行為をすることさえ知らず、恩も知らず、義務も知らず、ただ欲のままに動いて、他人に迷惑をかけ、ついには恐ろしい罪を犯すようになる。

3．人は互いに敬愛し、施しあわなければならないのに、

help one another in their difficulties; but, instead, they are selfish and hard-hearted; they despise one another for their failings and dislike others for their advantages. These aversions generally grow worse with time, and after a while, become intolerable.

These feelings of dislike do not soon end in acts of violence; yet they poison life with feelings of hatred and anger that become so deeply carved into the mind that people carry the marks into the cycle of reincarnation.

Truly, in this world of lust, a man is born alone and dies alone, and there is no one to share his punishment in the life after death.

The law of cause and effect is universal; each man must carry his own burden of sin and must go along to its retribution. The same law of cause and effect controls good deeds. A life of sympathy and kindness will result in good fortune and happiness.

4.   As years go by and people see how strongly they are bound by greed, habit and suffering, they become very sad and discouraged. Often in their discouragement they quarrel with others and sink deeper into sin and give up trying to walk the true path; often their lives come to some untimely end in the very midst of their wickedness

わずかな利害のために、互いに憎み争うことだけをしている。しかも、争う気持ちがほんのわずかでも、時の経過に従ってますます大きく激しくなり、大きな恨みになることを知らない。

この世の争いは、互いに害ないあっても、すぐに破滅に至ることはないけれども、毒を含み、怒りが積み重なり、憤（いきどお）りを心にしっかり刻みつけてしまい、生をかえ、死をかえて、互いに傷つけあうようになる。

人はこの愛欲の世界に、ひとり生まれ、ひとり死ぬ。未来の報いは代わって受けてくれるものがなく、おのれひとりでそれに当たらなければならない。

善と悪とはそれぞれその報いを異にし、善は幸いを、悪は災いをもたらし、動かすことのできない道理によって定まっている。しかも、それぞれが、おのれの業（ごう）をにない、報いの定まっているところへ、ひとり赴く。

4. 恩愛のきずなにつながれては憂いに閉ざされ、長い月日を経ても、いたましい思いを解くことができない。それとともに、激しい貪（むさぼ）りにおぼれては、悪意に包まれ、でたらめに事を起こし、他人と争い、真実の道に親しむことができず、寿命も尽きないうちに、死に追いやられ、永劫（えいごう）に苦しまなけ

and they suffer forever.

This falling into discouragement because of one's misfortunes and sufferings is most unnatural and contrary to the law of heaven and earth and, therefore, one will suffer both in this world and in the worlds after death.

It is true that everything in this life is transitory and filled with uncertainty, but it is lamentable that anyone should ignore this fact and keep on trying to seek enjoyment and satisfaction of his desires.

5.   It is natural in this world of suffering for people to think and act selfishly and egoistically and, because of it, it is equally natural for suffering and unhappiness to follow.

People favor themselves and neglect others. People let their own desires run into greed and lust and all manner of evil. Because of these they must suffer endlessly.

Times of luxury do not last long, but pass away very quickly; nothing in this world can be enjoyed forever.

6.   Therefore, people should cast away, while they are young and healthy, all their greed and attachment to worldly affairs, and should seek earnestly for true Enlight-

ればならない。

　このような人の仕業(しわざ)は、自然の道に逆らい、天地の道理に
そむいているので、必ず災いを招くようになり、この世でも、
後の世でも、ともに苦しみを重ねなければならない。

　まことに、世俗の事はあわただしく過ぎ去ってゆき、頼り
とすべきものは何一つなく、力になるものも何一つない。こ
の中にあって、こぞってみな快楽のとりことなっていること
は、嘆かわしい限りといわなければならない。

　5．このような有様が、まことにこの世の姿であり、人び
とは苦しみの中に生まれてただ悪だけを行い、善を行うこと
を少しも知らない。だから自然の道理によって、さらに苦し
みの報いを受けることを避けられない。

　ただおのれにのみ何でも厚くして、他人に恵むことを知ら
ない。そのうえ、欲に迫られてあらゆる煩悩(ぼんのう)*を働かせ、その
ために苦しみ、またその結果によって苦しむ。

　栄華の時勢(じせい)は永続せず、たちまちに過ぎ去る。この世の快
楽も何一つ永続するものはない。

　6．だから、人は世俗の事を捨て、健全なときに道を求め、
永遠の生を願わなければならない。道を求めることをほかに

enment, for there can be no lasting reliance or happiness apart from Enlightenment.

Most people, however, disbelieve or ignore this law of cause and effect. They go on in their habits of greed and selfishness, being oblivious of the fact that a good deed brings happiness and an evil deed brings misfortune. Nor do they really believe that one's acts in this life condition the following lives and implicate others with regard to the rewards and punishments for their sins.

They lament and cry about their sufferings, entirely misunderstanding the significance their present acts have upon their following lives and the relation their sufferings have to the acts of their previous lives. They think only of present desire and present suffering.

Nothing in the world is permanent or lasting; everything is changing and momentary and unpredictable. But people are ignorant and selfish, and are concerned only with the desires and sufferings of the passing moment. They do not listen to the good teachings nor do they try to understand them; they simply give themselves up to the present interest, to wealth and lust.

7.   From time immemorial, an incalculable number of people have been born into this world of delusion and suffering, and they are still being born. It is fortunate,

して、どんな頼み、どんな楽しみがあるというのか。

　ところが、人びとは善い行為をすれば善を得、道にかなった行為をすれば道を得るということを信じない。また、人が死んでまた生まれるということを知らず、施せば幸いを得るということを信じない。すべて善悪にかかわるすべてのことを信じない。

　ただ、誤った考えだけを持ち、道も知らず、善も知らず、心が暗くて、吉凶禍福が次々に起こってくる道理を知らず、ただ、眼前に起こることだけについて泣き悲しむ。

　どんなものでも永久に変わらないものはないのであるからすべてうつり変わる。ただこれについて苦しみ悲しむことだけを知っていて、教えを聞くことがなく、心に深く思うことがなく、ただ眼前の快楽におぼれて、財貨や色欲を貪って飽きることを知らない。

　7．人びとが、遠い昔から迷いの世界を経めぐり、憂いと苦しみに沈んでいたことは、ことばでは言い尽くすことができない。しかも、今日に至っても、なお迷いは絶えることがない。ところが、いま仏の教えに会い、仏の名を聞いて信ず

however, that the world has the Buddha's teachings and that men can believe in them and be helped.

Therefore, people should think deeply, should keep their minds pure and their bodies well, should keep away from greed and evil, and should seek good.

To us, fortunately, the knowledge of the Buddha's teachings has come; we should seek to believe in them and wish to be born in the Buddha's Pure Land. Knowing Buddha's teachings, we should not follow others into greedy and sinful ways, nor should we keep the Buddha's teachings to ourselves alone, but should practise the teachings and pass them on to others.

ることができたのは、まことにうれしいことである。

　だから、よく思いを重ね、悪を遠ざけ、善を選び、努め行わなければならない。

　いま、幸いにも仏の教えに会うことができたのであるから、どんな人も仏の教えを信じて、仏の国に生まれることを願わなければならない。仏の教えを知った以上は、人は他人に従って煩悩や罪悪のとりこになってはならない。また、仏の教えをおのれだけのものとすることなく、それを実践し、それを他人に教えなければならない。

CHAPTER FIVE

THE RELIEF OFFERED BY BUDDHA

I

AMIDA BUDDHA'S VOWS

1.   As already explained, people always yield to their worldly passions, repeating sin after sin, and carry burdens of intolerable acts, unable of their own wisdom or of their own strength to break these habits of greed and indulgence. If they are unable to overcome and remove worldly passions, how can they expect to realize their true nature of Buddhahood?

Buddha, who thoroughly understood human nature, had great sympathy for men and made a vow that He would do everything possible, even at the cost of great hardship to Himself, to relieve them of their fears and sufferings. To effect this relief He manifested himself as a Bodhisattva in the immemorable past and made the following ten vows:

(a) "Though I attain Buddhahood, I shall never be complete until everyone in my land is certain of entering Buddhahood and gaining Enlightenment.

第5章　仏の救い

第1節　仏の願い

1. 人びとの生活は、すでに説いたように、その煩悩は断ちにくいものであり、また、初めもわからない昔から、山のような罪業¹をになって、迷いに迷いを重ねてきている。だから、たとえ仏性²の宝をそなえていても、開き現わすことは容易ではない。

この人間の有様を見通された仏³は、はるかな昔に、ひとりの菩薩⁴となり、人びとを哀れみ、あらゆる恐れを抱くもののために大慈悲者となろうとして、次のような数多くの願いを起こした。たとえ、この身はどんな苦しみの毒の中にあっても、必ず努め励んでなしとげようと誓った。

(a)たとい、わたしが仏と成ったとしても、わたしの国に生まれる人びとが、確かに仏と成るべき身の上となり、必ずさとりに至らないならば、誓ってさとりを開かないであろう。

(b)たとい、わたしが仏と成ったとしても、わたしの光明に限りがあって、世界のはしばしまで照らすことがないならば、誓ってさとりを開かないであろう。

(b) "Though I attain Buddhahood, I shall never be complete until my affirming light reaches all over the world.

(c) "Though I attain Buddhahood, I shall never be complete until my life endures through the ages and saves innumerable numbers of people.

(d) "Though I attain Buddhahood, I shall never be complete until all the Buddhas in the ten directions unite in praising my name.

(e) "Though I attain Buddhahood, I shall never be complete until people with sincere faith endeavor to be reborn in my land by repeating my name in sincere faith ten times and actually do succeed in this rebirth.

(f) "Though I attain Buddhahood, I shall never be complete until people everywhere determine to attain Enlightenment, practise virtues, sincerely wish to be born in my land; thus, I shall appear at the moment of their death with a great company of Bodhisattvas to welcome them into my Pure Land.

(g) "Though I attain Buddhahood, I shall never be complete until people everywhere, hearing my name, think of my land and wish to be born there and, to that end, sincerely plant seeds of virture, and are thus able to (c)たとい、わたしが仏と成ったとしても、わたしの寿命に限りがあって、どんな数であってもかぞえられるほどの数であるならば、誓ってさとりを開かないであろう。

(d)たとい、わたしが仏と成ったとしても、十方の世界のあらゆる仏が、ことごとく称賛して、わたしの名前を称えないようなら、誓ってさとりを開かないであろう。

(e)たとい、わたしが仏と成ったとしても、十方のあらゆる人びとが真実の心をもって深い信心を起こして、わたしの国に生まれようと思って、十返わたしの名前を念じても、生まれないようなら、誓ってさとりを開かないであろう。

(f)たとい、わたしが仏と成ったとしても、十方のあらゆる人びとが、道を求める心を起こし、多くの功徳を修め、真実の心をもって願いを起こし、わたしの国へ生まれようと思っているのに、もしもその人の寿命が尽きるとき、偉大な菩薩たちにとりまかれて、その人の前に現われないようなら、誓ってさとりを開かないであろう。

(g)たとい、わたしが仏と成っても、十方のあらゆる人びとが、わたしの名前を聞いて、わたしの国に思いをかけ、多くの功徳のもとを植え、心をこめて供養して、わたしの国に生まれようと思っているのに、思いどおりに生まれることがで

accomplish all to their hearts' desire.

(h) "Though I attain Buddhahood, I shall never be complete until all those who are born in my Pure Land are certain to attain Buddhahood, so that they may lead many others to Enlightenment and to the practice of great compassion.

(i) "Though I attain Buddhahood, I shall never be complete until people all over the world are influenced by my spirit of loving compassion that will purify their minds and bodies and lift them above the things of the world.

(j) "Though I attain Buddhahood, I shall never be complete until people everywhere, hearing my name, learn right ideas about life and death, and gain that perfect wisdom that will keep their minds pure and tranquil in the midst of the world's greed and suffering.

"Thus I make these vows; may I not attain Buddhahood until they are fulfilled. May I become the source of unlimited Light, freeing and radiating the treasures of my wisdom and virtue, enlightening all lands and emancipating all suffering people."

2. Thus He, by accumulating innumerable virtues through many eons of time, became Amida or the

きないようなら、誓ってさとりを開かないであろう。

(h)わたしの国に来て生まれる者は、「次の生には仏と成るべき位」に到達するであろう。そして、彼らは思いのままに人びとを教え導き、それぞれの願いに従って、数多くの人びとを導いてさとりに入らせ、大悲の功徳を修めることができるであろう。たとい、わたしが仏と成ったとしても、もしもそれができないようなら、誓ってさとりを開かないであろう。

(i)たとい、わたしが仏と成ったとしても、十方の世界のあらゆる人びとが、わたしの光明に触れて、身も心も和らぎ、この世のものよりもすぐれたものになるようでありたい。もしもそうでないようなら、誓ってさとりを開かないであろう。

(j)たとい、わたしが仏と成ったとしても、十方の世界のあらゆる人びとが、わたしの名前を聞いて、生死にとらわれることのない深い信念と、さえぎられることのない深い智慧*とを得られないようなら、誓ってさとりを開かないであろう。

わたしは、いま、このような誓いを立てる。もしもこの願いを満たすことができないようなら、誓ってさとりを開かないであろう。限りのない光明の主となり、あらゆる国々を照らして世の中の悩みを救い、人びとのために、教えの蔵を開いて、広く功徳の宝を施すであろう。

Buddha of Infinite Light and Boundless Life, and perfected his own Buddha-land of Purity, wherein He is now living, in a world of peace, enlightening all people.

This Pure Land, wherein there is no suffering, is, indeed, most peaceful and happy. Clothing, food and all beautiful things appear when those who live there wish for them. When a gentle breeze passes through its jewel-laden trees, the music of its holy teachings fills the air and cleanses the minds of all who listen to it.

In this Pure Land there are many fragrant lotus blossoms, and each blossom has many precious petals, and each petal shines with ineffable beauty. The radiance of these lotus blossoms brightens the path of Wisdom, and those who listen to the music of the holy teaching are led into perfect peace.

3. Now all the Buddhas of the ten directions are praising the virtues of this Buddha of Infinite Light and Boundless Life.

Whoever hears this Buddha's Name magnifies and receives it with joy, his mind becomes one with Buddha's mind and he will be born in the Buddha's wondrous Land of Purity.

2．このように願いを立てて、はかり知れない長い間功徳を積み、清らかな国を作り、すでにはるかな昔に仏と成り、現にその極楽世界にいて、教えを説いている。

その国は清く安らかで、悩みを離れ、さとりの楽しみが満ちあふれ、着物も食物もそしてあらゆる美しいものも、みなその国の人びとの心の思うままに現われる。快い風がおもむろに吹き起こって、宝の木々をわたると、教えの声が四方に流れて、聞くものの心の垢を取り去っている。

また、その国にはさまざまな色の蓮の花が咲きにおい、花ごとにはかり知れない花びらがあり、花びらごとにその色の光が輝き、光はそれぞれ仏の智慧の教えを説いて、聞く人びとを仏の道に安らわせている。

3．いま十方のあらゆる仏たちから、この仏のすぐれた徳がたたえられている。

どんな人でも、この仏の名前を聞いて、信じ喜ぶ一念で、その仏の国に生まれることができるのである。

Those who are born in that Pure Land share in Buddha's boundless life; their hearts are immediately filled with sympathy for all sufferers and they go forward to manifest the Buddha's method of salvation.

In the spirit of these vows they cast away all worldly attachments and realize the impermanence of this world. And they devote their merits to the emancipation of all sentient life; they integrate their own lives with the lives of all others, sharing their illusions and sufferings but, at the same time, realizing their freedom from the bonds and attachments of this worldly life.

They know the hindrances and difficulties of worldly living but they know, also, the boundless potentialities of Buddha's compassion. They are free to go or come, they are free to advance or to stop as they wish, but they choose to remain with those upon whom Buddha has compassion.

Therefore, if anyone hearing the Name of this Amida Buddha is encouraged to call upon that Name in perfect faith, he shall share in Buddha's compassion. So all people should listen to the Buddha's teaching and should follow it even if it seems to lead them again through the flames that envelop this world of life and death.

　その仏の国に至る人びとは、みな寿命に限りがなく、また自らほかの人びとを救いたいという願いを起こし、その願いの仕事にいそしむことになる。

　これらの願いを立てることによって、執着を離れ、無常*をさとる。おのれのためになると同時に他人をも利する行為を実践し、人びととともに慈悲*に生き、この世俗の生活の足かせや執着にとらわれない。

　人びとはこの世の苦難を知りつつ、同時にまた、仏の慈悲の限りない可能性をも知っている。その人びとの心には、執着がなく、おのれとか、他人とかの区別もなく、行くも帰るも、進むも止まるも、こだわるところがなく、まさに心のあるがままに自由である。しかも、仏が慈悲をたれた人びととともにとどまることを選ぶのである。

　だから、もしもひとりの人がいて、この仏の名前を聞いて、喜び勇み、ただ一度でもその名を念ずるならば、その人は大いなる利益を得るであろう。たとえこの世界に満ちみちている炎の中にでも分け入って、この教えを聞いて信じ喜び、教えのとおりに行わなければならない。

If people truly and earnestly wish to attain Enlightenment, they must rely on the power of this Buddha. It is impossible for an ordinary person to realize his supreme Buddha-nature without the support of this Buddha.

4.   Amida Buddha is not far from anyone. His Land of Purity is described as being far away to the west but it is, also, within the minds of those who earnestly wish to be with him.

When some people picture in their minds the figure of Amida Buddha shining in golden splendor, the picture divides into eighty-four thousand figures or features, each figure or feature emitting eighty-four thousand rays of light and each ray of light, enlightening a world, never leaving in darkness a single person who is reciting the name of Buddha. Thus this Buddha helps people take advantage of the salvation He offers.

By seeing the image of Buddha, one is enabled to realize the mind of Buddha. The Buddha's mind has great compassion that includes all, even those who are ignorant of his compassion or forgetful of it, much more those who remember it in faith.

To those who have faith, He offers the opportunity to become one with Him. As this Buddha is the

　もしも、人びとが真剣にさとりを得ようと望むなら、どうしても、この仏の力によらなければならない。仏の力がなくてさとりを得ることは、普通の人間のできるところではない。

　４．いま、この仏は、ここよりはるか遠くのところにいるのではない。その仏の国ははるか遠くにあるけれども、仏を思い念じている者の心の中にもある。

　まず、この仏の姿を心に思い浮かべて見ると、千万の金色に輝き、八万四千の姿や特徴がある。一つ一つの姿や特徴には八万四千の光があり、一つ一つの光は、一つ残らず、念仏する人を見すえて、包容して捨てることがない。

　この仏を拝み見ることによって、また仏の心を拝み見ることになる。仏の心とは大いなる慈悲そのものであり、信心を持つ者を救いとるのはもちろん、仏の慈悲を知らず、あるいは忘れているような人びとをも救いとるのである。

　信あるものには仏は仏と一つになる機会を与える。この仏を思い念ずると、この仏は、あらゆるところに満ちみちる体

all-inclusive body of equality, whoever thinks of Buddha, Buddha thinks of him and enters his mind freely.

This means that, when a person thinks of Buddha, he has Buddha's mind in all its pure and happy and peaceful perfection. In other words, his mind is a Buddha-mind.

Therefore, each man in purity and sincerity of faith, should picture his own mind as being Buddha's mind.

5. Buddha has many forms of transfiguration and incarnation, and can manifest Himself in manifold ways according to the ability of each person.

He manifests his body in immense size to cover all the sky and stretches away into the boundless stellar spaces. He also manifests Himself in the infinitesimals of nature, sometimes in forms, sometimes in energy, sometimes in aspects of mind, and sometimes in personality.

But in some manner or other, He will surely appear to those who recite the name of Buddha with faith. To such, Amida always appears accompanied by two Bodhisattvas: Avalokitesvara, the Bodhisattva of Compassion and Mahasthama-prapta, the Bodhisattva of Wisdom. His

であるから、あらゆる人びとの心の中に入る。

だからこそ、心に仏を思うとき、その心は、実に円満な姿や特徴をそなえた仏であり、この心は仏そのものとなり、この心がそのまま仏となる。

清く正しい信心をもつものは、心が仏の心そのままであると思い描くべきである。

5. 仏の体にはさまざまの相(すがた)があり、人びとの能力に応じて現われ、この世界に満ちみちて、限りがなく、人の心の考えおよぶところではない。それは宇宙、自然、人間のそれぞれの姿の中で仰ぎ見ることができる。

しかし、仏の名を念ずるものは、必ずその姿を拝むことができる。この仏は常にふたりの菩薩(ぼさつ)を従えて、念仏する人のもとに迎えに来る。

仏の化身はあらゆる世界に満ちみちているけれども、信心を

manifestations fill up the world for everyone to see but only those who have faith notice them.

Those who are able to see His temporal manifestations acquire abiding satisfaction and happiness. Moreover, those who are able to see the real Buddha realize incalculable fortunes of joy and peace.

6.   Since the mind of Amida Buddha with all its boundless potentialities of love and wisdom is compassion itself, Buddha can save all.

The most wicked of people — those who commit unbelievable crimes, whose minds are filled with greed, anger and infatuation; those who lie, chatter, abuse and cheat; those who kill, steal and act lasciviously; those who are near the end of their lives after years of evil deeds — they are destined to long ages of punishment.

A good friend comes to them and pleads with them at their last moment, saying, "You are now facing death; you cannot blot out your life of wickedness, but you can take refuge in the compassion of the Buddha of Infinite Light by reciting His Name.

If these wicked men recite the holy name of Amida Buddha with singleness of mind, all the sins which would

もつ者だけが、それを拝み見ることができる。

　仏の仮の姿を思うことさえ、限りない幸福を得るのであるから、真実の仏を拝み見ることの功徳には、はかり知れないものがある。

　6．この仏の心は、大いなる慈悲と智慧そのものであるから、どんな人をも救う。

　愚かさのために恐ろしい罪を犯し、心の中では貪り、瞋り、愚かな思いを抱き、口では偽り、むだ口、悪口、二枚舌を使い、身では殺生し、盗み、よこしまな愛欲を犯すという十悪をなす者は、その悪い行いのために、永遠に未来の苦しみを受けることとなる。

　その人の命の終わるとき、善い友が来てねんごろに、「あなたはいま苦しみが迫っていて、仏を思うこともできないであろう。ただこの仏の名を称えるがよい。」と教える。

　この人が心を一つにして仏の名を称えると、ひと声ひと声

have destined them to the evil world will be cleared away.

If simply repeating the holy name can do this, how much more would be possible if one is able to concentrate his mind upon this Buddha!

Those who are thus able to recite the holy name, when they come to the end of life, will be met by Amida Buddha and the Bodhisattvas of Compassion and Wisdom and will be led by them into the Buddha's Land, where they will be born in all purity of the white lotus.

Therefore, everyone should keep in mind the words, "Namu-Amida-Butsu" or Whole-hearted Reliance upon the Buddha of Infinite Light and Boundless Life!

II
AMIDA BUDDHA'S LAND OF PURITY

1.   The Buddha of Infinite Light and Boundless Life is ever living and ever radiating His Truth. In His Pure Land there is no suffering and no darkness, and every hour is passed in joy; therefore, it is called the Land of Bliss.

In the midst of this Land there is a lake of pure water, fresh and sparkling, whose waves lap softly on shores of golden sands. Here and there are huge lotus

のうちに、はかり知れない迷いの世界に入る罪を除いて救う。

　もし人が、この仏の名を称えるならば、永遠に尽きることのない迷いの世界に入る罪をも除くのである。ましてや一心に思うに至っては、なおさらのことである。

　まことに念仏する人は、白蓮花のようなすばらしい人である。慈悲と智慧との二菩薩はその友となり、また、常に道を離れることなく、ついに浄土に生まれることになるであろう。

　だから、人びとはこのことばを身につけなければならない。このことばを身につけるということは、この仏の名を身につけることである。

第2節　清らかな国土

1．この仏はいま、現にいて、法を説いている。その国の人びとはみな苦しみを知らず、ただ楽しみの日のみを送るので、極楽というのである。

　その国には七つの宝でできた池があり、中には清らかな水をたたえ、池の底には黄金の砂が敷かれ、車の輪のように大

blossoms as large as chariot wheels of many and various lights and colors — blue lights from blue color, yellow for yellow, red for red, white for white — whose fragrance fills the air.

At different places on the margin of the lake there are pavilions decorated with gold and silver, lapis lazuli and crystal, with marble steps leading down to the water's edge. At other places there are parapets and balustrades hanging over the water and enclosed with curtains and networks of precious gems, and in between there are groves of spices trees and flowering shrubs.

The ground is shining with beauty and the air is vibrant with celestial harmonies. Six times during the day and night, delicately tinted flower petals fall from the sky and people gather them and carry them in flower vessels to all the other Buddah-lands and make offerings of them to the myriad Buddhas.

2.   In this wondrous Land there are many birds. There are snow-white storks and swans, and gaily colored peacocks and tropical birds of paradise, and flocks of little birds, softly singing. In the Buddha's Pure Land these sweetly singing birds are voicing Buddha's teachings and praising His virtues.

Whoever hears and listens to the music of these

きい蓮花が咲いている。その蓮花は、青い花には青い光が、黄色の花には黄色の光が、赤い花には赤い光が、白い花には白い光があり、清らかな香りをあたりに漂わせている。

また、その池の周囲のあちこちには、金・銀・青玉・水晶の四つの宝で作った楼閣があり、そこには大理石で作った階段がある。また、別の場所には池の上につき出た欄干があり、宝玉で飾られた幕で取り囲まれている。また、その間にはよいにおいのする木々や花がいっぱいに咲いた茂みがある。

空には神々しい音楽が鳴り、大地には黄金の色が照り映えて、夜昼六度も天の花が降り、その国の人びとはそれを集め花皿に盛って、ほかのすべての仏国へ持ってゆき、無数の仏に供養する。

2. また、この国の園には、白鳥、孔雀、おうむ、百舌鳥、迦陵頻伽など数多くの鳥が、常に優雅な声を出し、あらゆる徳と善とをたたえ、教えを宣布している。

人びとはこの声を聞いて、みな仏を念じ、教えを思い、人

—221—

voices, listens to the Buddha's voice and awakens to a newness of faith, joy and peace in fellowship with the brotherhood of followers everywhere.

Soft zephyrs pass through the trees of that Pure Land and stir the fragrant curtains of the Pavilions and pass away in sweet cadences of music.

People hearing faint echoes of this heavenly music think of the Buddha, of the Dharma (teaching), and of the Samgha (brotherhood). All these excellences are but reflections of the Pure Land.

3.   Why is Buddha in this land called Amida, indicating the Buddha of Infinite Light and Boundless Life? It is because the splendor of His Truth radiates unimpeded to the outermost and innermost limits of the Buddha-lands; it is because the vitality of His living compassion never wanes through the incalculable lives and eons of time.

It is because the number of those who are born in His Pure Land and are perfectly enlightened is incalculable and they will never again return to the world of delusions and death.

It is because the number of those who are awakened into the newness of Life by His Light is also incalculable.

の和合を念ずる。だれでもこの声の音楽を聞くものは、仏の声を聞く思いがし、仏への信心を新たにし、教えを聞く喜びを新たにして、あらゆる国の仏の教えを受ける者との友情を新たにする。

そよ風が吹き、宝の木々の並木をよぎり、輝く鈴をつけた網に触れると、微妙な音を出し、一時に百千の音楽がかなでられる。

この音を聞く者は、また自然に仏を念じ、教えを思い、人の和合を念ずるようになる。その仏の国は、このような功徳と美しい飾りとをそなえている。

3．どういうわけで、この国の仏は無量光仏、無量寿仏と名づけられるのであろうか。かの仏の光は量ることができず、十方の国々を照らして少しもさえぎられない。またその寿命も限りがないから、そう名づけるのである。

そして、その国に生まれる人びとも、みな、ふたたび迷いの世界にもどらない境地に至り、その数はかぞえ尽くすことができないからである。

また、この仏の光によって新しい命に目覚める人びとの数は無量だからである。

Therefore, should all people concentrate their minds on His Name and, as they come toward the end of life, even for one day or seven days, recite Amida Buddha's Name in perfect faith, and they do this with undisturbed mind, they will be born in the Buddha's Land of Purity, being led by Amida Buddha and many other holy ones who appear at this last moment.

If any man hears Amida Buddha's Name, awakens his faith in His teachings, he will be able to attain unsurpassed perfect Enlightenment.

　ただ、この仏の名を心に保ち、一日または七日にわたって、心を一つにして動揺することがないならば、その人の命が終わるとき、この仏は、多くの聖たちとともに、その人の前に現われる。その人の心はうろたえることなく、ただちにその国に生まれることができる。

　もし人が、この仏の名を聞き、この教えを信ずるならば、仏たちに守られ、この上もない正しいさとりを得ることができるのである。

THE WAY OF PRACTICE

は げ み

THE WAY OF PURIFICATION

I
PURIFICATION OF THE MIND

1. People have worldly passions which lead them into delusions and sufferings. There are five ways to emancipate themselves from the bond of worldly passions.

First, they should have right ideas of things, ideas that are based on careful observation, and understand causes and effects and their significance correctly. Since the cause of suffering is rooted in the mind's desires and attachments, and since desire and attachment are related to mistaken observations by an ego-self, neglecting the significance of the law of cause and effect, and since it is from these wrong observations, there can be peace only if the mind can be rid of these worldly passions.

Second, people can get rid of these mistaken observations and resulting worldly passions by careful and patient mind-control. With efficient mind-control they can avoid desires arising from the stimulation of the eyes, ears, nose, tongue, skin and the subsequent mental processes and, by so doing, cut off the very root of

第1章　さとりへの道

第1節　心を清める

1.　人には、迷いと苦しみのもとである煩悩*がある。この煩悩のきずなから逃れるには五つの方法がある。

第一には、ものの見方を正しくして、その原因と結果とをよくわきまえる。すべての苦しみのもとは、心の中の煩悩であるから、その煩悩がなくなれば、苦しみのない境地が現われることを正しく知るのである。

見方を誤るから、我という考えや、原因・結果の法則を無視する考えが起こり、この間違った考えにとらわれて煩悩を起こし、迷い苦しむようになる。

第二には、欲をおさえしずめることによって煩悩をしずめる。明らかな心によって、眼・耳・鼻・舌・身・意の六つに起こる欲をおさえしずめて、煩悩の起こる根元を断ち切る。

all worldly passions.

Third, they should have correct ideas with regard to the proper use of all things. That is, with regard to articles of food and clothing, they should not think of them in relation to comfort and pleasure, but only in their relation to the body's needs. Clothing is necessary to protect the body against extremes of heat and cold, and to conceal the shame of the body; food is necessary for the nourishment of the body while it is training for Enlightenment and Buddhahood. Worldly passions can not arise through such thinking.

Fourth, people should learn endurance; they should learn to endure the discomforts of heat and cold, hunger and thirst; they should learn to be patient when receiving abuse and scorn; for it is the practice of endurance that quenches the fire of worldly passions which is burning up their bodies.

Fifth, people should learn to see and so avoid all danger. Just as a wise man keeps away from wild horses or mad dogs, so one should not make friends with evil men, nor should he go to places that wise men avoid. If one practises caution and prudence, the fire of worldly passions which is burning in their vitals will die down.

2. There are five groups of desires in the world.

第三には、物を用いるに当たって、考えを正しくする。着物や食物を用いるのは享楽のためとは考えない。着物は暑さや寒さを防ぎ羞恥を包むためであり、食物は道を修めるもととなる身体を養うためにあると考える。この正しい考えのために、煩悩は起こることができなくなる。

第四には、何ごとも耐え忍ぶことである。暑さ・寒さ・飢え・渇きを耐え忍び、ののしりや謗りを受けても耐え忍ぶことによって、自分の身を焼き滅ぼす煩悩の火は燃え立たなくなる。

第五には、危険から遠ざかることである。賢い人が、荒馬や狂犬の危険に近づかないように、行ってはならない所、交わってはならない友は遠ざける。このようにすれば煩悩の炎は消え去るのである。

　2．世には五つの欲がある。

Desires arising from the forms the eyes see; from the sounds the ears hear; from the fragrances the nose smells; from tastes pleasant to the tongue; from things that are agreeable to the sense of touch. From these five doors to desire come the body's love of comfort.

Most people, being influenced by the body's love of comfort, do not notice the evils that follow comfort, and they are caught in a devil's trap like a deer in the forest caught in a hunter's trap. Indeed, these five doors of desires arising from the senses are the most dangerous traps. When caught by them, people are entangled in worldly passions and suffer. They should know how to get rid of these traps.

3.   There is no one way to get free from the trap of worldly passions. Suppose you caught a snake, a croco-dile, a bird, a dog, a fox and a monkey, six creatures of very different natures, and you tie them together with a strong rope and let them go. Each of these six creatures will try to go back to its own lair by its own method: the snake will seek a covering of grass, the crocodile will seek water, the bird will want to fly in the air, the dog will seek a village, the fox will seek the solitary ledges, and the monkey will seek the trees of a forest. In the attempt of each to go its own way there will be a struggle, but, being tied together by a rope, the strongest at any

眼に見るもの、耳に聞く声、鼻にかぐ香り、舌に味わう味、身に触れる感じ、この五つのものをここちよく好ましく感ずることである。

多くの人は、その肉体の好ましさに心ひかれて、これにおぼれ、その結果として起こる災いを見ない。これはちょうど、森の鹿が猟師のわなにかかって捕らえられるように、悪魔のしかけたわなにかかったのである。まことにこの五欲はわなであり、人びとはこれにかかって煩悩を起こし、苦しみを生む。だから、この五欲の災いを見て、そのわなから免れる道を知らなければならない。

3．その方法は一つではない。例えば、蛇と鰐と鳥と犬と狐と猿と、その習性を別にする六種の生きものを捕らえて強いなわで縛り、そのなわを結び合わせて放つとする。

このとき、この六種の生きものは、それぞれの習性に従って、おのおのその住みかに帰ろうとする。蛇は塚に、鰐は水に、鳥は空に、犬は村に、狐は野に、猿は森に。このためにお互いに争い、力のまさったものの方へ、引きずられていく。

one time will drag the rest.

Like the creatures in this parable, man is tempted in different ways by the desires of his six senses, eyes, ears, nose, tongue, touch and mind, and is controlled by the predominant desire.

If the six creatures are all tied to a post, they will try to get free until they are tired out, and then will lie down by the post. Just like this, if people will train and control the mind there will be no further trouble from the other five senses. If the mind is under control people will have happiness both now and in the future.

4.   People love their egoistic comfort, which is a love of fame and praise. But fame and praise are like incense that consumes itself and soon disappears. If people chase after honors and public acclaim and leave the way of truth, they are in serious danger and will soon have cause for regret.

A man who chases after fame and wealth and love affairs is like a child who licks honey from the blade of a knife. While he is tasting the sweetness of honey, he has to risk hurting his tongue. He is like a man who carries a torch against a strong wind; the flame will surely burn his hands and face.

　ちょうどこのたとえのように、人びとは目に見たもの、耳に聞いた声、鼻にかいだ香り、舌に味わった味、身に触れた感じ、及び、意に思ったもののために引きずられ、その中の誘惑のもっとも強いものの方に引きずられてその支配を受ける。

　またもし、この六種の生きものを、それぞれなわで縛り、それを丈夫な大きな柱に縛りつけておくとする。はじめの間は、生きものたちはそれぞれの住みかに帰ろうとするが、ついには力尽き、その柱のかたわらに疲れて横たわる。

　これと同じように、もし、人がその心を修め、その心を鍛練しておけば、他の五欲に引かれることはない。もし心が制御されているならば、人びとは、現在においても未来においても幸福を得るであろう。

　4.　人びとは欲の火の燃えるままに、はなやかな名声を求める。それはちょうど香が薫りつつ自らを焼いて消えてゆくようなものである。いたずらに名声を求め、名誉を貪って、道を求めることを知らないならば、身はあやうく、心は悔いにさいなまれるであろう。

　名誉と財と色香とを貪り求めることは、ちょうど、子供が刃に塗られた蜜をなめるようなものである。甘さを味わっているうちに、舌を切る危険をおかすこととなる。

One must not trust his own mind that is filled with greed, anger and foolishness. One must not let his mind run free, but must keep it under strict control.

5.   To attain perfect mind-control is a most difficult thing. Those who seek Enlightenment must first rid themselves of the fire of all desires. Desire is a raging fire, and one seeking Enlightenment must avoid the fire of desire as a man carrying a load of hay avoids sparks.

But it would be foolish for a man to put out his eyes for fear of being tempted by beautiful forms. The mind is master and if the mind is under control, the weaker desires will disappear.

It is difficult to follow the way to Enlightenment, but it is more difficult if people have no mind to seek such a way. Without Enlightenment, there is endless suffering in this world of life and death.

When a man seeks the way to Enlightenment, it is like an ox carrying a heavy load through a field of mud. If the ox tries to do its best without paying attention to other things, it can overcome the mud and take a rest. Just so, if the mind is controlled and kept on the right path, there will be no mud of greed to hinder it and all its suffering will disappear.

　愛欲を貪り求めて満足を知らない者は、たいまつをかかげて風に逆らいゆくようなものである。手を焼き、身を焼くのは当然である。

　貪りと瞋りと愚かさという三つの毒に満ちている自分自身の心を信じてはならない。自分の心をほしいままにしてはならない。心をおさえ欲のままに走らないように努めなければならない。

　5．さとりを得ようと思うものは、欲の火を去らなければならない。干し草を背に負う者が野火を見て避けるように、さとりの道を求める者は、必ずこの欲の火から遠ざからなければならない。

　美しい色を見、それに心を奪われることを恐れて眼をくり抜こうとする者は愚かである。心が主であるから、よこしまな心を断てば、従者である眼の思いは直ちにやむ。

　道を求めて進んでゆくことは苦しい。しかし、道を求める心のないことは、さらに苦しい。この世に生まれ、老い、病んで、死ぬ。その苦しみには限りがない。

　道を求めてゆくことは、牛が重荷を負って深い泥の中を行くときに、疲れてもわき目もふらずに進み、泥をはなれてはじめて一息つくのと同じでなければならない。欲の泥はさら

6. Those who seek the path to Enlightenment must first remove all egoistic pride and be humbly willing to accept the light of Buddha's teachings. All the treasures of the world, all its gold and silver and honors, are not to be compared with wisdom and virtue.

To enjoy good health, to bring true happiness to one's family, to bring peace to all, one must first discipline and control one's own mind. If a man can control his mind he can find the way to Enlightenment, and all wisdom and virtue will naturally come to him.

Just as treasures are uncovered from the earth, so virtue appears from good deeds, and wisdom appears from a pure and peaceful mind. To walk safely through the maze of human life, one needs the light of wisdom and the guidance of virtue.

The Buddha's teaching, which tells people how to eliminate greed, anger and foolishness, is a good teaching and those who follow it attain the happiness of a good life.

7. Human beings tend to move in the direction of their thoughts. If they harbor greedy thoughts, they become more greedy; if they think angry thoughts, they become more angry; if they hold thoughts of revenge, their feet move in that direction.

に深いが、心を正しくして道を求めてゆけば、泥を離れて苦しみはうせるであろう。

6．道を求めてゆく人は、心の高ぶりを取り去って、教えの光を身に加えなければならない。どんな金銀・財宝の飾りも、徳の飾りには及ばない。

身を健やかにし、一家を栄えさせ、人びとを安らかにするには、まず、心をととのえなければならない。心をととのえて道を楽しむ思いがあれば、徳はおのずからその身にそなわる。

宝石は地から生まれ、徳は善から現われ、智慧は静かな清い心から生まれる。広野のように広い迷いの人生を進むには、この智慧の光によって、進むべき道を照らし、徳の飾りによって身をいましめて進まなければならない。

貪りと瞋りと愚かさという三つの毒を捨てよ、と説く仏の教えは、よい教えであり、その教えに従う人は、よい生活と幸福を得る人である。

7．人の心は、ともすればその思い求める方へと傾く。貪りを思えば貪りの心が起こる。瞋りを思えば瞋りの心が強くなる。損なうことを思えば損なう心が多くなる。

At harvest time farmers keep their herds confined, lest they break through the fences into the field and give cause for complaint or for being killed; so people must closely guard their minds against dishonesty and misfortune. They must eliminate thoughts that stimulate greed, anger and foolishness, but encourage thoughts that stimulate charity and kindness.

When spring comes and the pastures have an abundance of green grass, farmers turn their cattle loose; but even then they keep a close watch over them. It is so with the minds of people: even under the best of conditions the mind will bear watching.

8.   At one time Shakyamuni Buddha was staying in the town of Kausambi. In this town there was one who resented Him and who bribed wicked men to circulate false stories about Him. Under these circumstances it was difficult for His disciples to get sufficient food from their begging and there was much abuse in that town.

Ananda said to Shakyamuni: "We had better not stay in a town like this. There are other and better towns to go to. We had better leave this town."

The Blessed One replied: "Suppose the next town is like this, what shall we do then?"

　牛飼いは、秋のとり入れ時になると、放してある牛を集め
て牛小屋に閉じこめる。これは牛が穀物を荒して抗議を受け
たり、または殺されたりすることを防ぐのである。

　人もそのように、よくないことから起こる災いを見て、心
を閉じこめ、悪い思いを破り捨てなければならない。貪り
と瞋りと損なう心を砕いて、貪らず、瞋らず、損なわない
心を育てなければならない。

　牛飼いは、春になって野原の草が芽をふき始めると牛を放
す。しかし、その牛の群れの行方を見守り、その居所に注意
を怠らない。

　人もまた、これと同じように、自分の心がどのように動い
ているか、その行方を見守り、行方を見失わないようにしな
ければならない。

　8．釈尊がコーサンビーの町に滞在していたとき、釈尊に
怨みを抱く者が町の悪者を買収し、釈尊の悪口を言わせた。
釈尊の弟子たちは、町に入って托鉢しても一物も得られず、
ただそしりの声を聞くだけであった。

　そのときアーナンダは釈尊にこう言った。「世尊よ、この
ような町に滞在することはありません。他にもっとよい町が
あると思います。」「アーナンダよ、次の町もこのようであっ

"Then we move to another."

The Blessed One said: "No, Ananda, there will be no end in that way. We had better remain here and bear the abuse patiently until it ceases, and then we move to another place.

"There are profit and loss, slander and honor, praise and abuse, suffering and pleasure in this world; the Enlightened One is not controlled by these external things; they will cease as quickly as they come."

II
THE GOOD WAY OF BEHAVIOR

1. Those who seek the way of Enlightenment must always bear in mind the necessity of constantly keeping their body, speech and mind pure. To keep the body pure one must not kill any living creature, one must not steal or commit adultery. To keep speech pure one must not lie, or abuse, or deceive, or indulge in idle talk. To keep the mind pure one must remove all greed, anger and false judgement.

If the mind becomes impure, for sure, one's deeds will be impure; if the deeds are impure, there will be suffering. So it is of the greatest importance that the mind and the body be kept pure.

たらどうするのか。」「世尊よ、また他の町へ移ります。」

　「アーナンダよ、それではどこまで行ってもきりがない。わたしはそしりを受けたときには、じっとそれに耐え、そしりの終わるのを待って、他へ移るのがよいと思う。アーナンダよ。仏は、利益・害・中傷・ほまれ・たたえ・そしり・苦しみ・楽しみという、この世の八つのことによって動かされることがない。こういったことは、間もなく過ぎ去るであろう。」

第2節　善　い　行　い

　1.　道を求めるものは、常に身と口と意の三つの行いを清めることを心がけなければならない。身の行いを清めるとは、生きるものを殺さず、盗みをせず、よこしまな愛欲を犯さないことである。口の行いを清めるとは、偽りを言わず、悪口を言わず、二枚舌を使わず、むだ口をたたかないことである。意の行いを清めるとは、貪らず、瞋らず、よこしまな見方をしないことである。

　心が濁れば行いが汚れ、行いが汚れると、苦しみを避けることができない。だから、心を清め、行いを慎しむことが道のかなめである。

2.   Once there was a rich widow who had a reputation for kindness, modesty and courtesy. She had a housemaid who was wise and diligent.

One day the maid thought: "My mistress has a very good reputation; I wonder whether she is good by nature, or is good because of her surroundings. I will try her and find out."

The following morning the maid did not appear before her mistress until nearly noon. The mistress was vexed and scolded her impatiently. The maid replied:

"If I am lazy for only a day or two, you ought not to become impatient." Then the mistress became angry.

The next day the maid got up late again. This made the mistress very angry and she struck the maid with a stick. This incident became widely known and the rich widow lost her good reputation.

3.   Many people are like this woman. While their surroundings are satisfactory they are kind, modest and quiet, but it is questionable if they will behave likewise when the conditions change and become unsatisfactory.

It is only when a person maintains a pure and peaceful mind and continues to act with goodness when unpleasant words enter his ears, when others show ill-will toward him or when he lacks sufficient food, clothes and

2．昔、ある金持ちの未亡人がいた。親切で、しとやかで、謙遜_{けんそん}であったため、まことに評判のよい人であった。その家にひとりの女中がいて、これも利口でよく働く女であった。

あるとき、その女中がこう考えた。「うちの主人は、まことに評判のよい人であるが、腹からそういう人なのか、または、よい環境がそうさせているのか、一つ試してみよう。」

そこで、女中は、次の日、なかなか起きず、昼ごろにようやく顔を見せた。主人はきげんを悪くして、「なぜこんなに遅いのか。」ととがめた。

「一日や二日遅くても、そうぷりぷり怒るものではありません。」とことばを返すと、主人は怒った。

女中はさらに次の日も遅く起きた。主人は怒り、棒で打った。このことが知れわたり、未亡人はそれまでのよい評判を失った。

3．だれでもこの女主人と同じである。環境がすべて心にかなうと、親切で謙遜_{けんそん}で、静かであることができる。しかし、環境が心に逆らってきても、なお、そのようにしていられるかどうかが問題なのである。

自分にとって面白くないことばが耳に入ってくるとき、相

shelter, that we may call him good.

Therefore, those who do good deeds and maintain a peaceful mind only when their surroundings are satisfactory are not really good people. Only those who have received the Buddha's teachings and are training their minds and bodies by those teachings can be called truly good, modest and peaceful people.

4. As to the suitability of words to be used there are five pairs of antonyms: words that are suitable to their occasions and those not so suitable to theirs; words that fit the facts and those that don't fit; words that sound pleasant and those that sound rude; words that are beneficial and those that are harmful; and words that are sympathetic and those that are hateful.

Whatever words we utter should be chosen with care for people will hear them and be influenced by them for good or ill. If our minds are filled with sympathy and compassion, they will be resistant to the evil words we hear. We must not let wild words pass our lips lest they arouse feelings of anger and hatred. The words we speak should always be words of sympathy and wisdom.

Suppose there is a man who wants to remove all the

手が明らかに自分に敵意を見せて迫ってくるとき、衣食住が
容易に得られないとき、このようなときにも、なお静かな心
と善い行いとを持ち続けることができるであろうか。

　だから、環境がすべて心にかなうときだけ、静かな心を持
ちよい行いをしても、それはまことによい人とはいえない。
＊仏の教えを喜び、教えに身も心も練り上げた人こそ、静かに
して、謙遜な、よい人といえるのである。

　4. すべてことばには、時にかなったことばとかなわない
ことば、事実にかなったことばとかなわないことば、柔らか
なことばと粗いことば、有益なことばと有害なことば、慈し
みあることばと憎しみのあることば、この五対がある。
　この五対のいずれによって話しかけられても、
　「わたしの心は変わらない。粗いことばはわたしの口から
漏れない。同情と哀れみとによって慈しみの思いを心にたく
わえ、怒りや憎しみの心を起こさないように。」と努めなけ
ればならない。

　例えばここに人がおり、鋤と鍬を持って、この大地の土を

dirt from the ground. He uses a spade and a winnow and works perseveringly scattering the dirt all about, but it is an impossible task. Like this foolish man we can not hope to eliminate all words. We must train our mind and fill our hearts with sympathy so that we will be undisturbed by the words spoken by others.

One might try to paint a picture with water colors on the blue sky, but it is impossible. And it is also impossible to dry up a great river by the heat of a torch made of hay, or to produce a crackling noise by rubbing together two pieces of well-tanned leather. Like these examples, people should train their minds so that they would not be disturbed by whatever kinds of words they might hear.

They should train their minds and keep them broad as the earth, unlimited as the sky, deep as a big river and soft as well-tanned leather.

Even if your enemy catches and tortures you, if you feel resentment, you are not following the Buddha's teachings. Under every circumstance you should learn to think: "My mind is unshakable. Words of hatred and anger shall not pass my lips. I will surround my enemy with thoughts of sympathy and pity that flow out from a mind filled with compassion for all sentient life."

なくそうと、土を掘ってはまき散らし、土よなくなれと言っ
たとしても、土をなくすことはできない。このようにすべて
のことばをなくしてしまうことはのぞみ得ない。

　だから、どんなことばで語られても、心を鍛えて慈しみの
心をもって満たし、心の変わらないようにしておかなければ
ならない。

　また、絵の具によって、空に絵を描こうとしても、物の姿
を現わすことはできないように、また、枯草のたいまつによ
って、大きな河の水を乾かそうとしてもできないように、ま
た、よくなめした柔らかな皮を摩擦して、ざらざらした音を
立てようとしてもできないように、どんなことばで話しかけ
られても、決して心の変わらないように、心を養わなければ
ならない。

　人は、心を大地のように広く、大空のように限りなく、大
河のように深く、なめした皮のように柔らかに養わなければ
ならない。

　たとえ、かたきに捕らえられて、苦しめられるようなこと
があっても、そのために心を暗くするのは、真に仏の教えを
守った者とはいえない。どんな場合に当たっても、

　「わたしの心は動かない。憎しみ怒ることばは、わたしの

5.   There is a fable told of a man who found an anthill which burned in the daytime and smoked at night. He went to a wise man and asked his advice as to what he should do about it. The wise man told him to dig into it with a sword. This the man did. He found in succession a gate-bar, some bubbles of water, a pitchfork, a box, a tortoise, a butcher-knife, a piece of meat and, finally, a dragon which came out. The man reported to the wise man what he had found. The wise man explained the significance of it and said, "Throw away everything but the dragon; leave the dragon alone and do not disturb him."

This is a fable in which "anthill" represents the human body. "Burned in the daytime" represents the fact that during the day people turn into acts the things they thought about the previous night. "Smoked at night" indicates the fact that people during the night recall with pleasure or regret the things they did the previous day.

In the same fable, "a man" means a person who seeks Enlightenment. "A wise man" means Buddha. "A sword" means pure wisdom. "Dig into it" refers to the effort he must make to gain Enlightenment.

口を漏れない。同情と哀れみのある慈しみの心をもって、その人を包むように。」と学ばなければならない。

5．ある人が、「夜は煙って、昼は燃える蟻塚。」を見つけた。ある賢者にそのことを語ると、「では、剣をとって深く掘り進め。」と命ぜられ、言われるままに、その蟻塚を掘ってみた。

はじめにかんぬきが出、次は水泡、次には刺又、それから箱、亀、牛殺しの刀、一片の肉が次々と出、最後に龍が出た。

賢者にそのことを語ると、「それらのものをみな捨てよ。ただ龍のみをそのままにしておけ。龍を妨げるな。」と教えた。

これはたとえである。ここに「蟻塚」というのはこの体のことである。「夜は煙って」というのは、昼間したことを夜になっていろいろ考え、喜んだり、悔やんだりすることをいう。「昼は燃える」というのは、夜考えたことを、昼になってから体や口で実行することをいう。

「ある人」というのは道を求める人のこと、「賢者」とは仏のことである。「剣」とは清らかな智慧のこと、「深く掘り進む」とは努力のことである。

Further in the fable, "gate-bar" represents ignorance; "bubbles" are puffs of suffering and anger;
"pitchfork" suggests hesitation and uneasiness; "box"
suggests the storage of greed, anger, laziness, fickleness,
repentance and delusion; "tortoise" means the body and
the mind; "butcher-knife" means the synthesis of the five
sensory desires, and "a piece of meat" means the resulting desire that causes a man to covet after satisfaction.
These things are all harmful to man and so Buddha said,
"Throw away everything."

Still further, "dragon" indicates a mind that has
eliminated all worldly passions. If a man digs into the
things about him with the sword of wisdom he will
finally come to his dragon. "Leave the dragon alone and
do not disturb him" means to go after and dig up a mind
free of worldly desires.

6.   Pindola, a disciple of Buddha, after gaining Enlightenment, returned to his native place of Kausambi to
repay the people there for the kindness they had shown
him. In so doing he prepared the field for the sowing of
Buddha-seeds.

On the outskirts of Kausambi there is a small park
that runs along the bank of the Ganges River shaded by
endless rows of coconut trees and where a cool wind
continually blows.

「かんぬき」とは※無明のこと、「水泡」とは怒りと悩み、「刺又」とはためらいと不安、「箱」とは貪り・瞋り・怠り・浮わつき・悔い・惑いのこと、「亀」とは身と心のこと、「牛殺しの刀」とは五欲のこと、「一片の肉」とは楽しみを貪り求める欲のことである。これらは、いずれもこの身の毒となるものであるから、「みな捨てよ」というのである。

　最後の「龍」とは、※煩悩の尽きた心のことである。わが身の足下を掘り進んでゆけば、ついにはこの龍を見ることになる。
　掘り進んでこの龍を見いだすことを、「龍のみをそのままにしておけ、龍を妨げるな。」というのである。

　6．釈尊の弟子ピンドーラは、さとりを得て後、故郷の恩に報いるために、コーサンビーの町に帰り、努力して仏の種をまく田地の用意をしようとした。コーサンビーの郊外に、小公園があり、椰子の並木は果てもなく続き、ガンジスの洋洋たる河波は、涼しい風を絶え間なく送っていた。

One hot summer day, Pindola sat in meditation in the cool shade of a tree when Lord Udyana came to this park with his consorts for recreation and, after music and pleasure, he took a nap in the shade of another tree.

While their Lord was asleep, his wives and ladies-in-waiting took a walk and suddenly came upon Pindola sitting in meditation. They recognized him as a holy-man and asked him to teach them, and they listened to his sermon.

When the Lord awoke from his nap, he went in search of his ladies and found them surrounding this man and listening to his teaching. Being of a jealous and lascivious mind, the Lord became angry and abused Pindola, saying: "It is inexcusable that you, a holy-man, should be in the midst of women and enjoy idle talking with them." Pindola quietly closed his eyes and remained silent.

The angry Lord drew his sword and threatened Pindola, but the holy-man remained silent and was as firm as a rock. This made the Lord still more angry so he broke open an anthill and threw some of the ant-filled dirt upon him, but still Pindola remained sitting in meditation, quietly enduring the insult and pain.

　夏のある日、昼の暑い日盛りを避けて、ピンドーラは、並木の木陰の涼しいところで坐禅していた。ちょうどこの日、城主ハウドャキ王も、妃たちを連れて公園に入り、管弦の遊びに疲れて、涼しい木陰にしばしの眠りにおちいった。

　妃たちは、王の眠っている間、あちらこちらとさまよい歩き、ふと、木陰に端坐するピンドーラを見た。彼女らはその姿に心うたれ、道を求める心を起こし、説法することを求めた。そして、彼の教えに耳を傾けた。

　目を覚ました王は、妃たちのいないのに不審をいだき、後を追って、木陰で妃たちにとりまかれているひとりの出家を見た。淫楽に荒んだ王は、前後の見境もなく、心中にむらむらと嫉妬の炎を燃やし、「わが女たちを近づけて雑談にふけるとはふらちな奴だ。」と悪口を浴びせた。ピンドーラは眼を閉じ、黙然として、一語も発しない。

　怒り狂った王は、剣を抜いて、ピンドーラの頭につきつけたが、彼はひとことも語らず、岩のように動かない。

　いよいよ怒った王は、蟻塚をこわして、無数の赤蟻を彼の体のまわりにまき散らしたが、それでもピンドーラは、端然と坐ったままそれに耐えていた。

Thereupon, the Lord became ashamed of his ferocious conduct and begged Pindola's pardon. As a result of this incident, the Buddha's teaching found its way into the Lord's castle and from there it spread all over the country.

7. A few days later Lord Udyana visited Pindola in the forest retreat where he lived and asked him, "Honored teacher, how is it that the disciples of Buddha can keep their bodies and minds pure and untempted by lust, although they are mostly young men?"

Pindola replied: "Noble Lord, Buddha has taught us to respect all women. He has taught us to look upon all old women as our mothers, upon those of our own age as our sisters, and upon younger ones as our daughters. Because of this teaching the disciples of Buddha are able to keep their bodies and minds pure and untempted by lust although they are youthful."

"But, Honored teacher, one may have impure thoughts of a woman the age of a mother or a sister or a daughter. How do the disciples of Buddha control their desires?"

"Noble Lord, the Blessed One taught us to think of our bodies as secreting impurities of all kinds such as blood, pus, sweat and oils; by thinking thus, we, although

　ここに至って、王ははじめて自分の狂暴を恥じ、その罪を
わびて許しを請うた。これから仏の教えがこの王家に入り、
その国に広まるいとぐちが開けた。

　7．その後、幾日か過ぎて、ウドヤナ王はピンドーラをそ
の住む森に訪ね、その不審をただした。

　「大徳よ、仏の弟子たちは、若い身でありながら、どうし
て欲におぼれず、清らかにその身を保つことができるのであ
ろうか。」

　「大王よ、仏はわたしたちに向かって、婦人に対する考え
を教えられた。年上の婦人を母と見よ。中ほどの婦人を妹と
見よ。若い婦人を娘と見よと。この教えによって、弟子たち
は若い身でありながら、欲におぼれず、その身を清らかに保
っている。」

　「大徳よ、しかし、人は、母ほどの人にも、妹ほどの人に
も、娘ほどの人にもみだらな心を起こすものである。仏の弟
子たちはどのようにして欲を抑えることができるのであろう
か。」

　「大王よ、世尊は、人の体がいろいろの汚れ、血・うみ・
汗・脂など、さまざまの汚れに満ちていることを観よと教え
られた。このように見ることによって、われわれ若い者でも、

young, are able to keep our minds pure."

"Honored teacher," still pressed the Lord. "It may be easy for you to do this for you have trained your body and mind, and polished your wisdom, but it would be difficult for those who have not yet had such training. They may try to remember the impurities but their eyes will follow beautiful forms. They may try to see the ugliness but they will be tempted by the beautiful figures just the same. There must be some other reason that the young men among the Buddha's disciples are able to keep their actions pure."

"Noble Lord," replied Pindola, "the Blessed One teaches us to guard the doors of the five senses. When we see beautiful figures and colors with our eyes, when we hear pleasant sounds with our ears, when we smell fragrance with our nose, or when we taste sweet things with our tongue or touch soft things with our hands, we are not to become attached to these attractive things, neither are we to be repulsed by unattractive things. We are taught to carefully guard the doors of these five senses. It is by this teaching of the Blessed One that even young disciples are able to keep their minds and bodies pure."

"The teaching of Buddha is truly marvelous. From my own experience I know that if I confront anything

心を清らかに保つことができるのである。」

「大徳よ、体を鍛え、心を練り、智慧をみがいた仏弟子たちには容易であるかも知れない。しかし、いかに仏の弟子でも、未熟の人には、容易なことではないであろう。汚れたものを見ようとしても、いつしか清らかな姿に心ひかれ、醜さを見ようとしても、いつしか美しい形に魅せられてゆく。仏弟子が美しい行いを保つには、もっと他に理由があるのではあるまいか。」

「大王よ、仏は五官の戸口を守れと教えられる。目によって色・形を見、耳によって声を聞き、鼻によって香りをかぎ、舌によって味を味わい、体によって物に触れるとき、そのよい姿に心を奪われず、またよくない姿に心をいらだたせず、よく五官の戸口を守れと教えられる。この教えによって、若い者でも、心身を清らかに保つことができるのである。」

「大徳よ、仏の仰せは、まことにすばらしい。わたしの経験によってもそのとおりである。五官の戸締りをしないで、

beautiful or pleasing, without being on my guard, I am disturbed by the sense impressions. It is of vital importance that we be on guard at the doors of the five senses, at all times to keep our deeds pure."

8.   Whenever a person expresses the thought of his mind in action there is always a reaction that follows. If one abuses you, there is a temptation to answer back, or to be revenged. One should be on guard against this natural reaction. It is like spitting against the wind, it harms no one but oneself. It is like sweeping dust against the wind, it does not get rid of the dust but defiles oneself. Misfortune always dogs the steps of one who gives way to the desire for revenge.

9.   It is a very good deed to cast away greed and to cherish a mind of charity. It is still better to keep one's mind intent on respecting the Noble Path.

One should get rid of a selfish mind and replace it with a mind that is earnest to help others. An act to make another happy inspires the other to make still another happy, and so happiness is born from such an act.

Thousands of candles can be lighted from a single candle, and the life of the candle will not be shortened. Happiness never decreases by being shared.

ものに向かえば、すぐに卑しい心にとらわれる。五官の戸口を守ることは、わたしどもの行いを清らかにするうえに、まことに大切なことである。」

8. 人が心に思うところを動作に表わすとき、常にそこには反作用が起こる。人はののしられると、言い返したり、仕返ししたくなるものである。人はこの反作用に用心しなくてはならない。それは風に向かって唾（つばき）するようなものである。それは他人を傷つけず、かえって自分を傷つける。それは風に向かってちりを掃くようなものである。それはちりを除くことにならず、自分を汚すことになる。仕返しの心には常に災いがつきまとうものである。

9. せまい心を捨てて、広く他に施すことは、まことによいことである。それとともに、志を守り、道を敬うことは、さらによいことである。

人は利己的な心を捨てて、他人を助ける努力をすべきである。他人が施すのを見れば、その人はさらに別の人を幸せにし、幸福はそこから生まれる。

一つのたいまつから何千人の人が火を取っても、そのたいまつはもとのとおりであるように、幸福はいくら分け与えても、減るということがない。

Those who seek Enlightenment must be careful of their first steps. No matter how high one's aspiration may be, it must be attained step by step. The steps of the path to Enlightenment must be taken in our everyday life.

10. At the very beginning of the path to Enlightenment there are twenty difficulties for us to overcome in this world, and they are: 1. It is hard for a poor man to be generous. 2. It is hard for a proud man to learn the Way of Enlightenment. 3. It is hard to seek Enlightenment at the cost of self-sacrifice. 4. It is hard to be born while Buddha is in the world. 5. It is hard to hear the teaching of Buddha. 6. It is hard to keep the mind pure against the instincts of the body. 7. It is hard not to desire things that are beautiful and attractive. 8. It is hard for a strong man not to use his strength to satisfy his desires. 9. It is hard not to get angry when one is insulted. 10. It is hard to remain innocent when tempted by sudden circumstances.

11. It is hard to apply oneself to study widely and thoroughly. 12. It is hard not to despise a beginner. 13. It is hard to keep oneself humble. 14. It is hard to find good friends. 15. It is hard to endure the discipline that leads to Enlightenment. 16. It is hard not to be disturbed by external conditions and circumstances. 17. It is hard to teach others by knowing their abilities. 18. It is hard to

　道を修める者は、その一歩一歩を慎まなければならない。志がどんなに高くても、それは一歩一歩到達されなければならない。道は、その日その日の生活の中にあることを忘れてはならない。

　10.　この世の中に、さとりへの道を始めるに当たって成し難いことが二十ある。

1. 貧しくて、施すことは難く、
2. 慢心にして道を学ぶことは難く、
3. 命を捨てて道を求めることは難く、
4. 仏の在世に生を受けることは難く、
5. 仏の教えを聞くことは難く、
6. 色欲を耐え忍び、諸欲を離れることは難く、
7. よいものを見て求めないことは難く、
8. 権勢を持ちながら、勢いをもって人に臨まないことは難く、
9. 辱しめられて怒らないことは難く、
10. 事が起きても無心であることは難く、
11. 広く学び深く究めることは難く、
12. 初心の人を軽んじないことは難く、
13. 慢心を除くことは難く、
14. よい友を得ることは難く、
15. 道を学んでさとりに入ることは難く、
16. 外界の環境に動かされないことは難く、
17. 相手の能力を知って、教えを説くことは難く、

maintain a peaceful mind. 19. It is hard not to argue about right and wrong. 20. It is hard to find and learn a good method.

11. Good men and bad men differ from each other in their natures. Bad men do not recognize a sinful act as sinful; if its sinfulness is brought to their attention, they do not cease doing it and do not like to have anyone inform them of their sinful acts. Wise men are sensitive to right and wrong; they cease doing anything as soon as they see that it is wrong; they are grateful to anyone who calls their attention to such wrong acts.

Thus good men and bad men differ radically. Bad men never appreciate kindness shown them, but wise men appreciate and are grateful. Wise men try to express their appreciation and gratitude by some return of kindness, not only to their benefactor, but to everyone else.

III
TEACHING IN ANCIENT FABLES

1. Once upon a time there was a country which had the very peculiar custom of abandoning its aged people in remote and inaccessible mountains.

A certain minister of the State found it too difficult

18.　心をいつも平らかに保つことは難く、

19.　是非をあげつらわないことは難く、

20.　よい手段を学び知ることは難い。

11.　悪人と善人の特質はそれぞれ違っている。悪人の特質は、罪を知らず、それをやめようとせず、罪を知らされるのをいやがる。善人の特質は、善悪を知り、悪であることを知ればすぐやめ、悪を知らせてくれる人に感謝する。

このように、善人と悪人とは違っている。

愚かな人とは自分に示された他人の親切に感謝できない人である。

一方賢い人とは常に感謝の気持ちを持ち、直接自分に親切にしてくれた人だけではなく、すべての人に対して思いやりを持つことによって、感謝の気持ちを表わそうとする人である。

第三節　仏のたとえ

1.　遠い昔、棄老国と名づける、老人を棄てる国があった。その国の人びとは、だれしも老人になると、遠い野山に棄てられるのがおきてであった。

その国の王に仕える大臣は、いかにおきてとはいえ、年老

to follow this custom in the case of his own aged father, and so he built a secret underground cave where he hid his father and cared for him.

One day a god appeared before the king of that country and gave him a puzzling problem, saying that if he could not solve it satisfactorily, his country would be destroyed. The problem was: "Here are two serpents; tell me the sex of each."

Neither the king nor anyone in the palace was able to solve the problem; so the king offered a great reward to anyone in his kingdom who could.

The minister went to his father's hiding place and asked him for the answer to that problem. The old man said: "It is an easy solution. Place the two snakes on a soft carpet; the one that moves about is the male, and the other that keeps quiet is the female." The minister carried the answer to the king and the problem was successfully solved.

Then the god asked other difficult questions which the king and his retainers were unable to answer, but which the minister, after consulting his aged father, could always solve.

いた父を棄てることができず、深く大地に穴を掘ってそこに家を作り、そこに隠して孝養を尽くしていた。

ところがここに一大事が起きた。それは神が現われて、王に向かって恐ろしい難問を投げつけたのである。

「ここに二匹の蛇がいる。この蛇の雄・雌を見分ければよし、もしできないならば、この国を滅ぼしてしまう。」と。

王はもとより、宮殿にいるだれひとりとして蛇の雄・雌を見分けられる者はいなかった。王はついに国中に布告して、見分け方を知っている者には、厚く賞を与えるであろうと告げさせた。

かの大臣は家に帰り、ひそかに父に尋ねると、父はこう言った。

「それは易しいことだ。柔らかい敷物の上に、その二匹の蛇を置くがよい。そのとき、騒がしく動くのは雄であり、動かないのが雌である。」

大臣は父の教えのとおり王に語り、それによって蛇の雄・雌を知ることができた。

それから神は、次々にむずかしい問題を出した。王も家臣たちも、答えることができなかったが、大臣はひそかにその問題を父に尋ね、常に解くことができた。

Here are some of the questions and their answers. "Who is the one who, being asleep, is called the awakened one, and, being awake, is called the sleeping one?" The answer is this: — It is the one who is under training for Enlightenment. He is awake when compared with those who are not interested in Enlightenment; he is asleep when compared with those who have already attained Enlightenment.

"How can you weigh a large elephant?" "Load it on a boat and draw a line to mark how deep the boat sinks into the water. Then take out the elephant and load the boat with stones until it sinks to the same depth, and then weigh the stones."

What is the meaning of the saying, "A cupful of water is more than the water of an ocean?" This is the answer: "A cupful of water given in a pure and compassionate spirit to one's parents or to a sick person has an eternal merit, but the water of an ocean will some day come to an end."

Next the god made a starving man, reduced to skin and bones, complain, "Is there anyone in this world more hungry than I?" "The man who is so selfish and greedy that he does not believe in the Three Treasures of the Buddha, the Dharma and the Samgha, and who does not make offerings to his parents and teachers, is not only

その問いと答えとは次のようなものであった。

「眠っているものに対しては覚めているといわれ、覚めているものに対しては眠っているといわれるのはだれであるか。」

「それは、いま道を修行している人のことである。道を知らない、眠っている人に対しては、その人は覚めているといわれる。すでに道をさとった、覚めている人に対しては、その人は眠っているといわれる。」「大きな象の重さはどうして量るか。」「象を舟に乗せ、舟が水中にどれだけ沈んだか印をしておく。次に象を降ろして、同じ深さになるまで石を載せその石の重さを量ればよい。」

「一すくいの水が大海の水より多いというのは、どんなことか。」「清らかな心で一すくいの水を汲んで、父母や病人に施せば、その功徳は永久に消えない。大海の水は多いといっても、ついに尽きるときがある。これをいうのである。」

次に神は、骨と皮ばかりにやせた、飢えた人を出して、その人にこう言わせた。

「世の中に、わたしよりもっと飢えに苦しんでいるものがあるであろうか。」

「ある。世にもし、心がかたくなで貧しく仏法僧の三宝を信ぜず、父母や師匠に供養をしないならば、その人の心は飢

more hungry but he will fall into the world of hungry demons and there he will suffer from hunger forever."

"Here is a plank of Chandana wood; which end was the bottom of the tree?" "Float the plank in water; the end that sinks a little deeper was the end nearest the root."

"Here are two horses apparently of the same size and form; how can you tell the mother from the son?" "Feed them some hay; the mother horse will push the hay toward her son."

Every answer to these difficult questions pleased the god as well as the king. The king was grateful to find out that the answers had come from the aged father whom the minister had hidden in the cave, and he withdrew the law of abandoning aged people in the mountains and ordered that they were to be treated kindly.

2.   Queen of Videha in India once dreamed of a white elephant that had six ivory tusks. She coveted the tusks and besought the king to get them for her. Although the task seemed an impossible one, the king who loved the queen very much offered a reward to any hunter who would report if he found such an elephant.

えきっているだけでなく、その報いとして、後の世には餓鬼道に落ち、長い間飢えに苦しまなければならない。」

「ここに真四角な栴檀の板がある。この板はどちらが根の方であったか。」

「水に浮かべてみると、根の方がいくらか深く沈む。それによって根の方を知ることができる。」

「ここに同じ姿・形の母子の馬がいる。どうしてその母子を見分けるか。」

「草を与えると、母馬は、必ず子馬の方へ草を押しつけ与えるから、直ちに見分けることができる。」

これらの難問に対する答えはことごとく神を喜ばせ、また王をも喜ばせた。そして王は、この智慧が、ひそかに穴蔵にかくまっていた大臣の老いた父から出たものであることを知り、それより、老人を棄てるおきてをやめて、年老いた人に孝養を尽くすようにと命ずるに至った。

2. インドのヴィデーハ国の王妃は、六牙の白象の夢を見た。王妃は、その象牙をぜひ自分のものにしたいと思い、王にその牙を手に入れたいと願った。王妃を愛する王は、この無理な願いを退けることができず、このような象を知る者があれば届け出よ、と賞金をつけて国中に触れを出した。

It happened that there was just such an elephant with six tusks in the Himalayan Mountains who was training for Buddhahood. The elephant once had saved a hunter's life in an emergency in the depths of the mountains and the hunter could go back safely to his country. The hunter, however, blinded by the great reward and forgetting the kindness the elephant had shown him, returned to the mountains to kill the elephant.

The hunter, knowing that the elephant was seeking Buddhahood, disguised himself in the robe of a Buddhist monk and, thus catching the elephant off guard, shot it with a poisoned arrow.

The elephant, knowing that its end was near and that the hunter had been overcome by the worldly desire for the reward, had compassion upon him and sheltered him in its limbs to protect the hunter from the fury of the other revengeful elephants. Then the elephant asked the hunter why he had done such a foolish thing. The hunter told of the reward and confessed that he coveted its six tusks. The elephant immediately broke off the tusks by hitting them against a tree and gave them to the hunter saying: — "By this offering I have completed my training for Buddhahood and will be reborn in the Pure Land. When I become a Buddha, I will help you to get rid of your three poisonous arrows of greed, anger and foolishness."

　ヒマラヤ山の奥にこの六牙の象がいた。この象は仏に成るための修行をしていたのであるが、あるときひとりの猟師を危難から救ってやった。ようやく国へ帰ることのできたこの猟師は、この触れを見、賞金に眼がくらみ、恩を忘れて、六牙の象を殺そうと山へ向かっていった。

　猟師はこの象が仏に成るための修行をしていたので、象を安心させるために袈裟をかけて出家の姿になった。そして、山に入って象に近づき、象が心を許しているさまを見すまして毒矢を放った。

　激しい毒矢に射られて死期の近いことを知った象は、猟師の罪をとがめようともせずに、かえってその煩悩の過ちを哀れみ、猟師をその四つの足の間に入れて、報復しようとする大勢の仲間の象から守り、さらに、猟師がこの危険をおかすに至ったわけを尋ねて、彼が六つの牙を求めるためであることを知り、自ら牙を大木に打ちつけて折り、彼にこれを与えた。白象は、「この布施行によって仏道修行を成就した。わたしは仏の国に生まれるであろう。やがて仏と成ったら、まず、あなたの心の中にある貪り・瞋り・愚かさという三つの毒矢を抜き去るであろう。」と誓った。

3. In a thicket at the foot of the Himalayan Mountains there once lived a parrot together with many other animals and birds. One day a fire started in the thicket from the friction of bamboos in a strong wind and the birds and animals were in frightened confusion. The parrot, feeling compassion for their fright and suffering, and wishing to repay the kindness he had received in the bamboo thicket where he could shelter himself, tried to do all he could to save them. He dipped himself in a pond nearby and flew over the fire and shook off the drops of water to extinguish the fire. He repeated this diligently with a heart of compassion out of gratitude to the thicket.

This spirit of kindness and self-sacrifice was noticed by a heavenly god who came down from the sky and said to the parrot: — "You have a gallant mind, but what good do you expect to accomplish by a few drops of water against this great fire?" The parrot answered:— "There is nothing that can not be accomplished by the spirit of gratitude and self-sacrifice. I will try over and over again and then over in the next life." The great god was impressed by the parrot's spirit and together they extinguished the fire.

4. At one time there lived in the Himalayas a bird with one body and two heads. Once one of the heads noticed the other head eating some sweet fruit and felt jealous

3．ヒマラヤ山のふもとの、ある竹やぶに、多くの鳥や獣（けもの）と一緒に、一羽のおうむが住んでいた。あるとき、にわかに大風が起こり、竹と竹とが擦れあって火が起こった。火は風にあおられて、ついに大火となり、鳥も獣も逃げ場を失って鳴き叫んだ。おうむは、一つには、長い間住居を与えてくれた竹やぶの恩に報いるために、一つには、大勢の鳥や獣の災難を哀れんで、彼らを救うために、近くの池に入っては翼を水に浸し、空にかけのぼっては滴（しずく）を燃えさかる火の上にそそぎかけ、竹やぶの恩を思う心と、限りない慈愛の心で、たゆまずにこれを続けた。

*
慈悲と献身の心は天界の神を感動させた。神は空から下って来ておうむに語った。

「おまえの心はけなげであるが、この大いなる火を、どうして羽の滴で消すことができよう。」
おうむは答えて言う。

「恩を思う心と慈悲の心からしていることが、できないはずはない。わたしはどうしてもやる。次の生に及んでもやりとおす。」と。

神はおうむの偉大な志にうたれ、力を合わせてこのやぶの火を消し止めた。

4．ヒマラヤ山に共命鳥（ぐみょうちょう）という鳥がいた。体は一つ、頭は

and said to itself: — "I will then eat poison fruit." So it ate poison and the whole bird died.

5. At one time the tail and the head of a snake quarrelled as to which should be the front. The tail said to the head:— "You are always taking the lead; it is not fair, you ought to let me lead sometimes." The head answered; — "It is the law of our nature that I should be the head; I can not change places with you."

But the quarrel went on and one day the tail fastened itself to a tree and thus prevented the head from proceeding. When the head became tired with the struggle the tail had its own way, with the result that the snake fell into a pit of fire and perished.

In the world of nature there always exists an appropriate order and everything has its own function. If this order is disturbed, the functioning is interrupted and the whole order will go to ruin.

6. There was a man who was easily angered. One day two men were talking in front of the house about the man who lived there. One said to the other: — "He is a nice man but is very impatient; he has a hot temper and gets angry quickly." The man overheard the remark, rushed out of the house and attacked the two men, striking and kicking and wounding them.

二つであった。

あるとき、一つの頭がおいしい果実を食べるのを見て、もう一つの頭がねたみ心を起こし、「それならわたしは毒の果実を食べてやろう。」と毒を食べて、両方ともに死んでしまった。

5．ある蛇の頭と尾とが、あるとき、お互いに前に出ようとして争った。尾が言うには、

「頭よ、おまえはいつも前にあるが、それは正しいことではない。たまにはわたしを前にするがよい。」

頭が言うには、

「わたしがいつも前にあるのはきまったならわしである。おまえを前にすることはできない。」と。

互いに争ったが、やはり頭が前にあるので、尾は怒って木に巻きついて頭が前へ進むことを許さず、頭がひるむすきに、木から離れて前へ進み、ついに火の穴へ落ち、焼けただれて死んだ。

ものにはすべて順序があり、異なる働きがそなわっている。不平を並べてその順序を乱し、そのために、そのおのおのに与えられている働きを失うようになると、そのすべてが滅んでしまうのである。

6．非常に気が早く怒りっぽい男がいた。その男の家の前で、二人の人がうわさをした。

When a wise man is advised of his errors, he will reflect on them and improve his conduct. When his misconduct is pointed out, a foolish man will not only disregard the advice but rather repeat the same error.

7.   Once there was a wealthy but foolish man. When he saw the beautiful three-storied house of another man, he envied it and made up his mind to have one built just like it, thinking he was himself just as wealthy. He called a carpenter and ordered him to build it. The carpenter consented and immediately began to construct the foundation, the first story, the second story, and then the third story. The wealthy man noticed this with irritation and said: — "I don't want a foundation or a first story or a second story; I just want the beautiful third story. Build it quickly."

A foolish man always thinks only of the results, and is impatient without the effort that is necessary to get good results. No good can be attained without proper effort, just as there can be no third story without the foundation and the first and the second stories.

8.   A foolish man was once boiling honey. His friend suddenly appeared and the foolish man wanted to offer him some honey, but it was too hot, and so without removing it from the fire he fanned it to make it cool. In

「ここの人は大変よい人だが、気の早いのと、怒りっぽい
のが病である。」と。

その男は、これを聞くとすぐ家を飛び出してきて、二人の人
におそいかかり、打つ、ける、なぐるの乱暴をし、とうとう
二人を傷つけてしまった。

賢い人は、自分の過ちを忠告されると、反省してあらため
るが、愚かな者は、自分の過ちを指摘されると、あらためる
どころか、かえって過ちを重ねるものである。

7．金持ちではあるが愚かな人がいた。他人の家の三階づ
くりの高層が高くそびえて、美しいのを見てうらやましく思
い、自分も金持ちなのだから、高層の家を造ろうと思った。

大工を呼んで建築を言いつけた。大工は承知して、まず基
礎を作り、二階を組み、それから三階に進もうとした。主人
はこれを見て、もどかしそうに叫んだ。

「わたしの求めるのは土台ではない、一階でもない、二階
でもない、三階の高楼だけだ。早くそれを作れ。」と。

愚かな者は、努め励むことを知らないで、ただ良い結果だ
けを求める。しかし、土台のない三階はあり得ないように、
努め励むことなくして、良い結果を得られるはずがない。

8．ある人が蜜を煮ているところへ親しい友が来たので、
蜜をごちそうしようと思い、火にかけたまま扇であおぎ冷や

like manner, it is impossible to get the honey of cool wisdom without first removing it from the fire of worldly passions.

9. Once there were two demons who spent a whole day arguing and quarrelling about a box, a cane and a pair of shoes. A man, passing by, inquired, "Why are you arguing about these things? What magical power have they that you should be quarrelling about possessing them?"

The demons explained to him that from the box they could get anything they desired—food, clothing or treasure; with the cane they could subdue all their enemies; and with the pair of shoes they could travel through the air.

Upon hearing this, the man said: "Why quarrel? If you will go away for a few minutes, I can think of a fair division of the things between you." So the two demons retired and as soon as they were gone, the man put on the shoes, seized the box and the cane and was off through the air.

The "demons" represent men of heathen beliefs. "A box" means the gifts that are made in charity; they do not realize how many treasures can be produced from charity. "A cane" means the practice of concentration of the mind. Men do not realize that by the practice of

そうとした。これと同じく、煩悩の火を消さないで、清涼の
さとりの蜜を得ようとしても、ついに得られるはずはない。

　9．二匹の鬼が、一つの箱と一本の杖と一足の靴とを中に
して互いに争い、終日争ってついにきまらず、なおも互いに
争い続けた。

　これを見たひとりの人が、

　「どうしてそのように争うのか。この品々にどのような不
思議があって、そのように奪いあいをするのか。」と尋ねた。

　二匹の鬼はこう答えた。

　「この箱からは、食物でも、宝でも、何でも欲しいものを
自由に取り出すことができる。また、この杖を手に取るとす
ぐに敵をうち下すことができる。この靴をはくと、空を自由
に飛ぶことができる。」と。

　その人はこれを聞いて、

　「争うことなんかあるものか。おまえら二人は、しばらく
ここから離れているがよい。わたしが等分に分けてやろう。」

　と言って、二匹の鬼を遠ざけ、自ら箱を抱え、杖を取り、
靴をはいて空へ飛び去った。

　鬼とは異教の人、箱とは布施のことである。彼らは、布施
からもろもろの宝の生ずることを知らない。また、杖とは心

spiritual concentration of mind, they can subdue all worldly desires. "A pair of shoes" means the pure disciplines of thought and conduct, that will carry them beyond all desires and arguments. Without knowing these, they quarrel and argue about a box, a cane and a pair of shoes.

10. Once upon a time a man was travelling alone. He came to a vacant house toward the evening and decided to spend the night there. About midnight a demon brought in a corpse and left it on the floor. Shortly, another demon appeared and claimed the corpse as his and they quarrelled over it.

Then the first demon said it was useless to argue about it further and proposed that they refer it to a judge to decide the possessor. The other demon agreed to this and, seeing the man cowering in the corner, asked him to decide the ownership. The man was terribly frightened, for he well knew that whatever decision he might make would anger the demon that lost and that the losing demon would seek revenge and kill him, but he decided to tell truthfully just what he had witnessed.

As he expected, this angered the second demon who grabbed one of the man's arms and tore it off, but the first demon replaced the arm with one taken from the

の統一のこと。彼らは、心の統一によって煩悩の悪魔をうち下すことを知らない。

また、靴とは清らかな戒のこと。彼らはこの清らかな戒によって、あらゆる争いを超えられることを知らない。だから、この箱と杖と靴を取りあって、争ってやまないのである。

10. ひとりの人が旅をして、ある夜、ただひとりでさびしい空き屋に宿をとった。すると真夜中になって、一匹の鬼が人の死骸をかついで入ってきて、床の上にそれを降ろした。

間もなく、後からもう一匹の鬼が追って来て、「これはわたしのものだ。」と言い出したので、激しい争いが起こった。

すると、前の鬼が後の鬼に言うには、

「こうして、おまえと争っていても果てしがない。証人を立てて所有をきめよう。」

後の鬼もこの申し出を承知したので、前の鬼は、先ほどからすみに隠れて小さくなって震えていた男を引き出して、どちらが先にかついで来たかを言ってくれと頼んだ。

男はもう絶体絶命である。どちらの鬼に味方しても、もう一方の鬼に恨まれて殺されることはきまっているから、決心して正直に自分の見ていたとおりを話した。

案の定、一方の鬼は大いに怒ってその男の手をもぎ取った。

corpse. The angry demon tore away the man's other arm, but the first demon immediately replaced that with the other arm of the corpse. And so it went on until both arms, both legs, the head and the body had been successively torn away and replaced with the corresponding parts of the corpse. Then the two demons, seeing the parts of the man scattered about on the floor, picked them up and devoured them and went away chuckling.

The poor man who had taken refuge in the deserted house was very much upset by his misfortunes. The parts of his body which the demons had eaten were the parts his parents had given him, and the parts that he now had belonged to the corpse. Who was he, anyway? Realizing all the facts, he was unable to figure it out and, becoming crazy, he wandered out of the house. Coming to a temple, he went in and told his troubles to the monks. People could see the true meaning of selflessness in his story.

11.   Once a beautiful and well-dressed woman visited a house. The master of the house asked her who she was; and she replied that she was the goddess of wealth. The master of the house was delighted and so treated her nicely.

これを見た前の鬼は、すぐ死骸の手を取って来て補った。
後の鬼はますます怒ってさらに手を抜き足を取り、胴を取り
去り、とうとう頭まで取ってしまった。前の鬼は次々に、死
体の手、足、胴、頭を取って、みなこれを補ってしまった。

　こうして二匹の鬼は争いをやめ、あたりに散らばった手足
を食べて満腹し、口をぬぐって立ち去った。

　男はさびしい小屋で恐ろしい目にあい、親からもらった手
も足も胴も頭も、鬼に食べられ、いまや自分の手も足も胴も
頭も、見も知らぬ死体のものである。一体、自分は自分なの
か自分ではないのか、まったくわからなくなった男は、夜明
けに、気が狂って空き屋を立ち去ったが、途中で寺を見つけ
て喜び勇み、その寺に入って、昨夜の恐ろしいできごとをす
べて話し、教えを請うたのである。人びとは、この話の中に、
無我の理を感得し、まことに尊い感じを得た。

　11.　ある家に、ひとりの美しい女が、着飾って訪ねてきた。
その家の主人が、

　「どなたでしょうか。」

と尋ねると、その女は、

　「わたしは人に富を与える福の神である。」

と答えた。主人は喜んで、その女を家に上げ手厚くもてなした。

Soon after another woman appeared who was ugly looking and poorly dressed. The master asked who she was and the woman replied that she was the goddess of poverty. The master was frightened and tried to drive her out of the house, but the woman refused to depart, saying, "The goddess of wealth is my sister. There is an agreement between us that we are never to live separately; if you chase me out, she is to go with me." Sure enough, as soon as the ugly woman went out, the other woman disappeared.

Birth goes with death. Fortune goes with misfortune. Bad things follow good things. Men should realize this. Foolish people dread misfortune and strive after good fortune, but those who seek Enlightenment must transcend both of them and be free of worldly attachments.

12.   Once there lived a poor artist who left his home, leaving his wife, to seek his fortune. After three years of hard struggles he had saved three hundred pieces of gold and decided to return to his home. On his way he came to a great temple in which a grand ceremony of offering was in progress. He was greatly impressed by it and thought to himself: "Hitherto, I have thought only of the present; I have never considered my future happiness. It is a part of my good fortune that I have come to this place; I must take advantage of it to plant seeds of

　すると、すぐその後から、粗末なみなりをした醜い女が入ってきた。主人がだれであるかと尋ねると、貧乏神であると答えた。主人は驚いてその女を追い出そうとした。すると女は、

「先ほどの福の神はわたしの姉である。わたしたち姉妹はいつも離れたことはないのであるから、わたしを追い出せば姉もいないことになるのだ。」

　と主人に告げ、彼女が去ると、やはり美しい福の神の姿も消えうせた。

　生があれば死があり幸いがあれば災いがある。善いことがあれば悪いことがある。人はこのことを知らなければならない。愚かな者は、ただいたずらに、災いをきらって幸いだけを求めるが、道を求めるものは、この二つをともに超えて、そのいずれにも執着してはならない。

　12.　昔、貧しい絵かきがいた。妻を故郷に残して旅に出、三年の間苦労して多くの金を得た。いよいよ、故郷に帰ろうとしたところ、途中で、多くの僧に供養する儀式の行われているのを見た。彼は大いに喜び、

「わたしはまだ福の種をまいたことがない。いまこの福の種をまく田地に会って、どうしてこのまま見過ごすことがで

merit." Thinking thus, he gratefully donated all his savings to the temple and returned to his home penniless.

When he reached home, his wife reproached him for not bringing her some money for her support. The poor artist replied that he had earned some money but had put it where it would be safe. When she pressed him to tell where he had hidden it, he confessed that he had given it to the monks at a certain temple.

This made the wife angry and she scolded her husband and finally carried the matter to the local judge. When the judge asked the artist for his defence, the artist said that he had not acted foolishly, for he had earned the money during long and hard struggles and wanted to use it as seed for future good fortune. When he came to the temple it seemed to him that there was the field where he should plant his gold as seed for good fortune. Then he added: "When I gave the monks the gold, it seemed that I was throwing away all greed and stinginess from my mind, and I have realized that real wealth is not gold but mind."

The judge praised the artist's spirit, and those who heard of this manifested their approval by helping him in various ways. Thus the artist and his wife entered into permanent good fortune.

きよう。」と、惜しげもなく、その多くの金を投げ出して、供養し終えて家に帰った。

空手で帰った夫を見た妻は、大いに怒ってなじり問いつめたが、夫は、財物はみな堅固な蔵の中にたくわえておいたと答えた。その蔵とは何かと聞くと、それは尊い教団のことであると答えた。

腹を立てた妻はこのことをその筋に訴え、絵かきはとり調べを受けることになった。彼は次のように答えた。

「わたしは貴い努力によって得た財物をつまらなく費やしたのではない。わたしはいままで福の種を植えることを知らないで過ごしてきたが、福の種をまく田地というべき供養の機会を見て信仰心が起き、もの惜しみの心を捨てて施したのである。まことの富とは財物ではなく、心であることを知ったから。」

役人は絵かきの心をほめたたえ、多くの人びともこれを聞いて心をうたれた。それ以来、彼の信用は高まり、絵かき夫婦はこれによって、大きな富を得るようになった。

13. ある男が墓場の近くに住んでいた。ある夜、墓場の中から、しきりに自分を呼ぶ声がするので、恐れ震え上がって

13. A man living near a cemetery heard one night a voice calling him from a grave. He was too timid to investigate it himself but the next day he mentioned it to a brave friend, who made up his mind to trace the place whence the voice came the following night.

While the timid man was trembling with fear, his friend went to the cemetery and, sure enough, the same voice was heard coming from a grave. The friend asked who it was and what it wanted. The voice from under the ground replied: "I am a hidden treasure that has decided to give myself to someone. I offered it to a man last night but he was too timid to come after it, so I will give it to you who are worthy of it. Tomorrow morning I will come to your house with my seven followers."

The friend said: "I will be waiting for you, but please tell me how I am to treat you." The voice replied: "We will come in monk's robes. Have a room ready for us with water; wash your body and clean the room, and have seats for us and eight bowls of rice-porridge. After the meal, you are to lead us one by one into a closed room in which we will transform ourselves into crocks of gold."

The next morning this man washed his body and cleaned the room just as he had been told and waited for

いた。夜が明けてから、彼がそのことを友に話すと、友の中で勇気のある者が、次の夜にも呼ぶ声がしたら、その声をたずねて、そのもとをつきとめてみようと決心した。

次の夜も、前夜のように、しきりに呼ぶ声がする。呼ばれた男はおびえて震えていたが、勇気のある男は、その声をたよりに墓場に入り、声の出る場所をたずねて、おまえはだれかと聞いた。

すると、地の中から声がして、

「わたしは、地の中に隠されている宝である。わたしは、わたしの呼んだ男にわたしを与えようと思うが、彼は恐れて来ない。おまえは勇気があるからわたしを取るにふさわしい。あすの朝、わたしは七人の従者とともにおまえの家に行くであろう。」と言った。

その男はこのことばを聞いて、

「わたしの家へ来るなら待っているが、どのようにもてなしたらよいのか。」と尋ねる。

声は答えた。「わたしどもは出家の姿で行くから、まず体を清め、部屋を清めて、水を用意し、八つの器にかゆを盛って待つがよい。

食事が終わったら、ひとりひとり導いて、すみに囲った部屋

the eight monks to appear. In due time they appeared and he received them courteously. After they had eaten the food he led them one by one into the closed room, where each monk turned himself into a crock full of gold.

There was a very greedy man in the same village who learned of the incident and wanted the crocks of gold. He invited eight monks to his house. After their meal he led them into a closed room, but instead of turning themselves into crocks of gold, they became angry and rough and reported the greedy man to the police who eventually arrested him.

As for the timid man, when he heard that the voice from the grave had brought wealth to the brave man, he went to the house of the brave man and greedily demanded the gold, insisting that it was his, because the voice first addressed him. When the timid man tried to take the crocks away he found lots of snakes inside raising their heads ready to attack him.

The king heard about this and ruled that the crocks belonged to the brave man and uttered the following observation: "Everything in the world goes like this. Foolish people are avaricious for good results only, but are too timid to go after them and, therefore, are continually failing. They have neither faith nor

の中に入れれば、わたしどもはそのまま黄金のつぼになるだろう。」と。

あくる朝、この男は、体を清め、家を清めて待っていると、はたして八人の出家が托鉢にやって来た。部屋に通して、水とかゆとを供養し、終わってからひとりひとりをすみに囲った部屋に導いた。すると、八人が八人とも、黄金のいっぱい入ったつぼに変わってしまった。

このことを聞いた欲深い男が、自分も黄金のつぼが欲しいと思い、同じように部屋を清めて托鉢の出家を八人招いて供養し、食事の後、すみの部屋に閉じこめた。しかし八人の出家は黄金のつぼになるどころではなく、怒って暴れ出し、その男はついに訴えられ、捕らえられた。

はじめに名を呼ばれておびえていた憶病な男も、呼んだ声が黄金のつぼであると知ると、これも欲を起こし、あの声はもともと自分を呼んだのだから、あのつぼは自分のものだと言いはり、その家へ入ってつぼを取ろうとすると、つぼの中には蛇がいっぱいいて、首をもたげてその男に向かっていった。

その国の王はこれを聞いて、黄金のつぼはみな、この勇気のある男のものであるとして、「世の中のことは何ごともこ

courage to face the internal struggles of the mind by which alone true peace and harmony can be attained."

のとおりであって、愚かな者 はただその果報だけを望むが、それはそれだけで得られるも のではない。ちょうどそれは、うわべだけ戒を保っていても、心の中にまことの信心がなければ決して真の安らぎは得られないのと同じである。」と諭した。

THE WAY OF PRACTICAL ATTAINMENT

I
SEARCH FOR TRUTH

1. In the search for truth there are certain questions that are unimportant. Of what material is the universe constructed? Is the universe eternal? Are there limits or not to the universe? In what way is this human society put together? What is the ideal form of organization for human society? If a man were to postpone his searching and practicing for Enlightenment until such questions were solved, he would die before he found the path.

Suppose a man were pierced by a poisoned arrow, and his relatives and friends got together to call a surgeon to have the arrow pulled out and the wound treated.

If the wounded man objects, saying, "Wait a little. Before you pull it out, I want to know who shot this arrow. Was it a man or a woman? Was it someone of noble birth, or was it a peasant? What was the bow made

第2章　実　践　の　道

第1節　道　を　求　め　て

1．この宇宙の組み立てはどういうものであるか、この宇
宙は永遠のものであるか、やがてなくなるものであるか、こ
の宇宙は限りなく広いものであるか、それとも限りがあるも
のであるか、社会の組み立てはどういうものであるか、この
社会のどういう形が理想的なものであるか。これらの問題が
はっきりきまらないうちは、道を修めることはできないという
ならば、だれも道を修め得ないうちに死が来るであろう。

例えば、人が恐ろしい毒矢に射られたとする。親戚や友人
が集まり、急いで医者を呼び毒矢を抜いて、毒の手当てをし
ようとする。

ところがそのとき、その人が、

「しばらく矢を抜くのを待て。だれがこの矢を射たのか、
それを知りたい。男か、女か、どんな素性のものか、また弓

of? Was it a big bow, or a small bow, that shot the arrow? Was it made of wood or bamboo? What was the bow-string made of? Was it made of fiber, or of gut? Was the arrow made of rattan, or of reed? What feathers were used? Before you extract the arrow, I want to know all about these things." Then what will happen?

Before all this information can be secured, no doubt, the poison will have time to circulate all through the system and the man may die. The first duty is to remove the arrow, and prevent its poison from spreading.

When a fire of passion is endangering the world, the composition of the universe matters little; what is the ideal form for the human community is not so important to deal with.

The question of whether the universe has limits or is eternal can wait until some way is found to extinguish the fires of birth, old age, sickness and death; in the presence of misery, sorrow, suffering and agony, one should first search for a way to solve these problems and devote oneself to the practice of that way.

The Buddha's teaching contains what is important to know and not what is unimportant. That is, it teaches

は何であったか、大弓か小弓か、木の弓か竹の弓か、弦は何
であったか、藤蔓か、筋か、矢は籐か葦か、羽根は何か、そ
れらがすっかりわかるまじ矢を抜くのは待て。」と言ったら、
どうであろうか。

いうまでもなく、それらのことがわかってしまわないうち
に、毒は全身に回って死んでしまうに違いない。この場合に
まずしなければならないことは、まず矢を抜き、毒が全身に
回らないように手当てをすることである。

この宇宙の組み立てがどうであろうと、この社会のどうい
う形のものが理想的であろうとなかろうと、身に迫ってくる
火は避けなくてはならない。

宇宙が永遠であろうとなかろうと、限りがあろうとなかろ
うと、生と老と病と死、愁い、悲しみ、苦しみ、悩みの火は、
現に人の身の上におし迫っている。人はまず、この迫ってい
るものを払いのけるために、道を修めなければならない。

*
仏の教えは、説かなければならないことを説き、説く必要
のないことを説かない。すなわち、人に、知らなければなら

people that they must learn what they should learn, remove what they should remove, train for what they should become enlightened about.

Therefore, people should first discern what is the most important, what problem should be solved first and what is the most pressing issue for them. To do all this, they must first undertake to train their minds; that is, they must first seek mind-control.

2. Suppose a man goes to the forest to get some of the pith that grows in the center of a tree and returns with a burden of branches and leaves, thinking that he has secured what he went after; would he not be foolish, if he is satisfied with the bark, wood for the pith which he was after? But that is what many people are doing.

A person seeks a path that will lead him away from birth, old age, sickness and death, or from misery, sorrow, suffering and agony; and yet, he follows the path a little way, notices some little advance, and immediately becomes proud and conceited and domineering. He is like the man who sought pith and went away satisfied with a burden of branches and leaves.

ないことを知り、断たなければならないものを断ち、修めなければならないものを修め、さとらなければならないものをさとれと教えるのである。

　だから、人はまず問題を選ばなければならない。自分にとって何が第一の問題であるか、何が自分にもっともおし迫っているものであるかを知って、自分の心をととのえることから始めなければならない。

　2．また、樹木の芯を求めて林に入った者が、枝や葉を得て芯を得たように思うならば、まことに愚かなことである。ややもすると、人は、木の芯を求めるのが目的でありながら、木の外皮や内皮、または木の肉を得て芯を得たように思う。

　人の身の上に迫る生と老と病と死と、愁い、悲しみ、苦しみ、悩みを離れたいと望んで道を求める。これが芯である。それが、わずかな尊敬と名誉とを得て満足して心がおごり、自分をほめて他をそしるのは、枝葉を得ただけにすぎないのに芯を得たと思うようなものである。

Another man becoming satisfied with the progress he has made by a little effort, relaxes his effort and becomes proud and conceited; he is carrying away only a load of branches instead of the pith he was seeking.

Still another man finding that his mind is becoming calmer and his thoughts clearer, he, too, relaxes his effort and becomes proud and conceited; he has a burden of the bark instead of the pith he was looking for.

Then again, another man becomes proud and conceited because he notices that he has gained a measure of intuitive insight; he has a load of the woody fiber of the tree instead of the pith. All of these seekers, who become easily satisfied by their insufficient effort and become proud and over-bearing, relax their efforts and easily fall into idleness. All these people will inevitably face suffering again.

Those who seek the true path to Enlightenment must not expect an easy task or one made pleasant by offers of respect and honor and devotion. And further, they must not aim with a slight effort, at a trifling advance in calmness or knowledge or insight.

First of all, one should get clearly in mind the basic and essential nature of this world of life and death.

　また、自分のわずかな努力に慢心して、望んだものを得たように思い、満足して心が高ぶり、自分をほめて他をそしるのは、木の外皮を得て芯を得たと思うようなものである。

　また、自分の心がいくらか静まり安定を得たとして、それに満足して心が高ぶり、自分をほめて他をそしるのは、木の内皮を得て芯を得たと思うようなものである。

　また、いくらかものを明らかに見る力を得て、これに眼がくらんで心が高ぶり、自分をほめて他をそしるのは、木の肉を得て芯を得たと思うようなものである。これらのものはみなすべて、気がゆるんで怠り、ふたたび苦しみを招くに至るであろう。

　道を求める者にとっては、尊敬と名誉と供養を受けることがその目的ではない。わずかな努力や、多少の心の安定、またわずかな見る力が目的なのではない。

　まず最初に、人はこの世の生と死の根本的な性質を心に留めなければならない。

3.   The world has no substance of its own. It is simply a vast concordance of causes and conditions that have had their origin, solely and exclusively, in the activities of the mind that has been stimulated by ignorance, false imagination, desires and infatuation. It is not something external about which the mind has false conceptions; it has no substance whatever. It has come into appearance by the processes of the mind itself, manifesting its own delusions. It is founded and built up out of the desires of the mind, out of its sufferings and struggles incidental to the pain caused by its own greed, anger and foolishness. Men who seek the way to Enlightenment should be ready to fight such a mind to attain their goal.

4.   "Oh my mind! Why do you hover so restlessly over the changing circumstances of life? Why do you make me so confused and restless? Why do you urge me to collect so many things? You are like a plow that breaks in pieces before beginning to plow; you are like a rudder that is dismantled just as you are venturing out on the sea of life and death. Of what use are many rebirths if we do not make good use of this life?

"Oh my mind! Once you caused me to be born as a king, and then you caused me to be born as an outcast and to beg for my food. Sometimes you cause me to be born in heavenly mansions of the gods and to dwell in

3. 世界はそれ自体の実体を持っていない。心のはからいをなくす道を得なければならない。外の形に迷いがあるのではなく、内の心が迷いを生ずるのである。

心の欲をもととして、この欲の火に焼かれて苦しみ悩み、*無明をもととして、迷いの闇に包まれて、愁い悲しむ。迷いの家を造るものはこの心の他にないことを知って、道を求める人は、この心と戦って進んでゆかなければならない。

4. 「わが心よ、おまえはどうして、無益な境地に進んで少しの落着きもなく、そわそわとして静かでないのか。

どうしてわたしを迷わせて、いたずらに、ものを集めさせるのか。

大地を耕そうとして、鍬がまだ大地に触れないうちにこわれてしまっては耕すことができないように、生死の迷いの海にさまよっていたので、数知れない生命を捨てたのに、心の大地の耕されることはなかった。

心よ、おまえはわたしを王者に生まれさせたこともある。また貧しい者に生まれさせて、あちこちに食を乞い歩かせたこともある。

ときにはわたしを神々の国に生まれさせ、栄華の夢に酔わ

luxury and in ecstasy; then you plunge me into the flames of hell.

"Oh, my foolish, foolish mind! Thus you have led me along different paths and I have been obedient to you and docile. But now that I have heard the Buddha's teaching, do not disturb me any more or cause me further sufferings, but let us seek Enlightenment together, humbly and patiently.

"Oh, my mind! If you could only learn that every-thing is non-substantial and transitory; if you could only learn not to grasp after things, not to covet things, not to give way to greed, anger and foolishness; then we might journey in quietness. Then, by severing the bond of desires with the sword of wisdom, being undisturbed by changing circumstances — advantage or disadvantage, good or bad, loss or gain, praise or abuse — we might dwell in peace.

"Oh, my dear mind! It was you who first awakened faith in us; it was you who suggested our seeking Enlightenment. Why do you give way so easily to greed, love of comfort and pleasant excitement again?

"Oh, my mind! Why do you rush hither and thither with no definite purpose? Let us cross this wild sea of delusion. Hitherto I have acted as you wished, but now

せたこともあるが、また地獄の火で焼かせたこともある。

　愚かな心よ、おまえはわたしをさまざまな道に導いた。わたしはこれまで、常におまえに従ってそむくことはなかった。しかし、いまやわたしは仏の教えを聞く身となった。もはやわたしを悩ましたり、妨げたりしないでくれ。どうかわたしが、さまざまな苦しみから離れて、速やかにさとりを得られるように努めてくれ。

　心よ、おまえが、すべてのものはみな実体がなくうつり変わると知って、執着することなく、何ものもわがものと思うことがなく、貪り、瞋り、愚かさを離れさえすれば、安らかになるのである。

　＊智慧の剣をもって愛欲の蔓を断ち、利害と損得と、たたえとそしりとにわずらわされることがなくなれば、安らかな日を得ることができるのである。

　心よ、おまえは、わたしを導いて道を求めることを思い立たせた。ところがいま、どうしてまたふたたび、この世の利欲と栄華にひかれて、動き回ろうとするのであるか。

　形がなくて、どこまでも遠く駆けてゆく心よ。どうか、この超え難い迷いの海を渡らせてくれ、これまでわたしは、おまえの思うとおりに動いてきた。

you must act as I wish and, together, we will follow the Buddha's teaching.

"Oh, my dear mind! These mountains, rivers and seas are changeable and pain-producing. Where in this world of delusion shall we seek quietness? Let us follow the Buddha's teaching and cross over to the other shore of Enlightenment."

5.   Thus, those who really seek the path to Enlightenment dictate terms to their mind. Then they proceed with strong determination. Even though they are abused by some and scorned by others, they go forward undisturbed. They do not become angry if they are beaten by fists, or hit by stones, or gashed by swords.

Even if enemies cut their head from the body, the mind must not be disturbed. If they let their mind become darkened by the things they suffer, they are not following the teaching of Buddha. They must be determined, no matter what happens to them, to remain steadfast, unmovable, ever radiating thoughts of compassion and good-will. Let abuse come, let misfortune come, and yet one should resolve to remain unmoved and tranquil in mind, filled with Buddha's teaching.

For the sake of attaining Enlightenment, one should

　しかし、これからは、おまえはわたしの思うとおりに動かなければならない。我らはともに仏の教えに従おう。

　心よ、山も川も海も、すべてはみなうつり変わり、災いに満ちている。この世のどこに楽しみを求めることができようか。教えに従って、速やかにさとりの岸に渡ろうではないか。」

　5、このように心と戦って、真に道を求める人は、常に強い覚悟をもって進むから、あざけりそしる人に出会ってもそれによって心を動かすことはない。こぶしをもって打ち、石を投げつけ、剣をもって斬りかかる人があっても、そのために瞋(いか)りの心を起こすことはない。

　両刃の鋸(のこぎり)によって頭と胴とが切り放たれるとしても、心乱れてはならない。それによって心が暗くなるならば、仏の教えを守らない者である。

　あざけりも来れ、そしりも来れ、こぶしも来れ、杖(つえ)や剣の乱打も来れ、わが心はそのために乱れることはない。それによって、かえって仏の教えが心に満たされるであろうと、かたく覚悟しているのである。

　さとりのためには、成しとげ難いことでも成しとげ、忍び

try to accomplish the impossible and one should endure the unendurable. One must give what he has to the last of it. If he is told that to gain Enlightenment he must limit his food to a single grain of rice a day, he will eat only that. If the path to Enlightenment leads him through fire, he will go forward.

But one must not do these things for any ulterior purpose. One should do them because it is the wise thing, the right thing, to do. One should do them out of a spirit of compassion, as a mother does things for her little child, for her sick child, with no thought of her own strength or comfort.

6. Once there was a king who loved his people and his country and ruled them with wisdom and kindness and, because of it his country was prosperous and peaceful. He was always seeking for greater wisdom and enlightenment; he even offered rewards to anyone who could lead him to worthy teachings.

His devotion and wisdom finally came to the attention of the gods, but they determined to test him. A god in disguise as a demon appeared before the gates of the king's palace and asked to be brought before the king as he had a holy teaching for him.

難いことでもよく忍び、施し難いものでもよく施す。

　日に一粒の米を食べ、燃えさかる火の中に入るならば、必ずさとりを得るだろうという者があれば、そのとおりにすることを少しも辞さない。

　しかし、施しても施したという思いを起こさず、ことをなしてもなしたという思いを起こさない。ただそれが賢いことであり正しいことだからするのである。それは母親が一枚の着物を愛するわが子に与えても、与えたという心を起こさず、病む子を看護しても、看護したという思いを起こさないのと同じである。

　6、遠い昔、ある王があった。王は智慧明らかで慈悲深く、民を愛し、国は豊かに安らかに治まっていた。また、王は道を求める心があつく、常に財宝を用意して、どんな人でも、尊い教えを示してくれる者には、この財宝を施すであろうと、布告していた。

　この、王の道を求めるまごころには、神の世界も震え動いたが、神は王の心を確かめるために、鬼の姿となって、王の宮殿の門の前に立った。

「わたしは尊い教えを知っている。王にとりついでもらいたい。」

The king who was pleased to hear the message courteously received him and asked for instruction. The demon took on a dreadful form and demanded food, saying that he could not teach until he had the food he liked. Choice food was offered the demon, but he insisted that he must have warm human flesh and blood. The crown-prince gave his body and the queen also gave her body, but still the demon was unsatisfied and so demanded the body of the king.

The king expressed his willingness to give his body, but asked that he might first hear the teaching before he would offer his body.

The god uttered the following wise teaching: "Misery rises from lust and fear rises from lust. Those who remove lust have no misery or fear." Suddenly the god resumed his true form and the prince and the queen also reappeared in their original bodies.

7.   Once there was a person who sought the True Path in the Himalayas. He cared nothing for all the treasures of the earth or even for all the delights of heaven, but he sought the teaching that would remove all mental delusions.

The gods were impressed by the man's earnestness and sincerity and decided to test his mind. So one of the gods disguised himself as a demon and appeared in the

　王はこれを聞いて大いに喜び、うやうやしく奥殿に迎えて、教えを聞きたいと願った。すると鬼は、刃のように恐ろしい牙をむきだして、

「いまわたしは非常に飢えている。このままではとても教えを説くことはできない。」と言う。

　それでは食物をさし上げようというと、

「わたしの食物は、熱い人間の血と肉でなければならない。」と言う。そのとき、王子は、すすんでわが命を捨てて、鬼の飢えを満たそうと言い、王妃もまた進んでその身を餌食にしようとした。ここに鬼は二人の身を食べたが、なお飢えを満たすことができず、さらに王の身を食べたいと言う。

　そのとき王は静かに言った。

「わたしは命を惜しまない。ただ、この身がなくなれば教えを聞くことができないから、おまえが教えを説き終わったそのときにこの身を与えよう。」

　鬼はそのとき、

「愛欲より憂いは生じ、愛欲より恐れは生ずる。愛欲を離れし人に憂いなし、またいずこにか恐れあらん。」と説いて、たちまち神の姿にかえった。それと同時に、死んだはずの王子も、夫人も、もとの姿にたちかえった。

　7、昔、ヒマラヤ山に真実を求める行者がいた。ただ迷いを離れる教えを求めて、そのほかは何も求めるものがなく、

Himalayas, singing: "Everything changes, everything appears and disappears."

The seeker heard this song which pleased him very much. He was as delighted as if he had found a spring of cool water for his thirst or as if a slave had been unexpectedly set free. He said to himself, "At last I have found the true teaching that I have sought for so long." He followed the voice and at last came upon the frightful demon. With an uneasy mind he approached the demon and said: "Was it you who sang the holy song that I have just heard? If it was you, please sing more of it."

The demon replied: "Yes, it was my song, but I can not sing more of it until I have had something to eat; I am starving."

The man begged him very earnestly to sing more of it, saying: "It has a sacred meaning to me and I have sought its teaching for a long time. I have only heard a part of it; please let me hear more."

The demon said again: "I am starving, but if I can taste the warm flesh and blood of a man, I will finish the song."

The man, in his eagerness to hear the teaching, promised the demon that he could have his body after he

地上に満ちた財宝はもとより、神の世界の栄華さえ望むところではなかった。

神はこの行者の行いに感動し、その心のまことを試そうと鬼の姿となってヒマラヤ山に現われ、「ものみなはうつり変わり、現われては滅びる。」と歌った。

行者はこの歌声を聞き、渇いたものが水を得たように、また囚(とら)われたものが放たれたように喜んで、これこそまことの理(ことわり)である、まことの教えであると思い、彼はあたりを見まわして、だれがこの尊い詩を歌ったのであろうかとながめ、そこに恐ろしい鬼を見いだした。怪しみながらも鬼に近づいて、「先ほどの歌はおまえの歌ったものか。もしそうなら、続きを聞かせてもらいたい。」と願った。

鬼は答えた。

「そうだ、それはわたしの歌だ。しかし、わたしはいま飢えているから、何か食べなくては歌うことができない。」

行者はさらに願った。

「どうかそう言わずに、続きを聞かせてもらいたい。あの歌には、まことに尊い意味があり、わたしの求めているものがある。しかし、あれだけではことばは終わっていない。どうか歌の残りを教えていただきたい。」

鬼はさらに言う。

「いまわたしは空腹に耐えられない。もし人の温かい肉を食

had heard the teaching. Then the demon sang the complete song.

> Everything changes,
> Everything appears and disappears,
> There is perfect tranquility
> When one transcends both life and extinction.

Hearing this, the man, after he wrote the poem on rocks and trees around, quietly climbed a tree and hurled himself to the feet of the demon, but the demon had disappeared and, instead, a radiant god received the body of the man unharmed.

8. Once upon a time there was an earnest seeker of the true path named Sadaprarudita. He cast aside every temptation for profit or honor and sought the path at the risk of his life. One day a voice from heaven came to him, saying, "Sadaprarudita! Go straight toward the east. Do not think of either heat or cold, pay no attention to worldly praise or scorn, do not be bothered by discriminations of good or evil, but just keep on going east. In the far east you will find a true teacher and will gain Enlightenment."

Sadaprarudita was very pleased to get this definite instruction and immediately started on his journey eastward. Sometimes he slept where night found him in a lonely field or in the wild mountains.

べ、血をすすることができるならば、あの歌の続きを説くで
あろう。」

これを聞いた行者は、続きの歌を聞かせてもらえるならば、
聞き終わってから、自分の身を与えるであろうと約束した。

鬼はそこで、残りを歌い、歌は完全なものとなった。それ
はこうである。

「ものみなうつり変わり、現われては滅びる。生滅にとらわ
れることなくなりて、静けさと安らぎは生まれる。」

行者はこの歌を木や石に彫りつけ、やがて木の上にのぼり、
身をおどらせて鬼の前に投げ与えた。その瞬間、鬼は神の姿
にかえり、行者の身は神の手に安らかに受けとめられた。

8、昔、サダープラルディタ（常啼）という求道者があっ
た。ひたすらにまことのさとりを求め、名誉利欲に誘われず、
懸命であった。ある日、空中に声があり、

「サダープラルディタよ、ただ東に進め。わきめもふらず、
暑さ寒さを忘れ、世の毀誉にかかわらず、善悪のはからいに
とらわれず、ひたすらに東に進め。必ずまことの師を得て、
さとりを得るであろう。」と教えた。

彼は大いに喜び、声の教えたとおり、ただまっしぐらに東
に進んで道を求めた。野に伏し、山に眠り、また異国の旅の

Being a stranger in foreign lands, he suffered many humiliations; once he sold himself into slavery, selling his own flesh out of hunger, but at last he found the true teacher and asked for his instruction.

There is a saying, "Good things are costly," and Sadaprarudita found it true in his case, for he had many difficulties on his journey in search of the path. He had no money to buy some flowers and incense to offer the teacher. He tried to sell his services but could find no one to hire him. There seemed to be an evil spirit hindering him every way he turned. The path to Enlightenment is a hard one and it may cost a man his life.

At last Sadaprarudita reached the presence of the teacher himself and then he had a new difficulty. He had no paper on which to take notes and no brush or ink to write with. Then he pricked his wrist with a dagger and took notes in his own blood. In this way he secured the precious Truth.

9. Once there was a boy named Sudhana who also wished for Enlightenment and earnestly sought the way. From a fisherman he learned the lore of the sea. From a doctor he learned compassion toward sick people in their suffering. From a wealthy man he learned that saving pennies was the secret of his fortune and thought how

迫害と屈辱を忍び、ときには身を売って人に仕え、骨を削る
思いをしてその日の糧を得つつ、ようやくまことの師のもと
にたどりついて教えを請うた。

　世に、好事魔多しという。善いことをしようとすれば必ず
障りがでるものである。サダープラルディタの求道の旅にも、
この障りはいくたびとなく現われた。

　師に捧げる香華のもとでを得たいと思い、身を売って人に
仕え、賃金を得ようとしても、やとい手がいない。悪魔の妨
げの手は彼の赴くところ、どこにでも伸びていた。さとりへ
の道はまことに血を枯らし骨を削る苦難の旅であった。

師について教えを受け、尊いことばを記そうと思っても、紙
も墨も得ることができない。彼は刀をとって自分の腕を突き、
血を流して師のことばを記した。このようにして、彼は尊い
さとりのことばを得たのであった。

　9、昔、スダナ（善財）という童子があった。この童子も
また、ただひたすらに道を求め、さとりを願う者であった。
海で魚をとる漁師を訪れては、海の不思議から得た教えを聞
いた。人の病を診る医師からは、人に対する心は慈悲でなけ
ればならないことを学んだ。また、財産を多く持つ長者に会

necessary it was to conserve every trifling gained on the path to Enlightenment.

From a meditating monk he learned that the pure and peaceful mind had a miraculous power to purify and tranquilize other minds. Once he met a woman of exceptional personality and was impressed by her benevolent spirit, and from her he learned a lesson that charity was the fruit of wisdom. Once he met an aged wanderer who told him that to reach a certain place he had to scale a mountain of swords and pass through a valley of fire. Thus Sudhana learned from his experiences that there was true teaching to be gained from everything he saw or heard.

He learned patience from a poor, crippled woman; he learned a lesson of simple happiness from watching children playing in the street; and from some gentle and humble people, who never thought of wanting anything that anybody else wanted, he learned the secret of living at peace with all the world.

He learned a lesson of harmony from watching the blending of the elements of incense, and a lesson of thanksgiving from the arrangement of flowers. One day, passing through a forest, he took a rest under a noble tree and noticed a tiny seedling growing near by out of a fallen and decaying tree and it taught him a lesson of the

っては、あらゆるものはみなそれなりの価値をそなえている
ということを聞いた。

　また坐禅する出家を訪れては、その寂かな心が姿に現われ
て、人びとの心を清め、不思議な力を与えるのを見た。また
気高い心の婦人に会ってはその奉仕の精神にうたれ、身を粉
にして骨を砕いて道を求める行者にめぐり会っては、真実に
道を求めるためには、刃の山にも登り、火の中でもかき分け
てゆかなければならないことを知った。

　このように童子は、心さえあれば、目の見るところ、耳の
聞くところ、みなことごとく教えであることを知った。

　かよわい女にもさとりの心があり、街に遊ぶ子供の群れに
もまことの世界のあることを見、すなおな、やさしい人に会
っては、ものに従う心の明らかな智慧をさとった。

　香をたく道にも仏の教えがあり、華を飾る道にもさとりの
ことばがあった。ある日、林の中で休んでいたときに、彼は
朽ちた木から一本の若木が生えているのを見て 生命の無常
を教わった。

uncertainty of life.

Sunlight by day and the twinkling stars by night constantly refreshed his spirit. Thus Sudhana profited by the experiences of his long journey.

Indeed, those who seek for Enlightenment must think of their minds as castles and decorate them. They must open wide the gates of their minds for Buddha, and respectfully and humbly invite Him to enter the inmost chamber, there to offer Him the fragrant incense of faith and the flowers of gratitude and gladness.

II
THE WAYS OF PRACTICE

1.   For those who seek Enlightenment there are three ways of practice that must be understood and followed: First, disciplines for practical behavior; second, right concentration of mind; and third, wisdom.

What are disciplines? Everyone, whether he is a common man or a way-seeker, should follow the precepts for good behavior. He should control both his mind and body, and guard the gates of his five senses. He should be afraid of even a trifling evil and, from moment to moment, should endeavor to practise only good deeds.

昼の太陽の輝き、夜の星のまたたき、これらのものも善財<ruby>善財<rt>ぜんざい</rt></ruby>童子のさとりを求める心を教えの雨でうるおした。

童子はいたるところで道を問い、いたるところでことばを聞き、いたるところでさとりの姿を見つけた。

まことに、さとりを求めるには、心の城を守り、心の城を飾らなければならない。そして<ruby>敬虔<rt>けいけん</rt></ruby>に、この心の城の門を開いて、その奥に仏をまつり、信心の<ruby>華<rt>はな</rt></ruby>を供え、歓喜の香を<ruby>捧<rt>ささ</rt></ruby>げなければならないことを童子は学んだのである。

第2節　さまざまな道

1、さとりを求める者が学ばなければならない三つのことがある。それは戒律と心の統一（<ruby>定<rt>じょう</rt></ruby>）と智慧*<ruby>智慧<rt>ちえ</rt></ruby>の三学である。

戒とは何であるか。人として、また道を修める者として守らなければならない戒を保ち、心身を統制し、五つの感覚器官の入口を守って、小さな罪にも恐れを見、善い行いをして励み努めることである。

What is meant by the concentration of mind? It means to get quickly away from greedy and evil desires as they arise and to hold the mind pure and tranquil.

What is wisdom? It is the ability to perfectly understand and to patiently accept the Fourfold Noble Truth, to know the fact of suffering and its nature; to know the source of suffering, to know what constitutes the end of suffering, and to know the Noble Path that leads to the end of suffering.

Those who earnestly follow these three ways of practice may rightly be called the disciples of Buddha.

Suppose a donkey, that has no nice shape, no voice and no horns like those of the cow, was following a herd of cows and proclaiming, "Look, I am also a cow." Would any one believe him? It is just as foolish when a man does not follow the three ways of practice but boasts that he is a way-seeker or a disciple of Buddha.

Before a farmer gathers a harvest in the fall, he must first plow the ground, sow the seed, irrigate, and remove the weeds as they come up in the springtime. Likewise, the seeker of Enlightenment must follow the three ways of practice. A farmer can not expect to see the buds

心の統一とは何であるか。欲を離れ不善を離れて、次第に心の安定に入ることである。

智慧とは何であるか。四つの真理を知ることである。それは、これが苦しみである、これが苦しみの原因である、これが苦しみの消滅である、これが苦しみの消滅に至る道であると、明らかにさとることである。

この三学を学ぶものが、仏の弟子といわれる。

驢馬が、牛の形も声も角もないのに、牛の群れの後からついてきて、わたしも牛であると言っても、だれも信用しないように、この戒と心の統一と智慧の三学を学ばないでいて、わたしは道を求める者である、仏の弟子であると言っても、それは愚かなことである。

農夫が秋に収穫を得るために、まず春のうちに田を耕し、種をまき、水をかけ、草を取って育てるように、さとりを求める者は、必ずこの三学を学ばなければならない。農夫が、

today, to see the plants tomorrow, and to gather the harvest the day after. So a man who seeks Enlightenment can not expect to remove worldly desires today, to remove attachments and evil desires tomorrow, and to get Enlightenment the day after.

Just as plants receive the patient care of the farmer after the seed has been sown and during the changes of climate and during the growth from plant to fruit, so the seeker of Enlightenment must patiently and perseveringly cultivate the soil of Enlightenment by following the three ways of practice.

2. It is difficult to advance along the path that leads to Enlightenment so long as one is covetous of comforts and luxuries and his mind disturbed by the desires of the senses. There is a wide difference between the enjoyment of life and the enjoyment of the True Path.

As already explained, the mind is the source of all things. If the mind enjoys worldly affairs, illusions and suffering will inevitably follow, but if the mind enjoys the True Path, happiness, contentment and enlightenment will just as surely follow.

Therefore, those who are seeking Enlightenment should keep their minds pure, and patiently keep and

まいた種が今日のうちに芽を出し、明日中に穂が出て、明後日には刈り入れができるようにと願ってもそれはできないことであるように、さとりを求める者も、今日のうちに煩悩を離れ、明日中に執着をなくし、明後日にさとりを得るというような不思議は得られるものではない。

種はまかれてから、農夫の辛苦と、季節の変化を受けて芽が生じ、ようやく最後に実を結ぶ。さとりを得るのもそのように、戒と心の統一と智慧の三学を修めているうちに次第に煩悩が滅び、執着が離れ、ようやくさとりの時が来るのである。

2、この世の栄華にあこがれ、愛欲に心を乱していながら、さとりの道に入ろうとするのは難い。世を楽しむことと道を楽しむこととはおのずから別である。

すでに説いたように、何ごとも心がもとである。心が世の中のことを楽しめば、迷いと苦しみが生まれ、心が道を好めば、さとりと楽しみが生まれる。

だから、さとりを求める者は、心を清らかにして教えを守り、戒を保たなければならない。戒を保てば心の統一を得、

practise the three ways. If they keep the precepts they will naturally obtain concentration of mind; and if they obtain concentration of the mind it will be just as natural for them to grasp wisdom, and wisdom will lead them to Enlightenment.

Indeed, these three ways (keeping the precepts, practising‘ concentration of mind and always acting wisely) are the true path to Enlightenment.

By not following them, people have for a long time accumulated mental delusions. They must not argue with worldly people, but must patiently meditate in their inner world of a pure mind in order to attain Enlightenment.

3. If the three ways of practice are analysed, they will reveal the eightfold noble path, the four viewpoints to be considered, the four right procedures, the five faculties of power to be employed, and the perfection of six practices.

The Noble Eightfold Path refers to right view, right thought, right speech, right behavior, right livelihood, right effort, right mindfulness, and right concentration.

Right View means to thoroughly understand the Fourfold Truth, to believe in the law of cause and effect

心の統一を得れば智慧が明らかとなり、その智慧こそ人をさとりに導く。

　まことに、この三学はさとりへの道である。三学を学ばないために、人びとは久しく迷いを重ねてきた。道に入って、他人と争わず、静かに内に想いをこらして心を清め、速やかにさとりを得なければならない。

　3、この三学は、開けば八正道となり、四念住、四正勤、五力、六波羅蜜とも説かれる。

　八正道は、正しいものの見方、正しいものの考え方、正しいことば、正しい行い、正しい生活、正しい努力、正しい念い、正しい心の統一である。

　正しいものの見方とは、四つの真理（四諦）を明らかにして、原因・結果の道理を信じ、誤った見方をしないこと。

and not to be deceived by appearances and desires.

Right Thought means the resolution not to cherish desires, not to be greedy, not to be angry, and not to do any harmful deed.

Right Speech means the avoidance of lying words, idle words, abusive words, and double-tongues.

Right Behavior means not to destroy any life, not to steal, or not to commit adultery.

Right Livelihood means to avoid any life that would bring shame.

Right Effort means to try to do one's best diligently toward the right direction.

Right Mindfulness means to maintain a pure and thoughtful mind.

Right Concentration means to keep the mind right and tranquil for its concentration, seeking to realize the mind's pure essence.

4. The four view-points to be considered are: First, to consider the body impure, seeking to remove all attach-

正しい考え方とは、欲にふけらず、貪らず、瞋（いか）らず、害（そこ）なう心のないこと。

正しいことばとは、偽りと、むだ口と、悪口と、二枚舌を離れること。

正しい行いとは、殺生と、盗みと、よこしまな愛欲を行わないこと。

正しい生活とは、人として恥ずべき生き方を避けること。

正しい努力とは、正しいことに向かって怠ることなく努力すること。

正しい念（おも）いとは、正しく思慮深い心を保つこと。

正しい心の統一とは、誤った目的を持たず、智慧（ちえ）を明らかにするために、心を正しく静めて心の統一をすることである。

4、四念住（しねんじゅう）とは次の四つである。

わが身は汚れたもので執着すべきものではないと見る。

ment to it, second, to consider the senses as a source of suffering, whatever their feelings of pain or pleasure may be; third, to consider the mind to be in a constant state of flux, and fourth, to consider everything in the world as being a consequence of causes and conditions and that nothing remains unchanged forever.

5. The four right procedures are: First, to prevent any evil from starting; second, to remove any evil as soon as it starts; third, to induce the doing of good deeds; and fourth, to encourage the growth and continuance of good deeds that have already started. One must endeavor to keep these four procedures.

6. The five faculties of power are: First, the faith to believe; second, the will to make the endeavor; third, the faculty of alertness; fourth, the ability to concentrate one's mind; and fifth, the ability to maintain clear wisdom. These five faculties are necessary powers to attain Enlightenment.

7. The perfection of six practices for reaching the other shore of Enlightenment are: the path of offering, the path of keeping precepts, the path of endurance, the path of endeavor, the path of concentration of mind, and the path of wisdom. By following these paths, one can

どのような感じを受けても、それはすべて苦しみのもとであると見る。

わが心は常にとどまることがなく、絶えずうつり変わるものと見る。

すべてのものはみな原因と条件によって成り立っているから、一つとして永久にとどまるものはないと見る。

5、四正勤とは次の四つである。

これから起ころうとする悪は、起こらない先に防ぐ。

すでに起こった悪は、断ち切る。

これから起ころうとする善は、起こるようにしむける。

すでに起こった善は、いよいよ大きくなるように育てる。

この四つを努めることである。

6、五力とは、次の五つである。

信ずること。

努めること。

思慮深い心を保つこと。

心を統一すること。

明らかな智慧を持つこと。

この五つがさとりを得るための力である。

7、六波羅蜜とは、布施・持戒・忍辱・精進・禅定・智慧

surely pass from the shore of delusion over to the shore of Enlightenment.

The practice of Offering gets rid of selfishness; the practice of Precepts keeps one thoughtful of the rights and comforts of others; the practice of Endurance helps one to control a fearful or angry mind; the practice of Endeavor helps one to be diligent and faithful; the practice of Concentration helps one to control a wandering and futile mind; and the practice of Wisdom changes a dark and confused mind into a clear and penetrating insight.

Offering and keeping Precepts make the foundation necessary to build a great castle on. Endurance and Endeavor are the walls of the castle that protect it against enemies from outside. Concentration and Wisdom are the personal armour that protects one against the assaults of life and death.

If one gives away a gift only when convenient, or because it is easier to give than not to give, it is an offering, of course, but it is not a True Offering. A True Offering comes from a sympathetic heart before any request is made, and a True Offering is the one that gives not occasionally but constantly.

Neither is it a True Offering if after the act there are

の六つのことで、この六つを修めると、迷いの此の岸から、さとりの彼の岸へと渡ることができるので、六度ともいう。

　布施は、惜しみ心を退け、持戒は行いを正しくし、忍辱は怒りやすい心を治め、精進は怠りの心をなくし、禅定は散りやすい心を静め、智慧は愚かな暗い心を明らかにする。

　布施と持戒とは、城を作る礎のように、修行の基となり、忍辱と精進とは城壁のように外難を防ぎ、禅定と智慧とは、身を守って生死を逃れる武器であり、それは甲冑に身をかためて敵に臨むようなものである。

　乞う者を見て与えるのは施しであるが、最上の施しとはいえない。心を開いて、自ら進んで他人に施すのが最上の施しである。また、ときどき施すのも最上の施しではない。常に施すのが最上の施しである。

　施した後で悔いたり、施して誇りがましく思うのは、最上

feelings of regret or of self-praise; a True Offering is one that is given with pleasure, forgetting oneself as the giver, the one who receives it and the gift itself.

True Offering springs spontaneously from one's pure compassionate heart with no thought of any return, wishing to enter into a life of Englightenment together.

There are seven kinds of offering which can be practised by even those who are not wealthy. The first is the physical offering. This is to offer service by one's labor. The highest type of this offering is to offer one's own life as is shown in the following story. The second is the spiritual offering. This is to offer a compassionate heart to others. The third is the offering of eyes. This is to offer a warm glance to others which will give them tranquility. The fourth is the offering of countenance. This is to offer a soft countenance with smile to others. The fifth is the oral offering. This is to offer kind and warm words to others. The sixth is the seat offering. This is to offer one's seat to others. The seventh is the offering of shelter. This is to let others spend the night at one's home. These kinds of offering can be practised by anyone in everyday life.

の施しではない。施して喜び、施した自分と、施しを受けた人と、施した物と、この三つをともに忘れるのが最上の施しである。

正しい施しは、その報いを願わず、清らかな慈悲の心をもって、他人も自分も、ともにさとりに入るように願うものでなければならない。

世に無財の七施とよばれるものがある。財なき者にもなし得る七種の布施行のことである。一には身施、肉体による奉仕であり、その最高なるものが次項に述べる捨身行である。二には心施、他人や他の存在に対する思いやりの心である。三には眼施、やさしきまなざしであり、そこに居るすべての人の心がなごやかになる。四には和顔施、柔和な笑顔を絶やさないことである。五には言施、思いやりのこもったあたたかい言葉をかけることである。六には牀座施、自分の席をゆずることである。七には房舎施、わが家に一夜の宿を貸すことである。以上の七施ならば、だれにでも出来ることであり、日常生活の中で行えることばかりなのである。

8. Once there was a prince named Sattva. One day he and his two elder brothers went to a forest to play. There they saw a famished tigress which was evidently tempted to devour her own seven cubs to satisfy her hunger.

The elder brothers ran away in fear but Sattva climbed up a cliff and threw himself over it to the tigress in order to save the lives of the baby tigers.

Prince Sattva did this charitable act spontaneously but within his mind he was thinking: "This body is changing and impermanent; I have loved this body with no thought of throwing it away, but now I make it an offering to this tigress so that I may gain Enlightenment." This thought of Prince Sattva shows the true determination to gain Enlightenment.

9. There are Four Unlimited States of Mind that the seeker of Enlightenment should cherish. They are compassion, tenderness, gladness and equanimity. One can remove greed by cherishing compassion; one can remove anger by tenderness; one can remove suffering by gladness, and one can remove the habit of discrimination of enemies and friends by cherishing an equitable mind.

It is a great compassion that makes people happy and contented; it is a great tenderness that removes everything that does not make people happy and con-

8、昔、薩埵太子という王子がいた。ある日、二人の兄の王子と森に遊んで、七匹の子を産んだ虎が飢えに迫られて、あわやわが子を食べようとするのを見た。

二人の兄の王子は恐れて逃げたが、薩埵太子だけは身を捨てて飢えた虎を救おうと、絶壁によじのぼって、身を投げて虎に与え、その母の虎の飢えを満たし、虎の子の命を救った。

薩埵太子の心は、ただ一筋に道を求めることにあった。「この身は砕けやすく変わりやすい。いままで施すことを知らず、ただわが身を愛することにばかりかかわってきた自分は、いまこそこの身を施して、さとりを得るために捧げよう。」

この決心によって、王子は飢えた虎にその身を施したのである。

9、またここに、道を求める者の修めなければならない慈と悲と喜と捨の四つの大きな心（四無量心）がある。

慈を修めると貪りの心を断ち、悲を修めると瞋りの心を断ち、喜は苦しみを断ち、捨は、恩と恨みのいずれに対しても差別を見ないようになる。

多くの人びとのために、幸福と楽しみとを与えることは、大きな慈である。多くの人びとのために、苦しみと悲しみを

tented; it is a great gladness that makes everyone happy and contented with a mind of joy; there is a great peacefulness when everyone is happy and contented, and then one can have equal feelings toward everybody.

With care one may cherish these Four Unlimited States of Mind and may get rid of greed, anger, suffering, and the minds of love-hate, but it is not an easy thing to do. An evil mind is as hard to get rid of as a watchdog, and a right mind is as easy to lose as a deer in a forest; or an evil mind is as hard to remove as letters carved in stone, and a right mind is as easy to lose as words written in water. Indeed, it is the most difficult thing in life to train oneself for Enlightenment.

10.   There was a young man named Srona who was born in a wealthy family but was of delicate health. He was very earnest to gain Enlightenment and became a disciple of the Blessed One. On the path to Enlightenment, he tried so hard that finally his feet bled.

The Blessed One pitied him and said, "Srona my boy, did you ever study the harp at your home? You know that a harp does not make music if the strings are stretched too tight or too loose. It makes music only when the strings are stretched just right.

なくすことが大きな悲である。多くの人びとに歓喜の心をもって向かうのが大きな喜である。すべてのものに対して平等で、分け隔てをしないのが大きな捨である。

このように、慈と悲と喜と捨の四つの大きな心を育てて、貪りと瞋りと苦しみと愛憎の心を除くのであるが、悪心の去り難い心とは飼犬のようであり、善心の失われやすいことは林を走る鹿のようである。また、悪心は岩に刻んだ文字のように消えにくく、善心は水に画いた文字のように消えやすい。だから道を修めることはまことに困難なものといわなければならない。

10、世尊の弟子シュローナは富豪の家に生まれ、生まれつき体が弱かった。世尊にめぐり会ってその弟子となり、足の裏から血を出すほど痛々しい努力を続け、道を修めたけれども、なおさとりを得ることができなかった。

世尊はシュローナを哀れんで言われた。

「シュローナよ、おまえは家にいたとき、琴を学んだことがあるであろう。糸は張ること急であっても、また緩くても、よい音は出ない。緩急よろしきを得て、はじめてよい音を出すものである。

"The training for Enlightenment is just like adjusting the harp strings. You can not attain Enlightenment if you stretch the strings of your mind too loosely or too tightly. You must be considerate and act wisely."

Srona found these words very profitable and finally gained what he sought.

11. Once there was a prince who was skillful in the use of the five weapons. One day he was returning home from his practice and met a monster whose skin was invulnerable.

The monster started for him but nothing daunted the prince. He shot an arrow at him which fell harmless. Then he threw his spear which failed to penetrate the thick skin. Then he threw a bar and a javelin but they failed to hurt the monster. Then he used his sword but the sword broke. The prince attacked the monster with his fists and feet but to no purpose, for the monster clutched him in his giant arms and held him fast. Then the prince tried to use his head as a weapon but in vain.

The monster said, "It is useless for you to resist; I am going to devour you." But the prince answered, "You may think that I have used all my weapons and am helpless, but I still have one weapon left. If you devour me, I will destroy you from the inside of your stomach."

　さとりを得る道もこれと同じく、怠れば道を得られず、またあまり張りつめて努力しても、決して道は得られない。だから、人はその努力についても、よくその程度を考えなければならない。」

　この教えを受けて、シュローナはよく会得し、やがてさとりを得ることができた。

　11、昔、五武器太子とよばれる王子がいた。五種の武器を巧みにあやつることができたので、この名を得たのである。修行を終えて郷里に帰る途中、荒野の中で、脂毛という名の怪物に出会った。

　脂毛は、そろそろと歩いて王子に迫ってきた。王子はまず矢を放ったが、矢は脂毛に当たっても毛にねばりつくばかりで傷つけることができない。剣も鉾も棒も槍も、すべて毛に吸い取られるだけで役に立たない。

　武器をすべてなくした王子は、こぶしを上げて打ち、足を上げて蹴ったが、こぶしも足もみな毛に吸いつけられて、王子の身は脂毛の身にくっついて宙に浮いたままである。頭で脂毛の胸を打っても、頭もまた胸の毛について離れない。

　脂毛は、「もうおまえはわしの手の中にある。これからおま

The courage of the prince disturbed the monster and he asked, "How can you do that?" The prince replied, "By the power of the Truth."

Then the monster released him and begged for his instruction in the Truth.

The teaching of this fable is to encourage disciples to persevere in their efforts and to be undaunted in the face of many set backs.

12. Both odious self-assertion and shamelessness offend mankind, but dishonor and shame protect human beings. People respect their parents, elders, brothers and sisters because they are sensitive to dishonor and shame. After self-reflection it is meritorious to withhold honor from one's self and to feel ashamed by observing other people.

If a man possesses a repentant spirit his sins will disappear, but if he has an unrepentant spirit his sins will continue and condemn him forever.

It is only the one who hears the true teaching rightly and realizes its meaning and relation to oneself who can receive and profit by it.

If a man merely hears the true teaching but does not acquire it, he will fail in his search for Enlightenment.

えを餌食にする。」と言うと、王子は笑って、

「おまえはわたしの武器がすべて尽きたように思うかも知れないが、まだわたしには金剛の武器が残っている。おまえがもしわたしをのめば、わたしの武器はおまえの腹の中からおまえを突き破るであろう。」と答えた。

そこで脂毛は王子の勇気にくじけて尋ねた。

「どうしてそんなことができるのか。」「真理の力によって。」と王子は答えた。そこで脂毛は王子を離し、かえって王子の教えを受けて、悪事から遠ざかるようになった。

12、おのれに恥じず、他にも恥じないのは、世の中を破り、おのれに恥じ、他にも恥じるのは世の中を守る。慚愧の心があればこそ、父母・師・目上の人を敬う心も起こり、兄弟姉妹の秩序も保たれる。まことに、自ら省みて、わが身を恥じ、人の有様を見ておのれに恥じるのは、尊いことといわなければならない。

懺悔の心が起これば、もはや罪は罪でなくなるが、懺悔の心がないならば、罪は永久に罪として、その人をとがめる。

正しい教えを聞いて、いくたびもその味わいを思い、これを修め習うことによって、教えが身につく。思うこと修めることがなければ、耳に聞いても身につけることはできない。

Faith, modesty, humbleness, endeavor and widsom are the great sources of strength to him who is seeking Enlightenment. Among these, wisdom is the greatest of all and the rest are but the aspects of wisdom. If a man, while in his training, loves worldly affairs, enjoys idle talk or falls asleep, he will be retired from the path to Enlightenment.

13. In training for Enlightenment, some may succeed quicker than others. Therefore, one should not be discouraged to see others becoming enlightened first.

When a man is practising archery, he dose not expect quick success but knows that if he practises patiently, he will become more and more accurate. A river begins as a brook but grows ever larger until it flows into the great ocean.

Like these examples, if a man trains with patience and perseverance, he will surely gain Enlightenment.

As already explained, if one keeps his eyes open, he will see the teaching everywhere, and so his opportunities for Enlightenment are endless.

Once there was a man who was burning incense. He noticed that the fragrance was neither coming nor going; it neither appeared nor disappeared. This trifle incident led him to gain Enlightenment.

信と慚と愧と努力と智慧とは、この世の大きな力である。このうち、智慧の力が主であって、他の四つは、これに結びつく従の力である。

道を修めるのに、雑事にとらわれ、雑談にふけり、眠りを貪るのは、退歩する原因である。

13、同じく道を修めても、先にさとる者もあれば、後にさとる者もある。だから、他人が道を得たのを見て、自分がまだ道を得ていないことを悲しむには及ばない。

弓を学ぶのに、最初に当たることが少なくても、学び続けていればついには当たるようになる。また、流れは流れ流れてついには海に入るように、道を修めてやめることがなければ、必ずさとりは得られる。

前に説いたように、眼を開けば、どこにでも教えはある。同様に、さとりへの機縁も、どこにでも現われている。

香をたいて香気の流れたときに、その香気の、あるのでもなく、ないのでもなく、行くのでもなく、来るのでもないさまを知って、さとりに入った人もある。

Once there was a man who got a thorn stuck in his foot. He felt the sharp pain and a thought came to him, that pain was only a reaction of the mind. From this incident a deeper thought followed that the mind may get out of hand if one fails to control it, or it may become pure if one succeeds. From these thoughts, a little later, Enlightenment came to him.

There was another man who was very avaricious. One day he was thinking of his greedy mind when he realized that greedy thoughts were but shavings and kindlings that wisdom could burn and consume. That was the beginning of his Enlightenment.

There is an old saying: "Keep your mind level. If the mind is level, the whole world will be level." Consider these words. Realize that all the distinctions of the world are caused by the discriminating views of the mind. There is a path to Enlightenment in those very words. Indeed, the ways to Enlightenment are unlimited.

III
THE WAY OF FAITH

1.   Those who take refuge in the three treasures, the Buddha, the Dharma and the Samgha, are called the

　道を歩いて足に棘を立て、疼きの中から、疼きを覚えるのは、もともと定まった心があるのではなく、縁に触れていろいろの心となるのであって、一つの心も、乱せば醜い煩悩となり、おさめれば美しいさとりとなることを知って、さとりに入った人もある。

　欲の盛んな人が、自分の欲の心を考え、欲の薪がいつしか智慧の火となるものであることを知って、ついにはさとりに入った例もある。

　「心を平らにせよ。心が平らになれば、世界の大地もみなことごとく平らになる。」という教えを聞いて、この世の差別は心の見方によるものであると考えて、さとりに入った人もある。まことにさとりの縁には限りがない。

第3節　信仰の道

　1、仏と教えと教団に帰依する者を、仏教の信者という。

disciples of Buddha. The disciples of Buddha observe the four parts of mind-control — the precepts, faith, offering and wisdom.

The disciples of Buddha practise the five precepts: not to kill, not to steal, not to commit adultery, not to lie, and not to take intoxicants of any kind.

The disciples of Buddha have faith in the Buddha's perfect wisdom. They try to keep away from greediness and selfishness and to practise offering. They understand the law of cause and effect, keeping in mind the transiency of life and conform to the norm of wisdom.

A tree leaning toward the east will naturally fall eastward and so those who listen to the Buddha's teaching and maintain faith in it will surely be born in the Buddha's Pure Land.

2.　It has rightly been said that those who believe in the three treasures of the Buddha, the Dharma and the Samgha are called the disciples of Buddha.

The Buddha is the one who attained perfect Enlightenment and used His attainment to emancipate and bless all mankind. The Dharma is the truth, the spirit of Enlightenment and the teaching that explains it. The Samgha is the perfect brotherhood of believers in the Buddha and Dharma.

また、仏教の信者は、次に説く戒律と信仰と布施と智慧とを
持っている。

　生きものの命を取らず、盗みをなさず、よこしまな愛欲を
犯さず、偽りを言わず、酒を飲まない。この五つを守るのが
信者の戒である。

　仏の智慧を信ずるのが信者の信であり、貪り、もの惜しみ
する心を離れて常に他人への施しを好むのが信者の布施であ
る。さらに、因と縁の道理を知り、ものみながうつり変わる
道理を知るのが、信者の智慧である。

　東に傾いている木は、いつ倒れても必ず東に倒れるように、
平生、仏の教えに耳を傾けている信心の厚いものは、いつ、
どのように命を終わっても、仏の国に生まれることに定まっ
ている。

　2、いま、仏教の信者とは、仏と教えと教団とを信ずる者
をいう。

　仏とはさとりを開いて、人びとを恵み救う人をいう。教え
とは、その仏の説かれた教えをいう。教団とは、その教えに
よって正しく修行する和合の団体をいう。

We speak of Buddhahood, the Dharma and the Brotherhood as though they are three different things, but they are really only one. Buddha is manifested in His Dharma and is realized by the Brotherhood. Therefore, to believe in the Dharma and to cherish the Brotherhood is to have faith in the Buddha, and to have faith in the Buddha means to believe in the Dharma and to cherish the Brotherhood.

Therefore, people are emancipated and enlightened simply by having faith in the Buddha. Buddha is the perfectly Enlightened One and He loves everyone as though each were His only child. So if anyone regards Buddha as his own parent, he identifies himself with Buddha and attains Enlightenment.

Those who thus regard Buddha will be supported by His wisdom and perfumed by His grace.

3. Nothing in the world brings greater benefit than to believe in Buddha. Just hearing Buddha's name, believing and being pleased even for a moment, is incomparably rewarding.

Therefore, one must please oneself by seeking the teaching of Buddha in spite of the conflagration that fills all the world.

　仏と教えと教団の、この三つは、三つでありながら、離れた三つではない。仏は教えに現われ、教えは教団に実現されるから、三つはそのまま一つである。

　だから、教えと教団を信ずることは、そのまま仏を信ずることであり、仏を信ずれば、おのずから教えと教団とを信ずることになる。

　したがって、すべての人は、ただ仏を信ずること一つによって救われ、またさとりが得られる。仏はすべての人を、自分のひとり子のように愛するから、人もまた子が母を思うように、仏を信ずれば、現実に仏を見、仏の救いが得られる。

　仏を念ずる者は、常に仏の光明におさめられ、また自然に仏の香気に染まる。

　3、世に仏を信ずることほど大きな利益をもたらすものはない。もしただ一度だけでも仏の名を聞いて、信じ喜ぶならば、この上ない大きな利益を得たものといわなければならない。

　だから、この世界に満ちみちている炎の中に入って行ってでも、仏の教えを聞いて信じ喜ばなければならない。

It will be hard to meet a teacher who can explain the Dharma; it will be harder to meet a Buddha; but it will be hardest to believe in His teaching.

But now that you have met the Buddha, who is hard to meet, and have had it explained to you what is hard to hear, you ought to rejoice and believe and have faith in Buddha.

4.   On the long journey of human life, faith is the best of companions; it is the best refreshment on the journey; and it is the greatest possession.

Faith is the hand that receives the Dharma; it is the pure hand that receives all the virtues. Faith is the fire that consumes all the impurities of worldly desires, it removes the burden, and it is the guide that leads one's way.

Faith removes greed, fear and pride; it teaches courtesy and to respect others; it frees one from the bondage of circumstances; it gives one courage to meet hardship; it gives one power to overcome temptations; it enables one to keep one's deeds bright and pure; and it enriches the mind with wisdom.

　まことに、仏に会うことは難く、その教えを説く人に会うことも難く、その教えを信ずることはさらに難い。

　いま、会い難いこの教えを説く人に会い、聞き難いこの教えを聞くことができたのであるから、この大きな利益を失わないように、仏を信じ喜ばなければならない。

　1、信こそはまことに人の善き伴侶であり、この世の旅路の糧であり、この上ない富である。

　信は仏の教えを受けて、あらゆる功徳を受けとる清らかな手である。信は火である。人びとの心の汚れを焼き清め、同じ道に入らせ、その上、仏の道に進もうとする人びとを燃えたたせるからである。

　信は人の心を豊かにし、貪りの思いをなくし、おごる心を取り去って、へりくだり敬うことを教える。こうして、智慧は輝き、行いは明らかに、困難に破れず、外界にとらわれず、誘惑に負けない、強い力が与えられる。

Faith is the encouragement when one's way is long and wearisome, and it leads to Enlightenment.

Faith makes us feel that we are in the presence of Buddha and it brings us to where Buddha's arm supports us. Faith softens our hard and selfish minds and gives us a friendly spirit and a mind of understanding sympathy.

5.   Those who have faith gain the wisdom to recognize the Buddha's teaching in whatever they hear. Those who have faith gain the wisdom to see that everything is but the appearance that arises from the law of causes and conditions, and then faith gives them the grace of patient acceptance and the ability to conform to their conditions peacefully.

Faith gives them the wisdom to recognize the transiency of life and the grace not to be surprised or grieved at whatever comes to them or with the passing of life itself, knowing that, however conditions and appearances may change, the truth of life remains always unchanged.

Faith has three significant aspects: repentance, a rejoicing and sincere respect for the virtues of others, and a grateful acceptance of Buddha's appearance.

信は、道が長く退屈なときに励ましとなり、さとりに導く。

信は、常に仏の前にいるという思いを人に与え、仏に抱かれている思いを与え、身も心も柔らかにし、人びとによく親しみなじむ徳を与える。

5、この信のあるものは、耳に聞こえるどんな声でも、仏の教えとして味わい、喜ぶ智慧が得られ、どんなできごとでも、すべてみな因と縁によって現われたものであることを知って、すなおにこれを受け入れる智慧が得られる。

かりそめのたわごとにすぎないこの世のできごとの中にも永久に変わらないまことのあることを知って、栄枯盛衰(えいこせいすい)の変わりにも、驚かず悲しまない智慧が得られる。

信には、懺悔(ざんげ)と、随喜(ずいき)と、祈願の三つのすがたが現われてくる。

People should cultivate these aspects of faith; they should be sensitive to their failings and impurities; they should be ashamed of them and confess them; they should diligently practise the recognition of the good traits and good deeds of others and praise them for their sake; and they should habitually desire to act with Buddha and to live with Buddha.

The mind of faith is the mind of sincerity; it is a deep mind, a mind that is sincerely glad to be led to Buddha's Pure Land by His power.

Therefore, Buddha gives a power to faith that leads people to the Pure Land, a power that purifies them, a power that protects them from self-delusion. Even if they have faith only for a moment, when they hear Buddha's name praised all over the world, they will be led to His Pure Land.

6.   Faith is not something that is added to the worldly mind — it is the manifestation of the mind's Buddha-nature. One who understands Buddha is a Buddha himself; one who has faith in Buddha is a Buddha himself.

But it is difficult to uncover and recover one's Buddha nature; it is difficult to maintain a pure mind in the constant rise and fall of greed, anger and worldly passion; yet faith enables one to do it.

深くおのれを省みて、自分の罪と汚れを自覚し、懺悔する。他人の善いことを見るとわがことのように喜んでその人のために功徳を願う心が起きる。またいつも仏とともにおり、仏とともに行い、仏とともに生活することを願うのである。

この信ずる心は、誠の心であり、深い心であり、仏の力によって仏の国に導かれることを喜ぶ心である。

だから、すべての所でたたえられる仏の名を聞いて、信じ喜ぶ一念のあるところにこそ、仏は真心こめて力を与え、その人を仏の国に導き、ふたたび迷いを重ねることのない身の上にするのである。

6、この、仏を信ずる心は、人びとの心の底に横たわっている*仏性の表われである。なぜかといえば、仏を知るものは仏であり、仏を信ずるものは仏でなければならないからである。

しかし、たとえ仏性があっても、仏性は、*煩悩の泥の底深く沈んで、成仏の芽を吹き出し、花開くことはできない。貪り・瞋りの煩悩の逆巻く中に、どうして仏に向かう清い心が起こるであろうか。

Within the forest of the poisonous Eranda trees only Eranda trees are said to grow, but not the fragrant Chandana. It is a miracle if a Chandana tree grows in an Eranda forest. Likewise, it is often a miracle that faith in Buddha grows in the heart of the people.

Therefore, the faith to believe in Buddha is called a "rootless" faith. That is, it has no root by which it can grow in the human mind, but it has a root to grow in the compassionate mind of Buddha.

7. Thus faith is fruitful and sacred. But faith is hard to awaken in an idle mind. In particular, there are five doubts that lurk in the shadows of the human mind and tend to discourage faith.

First, there is doubt in the Buddha's wisdom; second, there is doubt in the Buddha's teaching; third, there is doubt in the person who explains the Buddha's teachings; fourth, there is doubt as to whether the ways and methods suggested for following the Noble Path are reliable; and fifth, there is a person who, because of his arrogant and impatient mind, may doubt the sincerity of others who understand and follow the Buddha's teachings.

エーランダという毒樹の林には、エーランダの芽だけが吹き出して、チャンダナ（栴檀）の香木は生えることはない。エーランダの林にチャンダナが生えたならば、これはまことに不思議である。いま人びとの胸のうちに、仏に向かい、仏を信ずる心の生じたのも、これと同じく不思議なことといわなければならない。

だから、人びとの仏を信ずる信の心を無根の信という。無根というのは、人びとの心の中には信の生え出る根はないが、仏の慈悲の心の中には、信の根があることをいうのである。

7、信はこのように尊く、まことに道のもとであり功徳の母であるが、それにもかかわらず、この信が道を求める人にも円満に得られないのは、次の五つの疑いが妨げているからである。

一つには、仏の智慧を疑うこと。

二つには、教えの道理に惑うこと。

三つには、教えを説く人に疑いを持つこと。

四つには、求道の道にしばしば迷いを生ずること。

五つには、同じく道を求める人びとに対して、慢心から相手を疑って、いらだつ思いがあるためである。

Indeed, there is nothing more dreadful than doubt. Doubt separates people. It is a poison that disintegrates friendships and breaks up pleasant relations. It is a thorn that irritates and hurts; it is a sword that kills.

The beginnings of faith were long ago planted by the compassion of Buddha. When one has faith, one should realize this fact and be very grateful to Buddha for His goodness.

One should never forget that it is not because of one's own compassion that one has awakened faith, but because of the Buddha's compassion which long ago threw its pure light of faith into human minds and dispelled the darkness of their ignorance. He who enjoys the present faith has entered into their heritage.

Even living an ordinary life, one can be born in the Pure Land, become one awakens faith through the Buddha's long continued compassion.

It is, indeed, hard to be born in this world. It is hard to hear the Dharma; it is harder to awaken faith; therefore, everyone should try one's best to hear the Buddha's teachings.

まことに世に疑いほど恐ろしいものはない。疑いは隔てる心であり、仲を裂く毒であり、互いの生命を損なう刃であり、互いの心を苦しめる棘である。

だから信を得た者は、その信が、遠い昔に、仏の慈悲によって、すでにその因縁が植えつけられていたものであることを知らなければならない。

人の胸の中にひそむ疑いの闇を破って、信の光をさし入れ給う仏の手のあることを知らなければならない。

信を得て、遠い昔に仏が与えられた深い因縁を喜び、厚い仏の慈悲を喜ぶ者は、この世の生活そのままに、仏の国に生まれることができるのである。

まことに、人の生まれることは難く、教えを聞くことも難く、信を得ることはさらに難い。だから、努め励んで、教えを聞かなければならない。

IV

SACRED SAYINGS

1. "He abused me, he laughed at me, he struck me." Thus one thinks and so long as one retains such thoughts one's anger continues.

Anger will never disappear so long as there are thoughts of resentment in the mind. Anger will disappear just as soon as thoughts of resentment are forgotten.

If a roof is improperly made or in disrepair, rain will leak into the house; so greed enters the mind that is improperly trained or out of control.

To be idle is a short road to death and to be diligent is a way of life; foolish people are idle, wise people are diligent.

An arrow-maker tries to make his arrows straight; so a wise man tries to keep his mind straight.

A disturbed mind is forever active, jumping hither and thither, and is hard to control; but a tranquil mind is peaceful; therefore, it is wise to keep the mind under control.

It is a man's own mind, not his enemy or foe, that lures him into evil ways.

第4節　仏のことば

1、わたしをののしった、わたしを笑った、わたしを打ったと思う者には、怨みは鎮まることがない。

怨みは怨みによって鎮まらない。怨みを忘れて、はじめて怨みは鎮まる。

屋根のふき方の悪い家に、雨が漏るように、よく修めていない心に、貪りのおもいがさしこむ。

怠るのは死の道、努め励むのは生の道である。愚かな人は怠り、智慧ある人は努め励む。

弓矢を作る人が、矢を削ってまっすぐにするように、賢い人は、その心を正しくする。

心は抑え難く、軽くたち騒いでととのえ難い。この心をととのえてこそ、安らかさが得られる。

怨みを抱く人のなすことよりも、かたきのなす悪よりも、この心は、人に悪事をなす。

The one who protects his mind from greed, anger and foolishness, is the one who enjoys real and lasting peace.

2.   To utter pleasant words without practising them is like a fine flower without fragrance.

The fragrance of a flower does not float against the wind; but the honor of a good man goes even against the wind into the world.

A night seems long to a sleepless man and a journey seems long to a weary traveler; so the time of delusion and suffering seems long to a man who does not know the right teaching.

On a trip a man should travel with a companion of equal mind or one who has a better mind; one had better travel alone than to travel with a fool.

An insincere and evil friend is more to be feared than a wild beast; a wild beast may wound your body, but an evil friend will wound your mind.

So long as a man can not control his own mind, how can he get any satisfaction from thinking such thoughts as, "This is my son" or "This is my treasure"? A

　この心を、貪^{むさぼ}りから守り、瞋^{いか}りから守り、あらゆる悪事から守る人に、まことの安らかさが得られる。

　2、ことばだけ美しくて、実行の伴わないのは、色あって香りのない花のようなものである。

　花の香りは、風に逆らっては流れない。しかし、善い人の香りは、風に逆らって世に流れる。

　眠られない人に夜は長く、疲れた者に道は遠い。正しい教えを知らない人に、その迷いは長い。

　道を行くには、おのれにひとしい人、またはまさった人と行くがよい。愚かな人とならば、ひとり行く方がまさっている。

　猛獣は恐れなくとも、悪友は恐れなくてはならない。猛獣はただ身を破るにすぎないが、悪友は心を破るからである。

　これはわが子、これはわが財宝と考えて、愚かな者は苦しむ。おのれさえ、おのれのものでないのに、どうして子と財

foolish man suffers from such thoughts.

To be foolish and to recognize that one is a fool, is better than to be foolish and imagine that one is wise.

A spoon cannot taste of the food it carries. Likewise, a foolish man cannot understand the wise man's wisdom even if he associates with a sage.

Fresh milk is often slow to curdle; so sinful actions do not always bring immediate results. Sinful actions are more like coals of fire that are hidden in the ashes and keep on smouldering, finally causing a greater fire.

A man is foolish to desire privileges, promotion, profits, or honor, for such desires can never bring happiness but will bring suffering instead.

A good friend who points out mistakes and imperfections and rebukes evil is to be respected as if he reveals the secret of some hidden treasure.

3. A man who is pleased when he receives good instruction will sleep peacefully, because his mind is thereby cleansed.

A carpenter seeks to make his beam straight; an arrow-maker seeks to make his arrows well-balanced; the

宝とがおのれのものであろうか。

愚かにして愚かさを知るのは、愚かにして賢いと思うよりもまさっている。

愚かな人は賢い人と交わってもちょうど匙が味を知らないように、賢い人の示す教えを知ることができない。

新しい乳が容易に固まらないように、悪い行いもすぐにはその報いを示さないが、灰に覆われた火のように、隠れて燃えつつ、その人に従う。

愚かな人は常に名誉と利益とに苦しむ。上席を得たい、権利を得たい、利益を得たいと、常にこの欲のために苦しむ。

過ちを示し、悪を責め、足らないところを責める人には、宝のありかを示す人のように、仰ぎ仕えなければならない。

3、教えを喜ぶ人は、心が澄んで、快く眠ることができる。教えによって心が洗われるからである。

大工が木をまっすぐにし、弓師が矢を矯め直し、溝つくり

digger of an irrigation ditch seeks to make the water run smoothly; so a wise man seeks to control his mind so that it will function smoothly and truly.

A great rock is not disturbed by the wind; the mind of a wise man is not disturbed by either honor or abuse.

To conquer oneself is a greater victory than to conquer thousands in a battle.

To live a single day and hear a good teaching is better than to live a hundred years without knowing such teaching.

Those who respect themselves must be on constant guard lest they yield to evil desires. Once in a lifetime, at least, they should awaken faith, either in their youth, or in middle age, or even in old age.

The world is always burning, burning with the fires of greed, anger and foolishness; one should flee from such dangers as soon as possible.

The world is like a bubble, it is like the gossamer web of a spider, it is like the defilement in a dirty jar; one should constantly protect the purity of his mind.

が水を導くように、賢い人は心をととのえ導く。

堅い岩が風に揺るがないように、賢い人はそしられてもほめられても心を動かさない。

おのれに勝つのは、戦場で千万の敵に勝つよりもすぐれた勝利である。

正しい教えを知らないで、百年生きるよりも、正しい教えを聞いて、一日生きる方がはるかにすぐれている。

どんな人でも、もしまことに自分を愛するならば、よく自分を悪から守れ。若いとき、壮んなとき、また老いた後も一度は目覚めよ。

世は常に燃えている。貪りと瞋りと愚かさの火に燃えている。この火の宅から、一刻も早く逃げ出さなければならない。

この世はまことにあわのような、くもの糸のような、汚れをもった瓶のようなものである。だから、人はそれぞれの尊い心を守らなければならない。

4.   To avoid any evil, to seek the good, to keep the mind pure: this is the essence of Buddha's teaching.

Endurance is one of the most difficult disciplines, but it is to him who endures that the final victory comes.

One must remove resentment when he is feeling resentful; one must remove sorrow while he is in the midst of sorrow; one must remove greediness while he is steeped in greed. To live a pure unselfish life, one must count nothing as one's own in the midst of abundance.

To be healthy is a great advantage; to be contented with what one has is better than the possession of great wealth; to be considered reliable is the truest mark of friendliness; to attain Enlightenment is the highest happiness.

When one has the feeling of dislike for evil, when one feels tranquil, when one finds pleasure in listening to good teachings, when one has these feelings and appreciates them, one is free of fear.

Do not become attached to the things you like, do not maintain aversion to the things you dislike. Sorrow, fear and bondage come from one's likes and dislikes.

4、どんな悪をもなさず、あらゆる善いことをし、おのおの心を清くする、それが仏の教えである。

耐え忍ぶことは、なし難い修行の一つである。しかしよく忍ぶ者にだけ最後の勝利の花が飾られる。

怨みのさ中にあって怨みなく、愁いのさ中にあって愁いがなく、貪りのさ中にあって貪りがなく、一物もわがものと思うことなく、清らかに生きなければならない。

病のないのは第一の利、足るを知るのは第一の富、信頼あるのは第一の親しみ、さとりは第一の楽しみである。

悪から遠ざかる味わい、寂けさの味わい、教えの喜びの味わい、この味わいを味わう者には恐れがない。

心に好悪を起こして執着してはならない。好むこと、きらうことから悲しみが起こり、恐れが起こり、束縛が起こる。

5.   Rust grows from iron and destroys it; so evil grows from the mind of man and destroys him.

A scripture that is not read with sincerity soon becomes covered with dust; a house that is not fixed when it needs repairing becomes filthy; so an idle man soon becomes defiled.

Impure acts defile a woman; stinginess defiles an offering; so evil acts defile not only this life but also the following lives.

But the defilement to be most dreaded is the defilement of ignorance. A man can not hope to purify either his body or mind until ignorance is removed.

It is easy to slip into shamelessness, to be pert and bold like a crow, to hurt others without any feeling of regret for such action.

It is hard, indeed, to feel humble, to know respect and honor, to get rid of all attachments, to keep pure in thought and deed, and to become wise.

It is easy to point out the mistakes of others, while it is hard to admit one's own mistakes. A man broadcasts the sins of others without thinking, but he hides his own

5、鉄の錆（さび）が鉄からでて鉄をむしばむように、悪は人から出て人をむしばむ。

経があっても読まなければ経の垢（あか）、家があっても破れてつくろわないのは家の垢、身があっても怠るのは身の垢である。

行いの正しくないのは人の垢、もの惜しみは施しの垢、悪はこの世と後の世の垢である。

しかし、これらの垢よりも激しい垢は無明（＊むみょう）の垢である。この垢を落とさなければ、人は清らかになることはできない。

恥じる心なく、烏（からす）のようにあつかましく、他人を傷つけて省みるところのない人の生活は、なしやすい。

謙遜（そん）の心があり、敬いを知り、執着を離れ、清らかに行い、智慧（ちえ）明らかな人の生活は、なし難い。

他人の過ちは見やすく、おのれの過ちは見難い。他人の罪は風のように四方に吹き散らすが、おのれの罪は、さいころを隠すように隠したがる。

sins as a gambler hides his extra dice.

The sky holds no trace of bird or smoke or storm; an evil teaching carries no Enlighenment; nothing in this world is stable; but an Enlightened mind is undisturbed.

6.   As a knight guards his castle gate, so one must guard one's mind from dangers outside and dangers inside; one must not neglect it for a moment.

Everyone is the master of himself, he is the oasis he can depend on; therefore, everyone should control himself above all.

The first steps toward spiritual freedom from the worldly bonds and fetters are to control one's mind, to stop idle talk, and to be somewhat pensive.

The sun makes the day bright, the moon makes the night beautiful, discipline adds to the dignity of a warrior; so quiet meditation distinguishes the seeker for Enlightenment.

He who is unable to guard his five senses of eyes, ears, nose, tongue and body, and becomes tempted by his surroundings, is not the one who can train for Enlightenment. He who firmly guards the gateways of his five senses and keeps his mind under control is the one who

空には鳥や煙や嵐(あらし)の跡なく、よこしまな教えにはさとりなく、りぶての（）ものには永遠ということがない。そして、さとりの人には動揺がない。

6、内も外も、堅固に城を守るように、この身を守らなければならない。そのためには、ひとときもゆるがせにしてはならない。

おのれこそはおのれの主(あるじ)、おのれこそはおのれの頼りである。だから、何よりもまずおのれを抑えなければならない。

おのれを抑えることと、多くしゃべらずにじっと考えることは、あらゆる束縛を断ち切るはじめである。

日は昼に輝き、月は夜照らす。武士は武装をして輝き、道を求める人は、静かに考えて輝く。

眼と耳と鼻と舌と身の、五官の戸口を守らず、外界に引かれる人は、道を修める人ではない。五官の戸口をかたく守って、心静かな人が、道を修める人である。

can successfully train for Enlightenment.

7.   He who is influenced by his likes and dislikes can not rightly understand the significance of circumstances and tends to be overcome by them; he who is free from attachments rightly understands circumstances and to him all things become new and significant.

Happiness follows sorrow, sorrow follows happiness, but when one no longer discriminates between happiness and sorrow, a good deed and a bad deed, one is able to realize freedom.

To worry in anticipation or to cherish regret for the past is like the reeds that are cut and wither away.

The secret of health for both mind and body is not to mourn for the past, not to worry about the future, or not to anticipate troubles, but to live wisely and earnestly for the present.

Do not dwell in the past, do not dream of the future, concentrate the mind on the present moment.

It is worthy to perform the present duty well and without failure; do not seek to avoid or postpone it till tomorrow. By acting now, one can live a good day.

7、執着があれば、それに酔わされて、ものの姿をよく見ることができない。執着を離れると、ものの姿をよく知ることができる。だから、執着を離れた心に、ものはかえって生きてくる。

悲しみがあれば喜びがあり、喜びがあれば悲しみがある。悲しみも喜びも超え、善も悪も超え、はじめてとらわれがなくなる。

まだこない未来にあこがれて、とりこし苦労をしたり、過ぎ去った日の影を追って悔いていれば、刈り取られた葦のように痩せしぼむ。

過ぎ去った日のことは悔いず、まだこない未来にはあこがれず、とりこし苦労をせず、現在を大切にふみしめてゆけば、身も心も健やかになる。

過去は追ってはならない、未来は待ってはならない。ただ現在の一瞬だけを、強く生きねばならない。

今日すべきことを明日に延ばさず、確かにしていくことこそ、よい一日を生きる道である。

Wisdom is the best guide and faith is the best companion. One must try to escape from the darkness of ignorance and suffering, and seek the light of Enlightenment.

If a man's body and mind are under control he should give evidence of it in virtuous deeds. This is a sacred duty. Faith will then be his wealth, sincerity will give his life a sweet savor, and to accumulate virtues will be his sacred task.

On life's journey faith is nourishment, virtuous deeds are a shelter, wisdom is the light by day and right mindfulness is the protection by night. If a man lives a pure life nothing can destroy him; if he has conquered greed nothing can limit his freedom.

One should forget oneself for the sake of one's family; one should forget one's family for the sake of one's village; one should forget one's village for the sake of the nation; and one should forget everything for the sake of Enlightenment.

Everything is changeable, everything appears and disappears; there is no blissful peace until one passes beyond the agony of life and death.

信は人のよき友、智慧は人のよい導き手である。さとりの光を求めて、苦しみの闇を免れるようにしなければならない。

信は最上の富、誠は最上の味、功徳を積むのは、この世の最上の営みである。教えの示すとおりに身と心とを修めて、安らかさを得よ。

信はこの世の旅の糧、功徳は人の貴い住みか、智慧はこの世の光、正しい思いは夜の守りである。汚れのない人の生活は滅びず、欲に打ち勝ってこそ、自由の人といわれる。

家のためにわが身を忘れ、村のためにわが家を忘れ、国のために村をも忘れ、さとりのためにはすべてを忘れよ。

ものみなうつり変わり、現われてはまた滅びる。生滅にわずらわされなくなって、静けさ安らかさは生まれる。

THE BROTHERHOOD

なかま

CHAPTER ONE

DUTIES OF THE BROTHERHOOD

I
HOMELESS BROTHERS

1.   A man who wishes to become My disciple must be willing to give up all direct relations with his family, the social life of the world and all dependence upon wealth.

A man who has given up all such relations for the sake of the Dharma and has no abiding place for either his body or mind has become My disciple and is to be called a homeless brother.

Though his feet leave their imprints in My footsteps and his hands carry My garment, if his mind is disturbed by greed, he is far from me. Though he dresses like a monk, if he does not accept the teaching, he does not see me.

But if he has removed all greed and his mind is pure and peaceful, he is very close to Me though he be thousands of miles away. If he receives the Dharma, he see me in it.

第1章　人のつとめ

第1節　出家の生活

1、わたしの弟子になろうとするものは家を捨て世間を捨て財を捨てなければならない。教えのためにこれらすべてを捨てたものはわたしの相続者であり、出家とよばれる。*

たとえ、わたしの衣の裾をとって後ろに従い、わたしの足跡を踏んでいても、欲に心が乱れているならば、その人はわたしから遠い。たとえ、姿は出家であっても、彼は教えを見ていない。教えを見ない者はわたしを見ないからである。

たとえ、わたしから離れること何千里であっても、心が正しく静かであり、欲を離れているなら、彼はわたしのすぐそばにいる。なぜかというと、彼は教えを見ており、教えを見る者はわたしを見るからである。

2.   My disciples, the homeless brothers must observe the four rules and about them build their lives.

First, they wear old and cast-off garments; second, they get their food through alms-begging; third, their home is where night finds them as under a tree or on a rock; and, fourth, they use only a special medicine made from urine laid down by the Brotherhood.

To carry a bowl in the hand and go from house to house is a begger's life, but a brother is not compelled to do so by others, he is not forced into it by circumstances or by temptation; he does it of his own free will because he knows that a life of faith will keep him away from the delusions of life, will help him to avoid suffering, and will lead him toward Enlightenment.

The life of a homeless brother is not an easy one; he ought not to undertake it if he can not keep his mind free from greed and anger or if he can not control his mind or his five senses.

3.   To believe himself to be a homeless brother and to be able to answer when he is asked about it, he must be able to say:

"I am willing to undertake whatever is necessary to

2．出家の弟子は次の四つの条件を生活の基礎としなければならない。

一つには古布をつづり合わせた衣を用いなければならない。二つには托鉢によって食を得なければならない。三つには木の下、石の上を住みかとしなければならない。四つには腐尿薬のみを薬として用いなければならない。

食物を入れる容器を手にして戸ごとに食を乞うのは乞食の行ではあるが、それは他人に脅かされたためでもなく、他人に誘われ欺かれたためでもない。ただこの世のあらゆる苦しみを免れ、迷いを離れる道がここで教えられることを信じてなったのである。

このように出家していながら、しかも欲を離れず、瞋りに心を乱され、五官を守ることができないとしたら、まことにふがいないことである。

3．自ら出家であると信じ、人に問われてもわたしは出家であると答える者は、次のように言うことができるに違いない。

「わたしは出家としてしなければならないことは必ず守る。

－387－

be a homeless brother. I will be sincere about it and will try to accomplish the purpose for becoming one. I will be grateful to those who help me by donations and will try to make them happy by my earnestness and good life."

To be a homeless brother he must train himself in many ways: He must be sensitive to shame and dishonor when he fails; he must keep his body, speech and mind pure if his life is to be pure; he must guard the gates of his five senses; he must not lose control of his mind for the sake of some passing pleasure; he must not praise himself or rebuke others; and he must not be idle or given to lengthy sleep.

In the evening he should have a time for quiet sitting and meditation and a short walk before retiring. For peaceful sleep he should rest on the right side with his feet together and his last thought should be of the time when he wishes to rise in the early morning. Early in the morning he should have another time for quiet sitting and meditation and a short walk afterwards.

During the whole day he should always maintain an alert mind, keeping both body and mind under control, resisting all tendency towards greed, anger, foolishness, sleepiness, inattention, regret, suspicion, and all worldly desires.

　この出家のまことをもって、わたしに施しをする人に、大きな幸いを得させ、同時に、わたし自身の出家した目的を果たすようにしよう。」と。

　さて、出家のしなければならないこととは何であるか。慚と愧をそなえ、身と口と意による三つの行為と生活を清め、よく五官の戸口を守って、享楽に心を奪われない。また、自分をたたえて他人をそしるということをせず、怠けて眠りにふけることがない。

　夕方には静坐や歩行をし、夜半には右わきを下に、足と足とを重ね、起きるときのことをよく考えて静かに眠り、明け方にはまた静坐したり歩行したりする。

　また日常生活においてもつねに正しい心でなければならない。静かなところを選んで座を占め、身と心とをまっすぐにし、貪り、瞋り、愚かさ、眠け、心の浮わつき、悔い、疑いを離れて心を清めなければならない。

Thus, with his mind concentrated, he should culti-vate excellent wisdom and aim only at perfect Enlighten-ment.

4.   If a homeless brother, forgetting himself, lapses into greed, anger, resentment, jealousy, conceit, self-praise, or insincerity, he is like one carrying a keen two-edged sword, covered only by a thin cloth.

He is not a homeless brother simply because he wears a monk's rags and carries a begging bowl; he is not a homeless brother just because he recites scriptures easily; he is only a man of straw and nothing more.

Even if his external appearance is that of a monk, he can not remove his worldly desires. He is not a homeless brother, he is no more than an infant clothed in a monk's robe.

Those who are able to concentrate and control the mind, who contain wisdom, who have removed all worldly desires, and whose only purpose is to attain Enlightenment — only these can be called the true homeless brothers.

A true homeless brother determines to reach his goal of Enlightenment even though he loses his last drop of blood and his bones crumble into powder. Such a man,

　このように心を統一して、すぐれた智慧*を起こし、煩悩*を断ち切って、ひたすらさとりに向かうのである。

　4．もし出家の身でありながら、貪りを捨てず、瞋りを離れず、怨み、そねみ、うぬぼれ、たぶらかし、といった過ちを覆い隠すことをやめないなら、ちょうど両刃*の剣を衣に包んでいるようなものである。

　衣を着ているから出家なのではなく、托鉢*しているから出家なのではなく、経を誦んでいるから出家なのではなく、外形がただ出家であるのみ、ただそれだけのことである。

　形がととのっても、煩悩をなくすことはできない。赤子に衣を着けさせても出家とよぶことはできない。

　心を正しく統一し、智慧を明らかにし、煩悩をなくして、ひたすらさとりに向かう出家本来の道を歩く者でなければ、まことの出家とはよばれない。

　たとえ血は涸れ、骨は砕けても、努力を加え、至るべきところへ至らなければならないと決心し、努め励んだならば、

trying his best, will finally attain the goal and give evidence of it by his ability to do the meritorious deeds of a homeless brother.

5. The mission of a homeless brother is to carry forward the light of the Buddha's teachings. He must preach to everyone; he must wake up sleeping people; he must correct false ideas; he must help people have a right viewpoint; he must go everywhere to spread the teaching even at the risk of his own life.

The mission of a homeless brother is not an easy one, so he who aspires to it should wear Buddha's clothes, sit on Buddha's seat and enter into Buddha's room.

To wear Buddha's clothes means to be humble and to practise endurance; to sit on Buddha's seat means to see matter as non-substantial and to have no attachments; to enter into Buddha's room means to share His all-embracing great compassion and to have sympathy for everyone.

ついには出家の目的を果たして、清らかな行いを成しとげることができる。

　5．出家の道は、また、教えを伝えることである。すべての人びとに教えを説き、眠っている人の目を覚まさせ、邪見な人の心を正しくし、身命を惜しまず、広く教えをしかなりればならない。

　しかし、この教えを説くということは容易でないから、教えを説くことを志す者は、みな仏の衣を着、仏の座に坐り、仏の室に入って説かなければならない。

　仏の衣を着るとは、柔和であって忍ぶ心を持つことである。仏の座に坐るとは、すべてのものを空と見て、執着を持たないことである。仏の室に入るとは、すべての人に対して大慈悲の心を抱くことである。

6. Those who wish to teach the Buddha's teaching acceptably must be concerned about four things: first, they must be concerned about their own behavior; second, they must be concerned about their choice of words when they approach and teach people; third, they must be concerned about their motive for teaching and the end they wish to accomplish; and fourth, they must be concerned about the great compassion.

To be a good teacher of the Dharma, then, a homeless brother must first of all have his feet well set on the ground of endurance; he must be modest; he must not be extreme or desire publicity; he must constantly think of the emptiness of things; and he must not become attached to anything. If he is thus concerned he will be capable of right conduct.

Secondly, he must exercise caution in approaching people and situations. He must avoid people who are living evil lives or people of authority; he must avoid opposite sex. Then he must approach people in a friendly way; he must always remember that things rise from a combination of causes and conditions, and, standing at that point, he must not blame or abuse them, or speak of their mistakes, or hold them in light esteem.

Thirdly, he must keep his mind peaceful, considering Buddha as his spiritual father, considering other

6．またこの教えを説こうと思う者は、次の四つのことに心をとどめなければならない。第一にはその身の行いについて、第二にはそのことばについて、第三にはその願いについて、第四にはその大悲についてである。

第一に、教えを説く者は、忍耐の大地に住し、柔和であって荒々しくなく、すべては空であって善悪のはからいを起こすべきものでもなく、また執着すべきものでもないと考え、ここに心のすわりを置いて、身の行いを柔らかにしなければならない。

第二には、さまざまな境遇の相手に心をくばって、権勢ある者や邪悪な生活をする者に近づかないようにし、また異性に親しまない。静かなところにあって心を修め、すべては因縁によって起こる道理を考えてこれを心のすわりとし、他人を侮らず、軽んぜず、他人の過ちを説かないようにしなければならない。

第三には、自分の心を安らかに保ち、仏に向かっては慈父

homeless brothers who are training for Enlightenment as his teachers, and looking upon everyone with great compassion. Then he must teach all equally.

Fourthly, he must let his spirit of compassion display itself, even as Buddha did, to the utmost degree. Especially he should let his spirit of compassion flow out to those who do not know enough to seek Enlightenment. He should wish that they might seek Enlightenment, and then he should follow his wishes with unselfish effort to awaken their interest.

II
LAY FOLLOWERS

1. It has already been explained that to become a disciple of Buddha one must believe in the three treasures: the Buddha, the Dharma, and the Samgha.

To become a lay follower one must have an unshakable faith in Buddha, must believe in His teachings, study and put precepts into practice, and must cherish the Brotherhood.

Lay followers should follow the five precepts: not to kill, not to steal, not to commit adultery, not to lie or deceive, and not to use intoxicants.

の思いをなし、道を修める人に対しては師の思いをなし、すべての人びとに対しては大悲の思いを起こし、平等に教えを説かなければならない。

第四には、仏と同様に慈悲の心を最大に発揮し、道を求めることを知らない人びとには、必ず教えを聞くことができるようになってほしいと心に願い、その願いに従って努力しなければならない。

第2節 信者の道

1. 仏教を信ずる者とは、三宝（さんぽう）、すなわち、仏と教えと教団を信ずる者のことであるということは、すでに説いた。

だから、仏教を信ずる者は、仏と教えと教団に対して、破れることのない信を抱き、教えが命じている信者としての戒律を守らなければならない。

在家者としての戒とは、ものの命を取らず、盗まず、よこしまな愛欲にふけらず、偽りを言わず、酒を飲まないことである。

Lay followers should not only believe in the three treasures and keep the precepts by themselves, but also they should, as far as they are able, help others observe them, especially their relatives and friends, trying to awaken in them an unshakable faith in the Buddha, the Dharma and the Samgha, so that they, too, may share in Buddha's compassion.

Lay followers should always remember that the reason they believe in the three treasures and keep the precepts is to enable themselves ultimately to attain Enlightenment, and for that reason they should, though living in the world of desires, avoid becoming attached to such desires.

Lay followers should always keep in mind that sooner or later they will be obliged to part with their parents and families and pass away from this life of birth and death; therefore, they should not become attached to things of this life but should set their minds on the world of Enlightenment, wherein nothing passes away.

2. If lay followers want to awaken an earnest and undisturbed faith in the Buddha's teachings, they should realize within their minds a quiet and undisturbed happiness, that will shine out on all their surroundings and will be reflected back to them.

　在家者はこの三宝に対する信と、在家者としての戒を保つとともに、他人にもこの信と戒を得させるようにしなければならない。親戚、友人、知人の間に同信の人をつくるように努めなければならない。そうすることによって彼らもまた仏の慈悲に浴することができる。

　三宝に対する信を持ち、在家としての戒を守ることは、さとりを得るためであるから、在家の愛欲の生活の中にあっても、愛着に縛られないようにしなければならない。

　父母ともついには別れなければならない。家族ともついには離れなければならない。この世もついには去らなければならない。別れなければならないもの、去らなければならないものに心を縛られず、別離というもののない涅槃に心を寄せなければならない。

　2．仏の教えを聞いて、信が厚く、退くことがなければ、喜びは自然にわき起こる。この境地に入れば、何ごとにも光を認め、喜びを見いだしてゆくことができる。

This mind of faith is pure and gentle, always patient and enduring, never arguing, never causing suffering to others but always pondering the three treasures: the Buddha, the Dharma and the Samgha. Thus happiness spontaneously rises in their minds, and the light for Enlightenment can be found everywhere.

Since they are resting in the bosom of Buddha by faith, they are kept far from having a selfish mind, from attachment to their possessions, and, therefore, they have no fear in their daily life or dread of being criticised.

They will have no fear about their future death since they believe in the birth in Buddha's Land. Since they have faith in the truth and the holiness of the teachings, they can express their thoughts freely and without fear.

Since their minds are filled with compassion for all people, they will make no distinctions among them but will treat all alike, and since their minds are free from likes and dislikes it will be pure and equitable and happy for them to do any good deed.

Whether they live in adversity or in prosperity, it will make no difference to the increase of their faith. If they cherish humility, if they respect the Buddha's teachings,

その心は清く柔らかに、常に耐え忍んで、争いを好まず、人びとを悩まさず、仏と教えと教団を思うから、喜びは自然にわきいで、光はどこにでも見いだされる。

信ずることによって仏と一体になり、我という思いを離れているから、わがものを貪らず、したがって、生活に恐れがなく、そしられることをいとわない。

仏の国に生まれることを信じているから死を恐れない。教えの真実と尊さを信じているから、人びとの前に出ても、恐れることなく自分の信ずるところを言うことができる。

また慈悲を心のもととするから、すべての人に対して好ききらいの思いがなく、心が正しく清らかであるから、進んであらゆる善を修める。

また順調の時も逆境のときも信仰を増し、恥を知り、教えを敬い、言ったとおりに行い、行うとおりに言い、ことばと

if they are consistent in speech and action, if they are guided by wisdom, if their mind is as immovable as a mountain, then they will make steady progress on the path to Enlightenment.

And though they are forced to live in a difficult situation and among people of impure minds, if they cherish faith in Buddha they can ever lead them toward better deeds.

3. Therefore, one should first have the wish of hearing the Buddha's teachings.

If anyone should tell him that it would be necessary for him to go through fire to gain Enlightenment, then he should be willing to pass through such a fire.

There is satisfaction in hearing the Buddha's name, that is worth passing through a world filled with fires.

If one wishes to follow the Buddha's teaching one must not be egoistic or self-willed, but should cherish feelings of good-will toward all alike; one should respect those who are worthy of respect; one should serve those who are worthy of service and treat everyone with uniform kindness.

行いとが一致し、明らかな*智慧をもってものを見、心は山の
ように動かず、ますますさとりへの道に進むことを願う。

　また、どんなできごとに出会っても、仏の心を心として人
びとを導き、濁った世の中にも、汚れた人びととの間にも交わ
って、その人びとが善にうつるように尽くすのである。

　3．だから、だれでもまず自ら教えを聞くことを願わなけ
ればならない。

　だれかが「この燃え立つ火の中へ入れば教えが得られる。」
と言うなら、その火の中に入る覚悟を持たなければならない。

　世界に満ちた火の中に分け入って仏の名を聞くことは、ま
ことにその人の救いだからである。

　このようにして自ら教えを得て、広く施し、敬うべき人を
敬い、仕えるべき人に仕え、深い慈悲の心をもって他人に向
かわなければならない。利己的であったり、思うままにふる
まうのは、道を行う人の行ではない。

Thus, lay followers are to train their own minds first and not be disturbed by the actions of others. In this manner, they are to receive the Buddha's teaching and put it into practice, not envying others, not being influenced by others, and not considering other ways.

Those who do not believe in the Buddha's teaching have a narrow vision and, consequently, a disturbed mind. But those who believe in the Buddha's teaching, believe that there is a great wisdom and a great compassion embracing everything and, in that faith, they are undisturbed by trifles.

4. Those who hear and receive the Buddha's teaching know that their lives are transient and that their bodies are merely the aggregation of sufferings and the source of all evils, and so they do not become attached to them.

At the same time, they do not neglect to take good care of their bodies, not because they wish to enjoy the physical pleasures of the body, but because the body is temporarily necessary for the attainment of wisdom and for their mission of explaining the path to others.

If they do not take good care of their bodies they can not live long. If they do not live long, they can not

　このようにして教えを聞き、教えを信じ、他人をうらやまず、他人のことばに迷うことなく、自分のするしないについて省みることが肝心であり、他人のするしないを心にかけてはならない。何よりも自分の心を修めることが大切なのである。

　仏を信じない人は、自分のことだけを思いわずらうから、心が狭く小さく、いつもこせこせと焦るのである。しかし、仏を信ずる人は、背後の力、背後の大悲を信ずるから、自然に心が広く大きくなり、焦らない。

　4．また、教えを聞く人は、もとよりこの身を無常なもの*と見、苦しみの集まるもとと見、悪の源と見るから、この身に執着しない。

　しかしまた、この身を大切に養うことを怠らない。それは楽しみを貪るためではなく、道を得、道を伝えるためである。

　この身を守らなければ命をまっとうすることができず、命をまっとうしなければ、教えを受けて身に行うことも、また

practise the teaching personally or transmit it to others.

If a man wishes to cross a river he is very careful of his raft. If he has a long journey to make, he takes good care of his horse. So, if a man seeks to attain Enlightenment he must take good care of his body.

Those who are the disciples of Buddha must wear clothing to protect the body from extremes of heat and cold and to cover its private parts, but they should not wear it for decoration.

They must eat food to nourish the body so that they may hear and receive and explain the teaching, but they should not eat for mere enjoyment.

They must live in the house of Enlightenment to be protected from the thieves of worldly passions and from the storms of evil teaching, and they should use the house for its real purpose and not for display or the concealment of selfish practices.

Thus, one should value things and use them solely in their relation to Enlightenment and the teaching. He should not possess them or become attached to them for selfish reasons but only as they serve a useful purpose in carrying the teaching to others.

教えを広く伝えることもできない。

　河を渡ろうとする者はよく筏を守り、旅をする人はよく馬を守るように、教えを聞く人はその身を大切に守らなければならない。

　また仏を信ずる者は、着物を着るにも虚飾のためにせず、ただ羞恥のためにし、寒さ暑さを防ぐためにしなければならない。

　食物をとるにも楽しみのためにせず、身をささえ養って教えを受け、または説くためにしなければならない。

　家に住むにも同じく、身のためにし、虚栄のためにしてはならない。さとりの家に住み、*煩悩の賊を防ぎ、誤った教えの風雨を避けるためと、思わなければならない。

　すべてこのように、何ごとも身のためを思わず、他人に対してもおごる思いをせず、たださとりのため、教えのため、他人のためと思ってしなければならない。

Therefore, his mind should always dwell on the teaching even when he is living with his family. He should care for them with a wise and sympathetic mind, seeking various means to awaken faith in their minds.

5. Lay members of the Buddha's Samgha should study the following lessons every day: How to serve their parents, how to live with their wives and children, how to control themselves, and how to serve Buddha.

To best serve their parents they must learn to practise kindness toward all animate life. To live happily with their wives and children they must keep away from lust and thoughts of selfish comfort.

While hearing the music of the family life they must not forget the sweeter music of the teaching, and while living in the shelter of the home, they should often seek the safer shelter of Zen practice, where wise men find refuge from all impurity and all disturbance.

When laymen are giving offerings they should remove all greed from their hearts; when they are in the midst of crowds, their minds should be in the company of wise men; when they face misfortune, they should keep their minds tranquil and free from hindrances.

　だから、家にあって家族と一緒にいても、その心はしばらくも教えを離れない。慈悲の心をもって家族に従っているが、手段を示して彼らに救いの道を教えるのである。

　5．またこの仏教教団の在家者には、日常、父母に仕え、家族に仕え、自分に仕え、仏に仕えるいろいろな心がけがある。

　すなわち、父母に仕えるときには、一切を守り養って、永く平和を得ようと思い、妻子と一緒にいるときには、愛着の牢獄（ろうごく）から脱しなければならないものと思わなければならない。

　音楽を聞いているときには、教えの楽しみを得ようと思い、室にいるときは、賢者の境地に入って永く汚れを離れようと思わなければならない。

　また、たまたま他人に施しをするときは、すべてを捨てて貪（むさぼ）る心をなくそうと思い、集いの中にあるときには、諸仏の集いに入ろうと思い、災難にあったときには、どんなことにも動揺しない心を得ようと願わなければならない。

Duties of the Brotherhood

When they take refuge in the Buddha, they should seek His wisdom.

When they take refuge in the Dharma, they should seek its truth which is like a great ocean of wisdom.

When they take refuge in the Samgha, they should seek its peaceful fellowship unobstructed by selfish interests.

When they wear clothes, they must not forget to put on also the garment of goodness and humility.

When they want to relieve themselves, they must wish to discharge all greed, anger and foolishness from their minds.

When they are toiling on an up-hill road, they should think of it as the road to Enlightenment that will carry them beyond the world of delusion. When they are following an easy road, they should take advantage of its easier conditions to make greater progress toward Buddhahood.

When they see a bridge, they must wish to construct the bridge of the teaching to let the people cross.

また仏に帰依するときには、人びととともに大道を体得して、道を求める心を起こそうと願い、

教えに帰依しては、人びととともに深く教えの蔵に入って、海のように大きい智慧を得ようと願い、

教団に帰依しては、人びととともに大衆を導いて、すべての障害を除こうと願うがよい。

また、着物を着るなら、善根と慚愧を衣服とすることを忘れず、

大小便をするときは、心の貪りと瞋りと愚かさの汚れを除こうと願い、

高みに昇る道を見ては、無上の道へ昇って迷いの世界を超えようと思い、低きに下る道を見ては、優しくへり下って奥深い教えへ入ろうと願うがよい。

また、橋を見ては、教えの橋を作って人を渡そうと願い、

When they meet a sorrowful man, they should lament the bitterness of this ever-changing world.

When they see a greedy man, they should have a great longing to keep free from the illusions of this life and to attain the true riches of Enlightenment.

When they see savory food, they must be on guard; when they see distasteful food, they should wish that greed might never return.

During the intense heat of summer, they must wish to be away from the heat of worldly desires and gain the fresh coolness of Enlightenment. During the unbearable cold of winter, they must think of the warmth of Buddha's great compassion.

When they recite the sacred scriptures, they should be determined not to forget them and resolve to put their teaching into practice.

When they think of Buddha, they should cherish a deep wish to have eyes like Buddha.

As they fall asleep at night, they should wish that their body, speech and mind might be purified and refreshed; when they awake in the morning, their first wish should be that during that day their minds might be

　なげき悲しむ人を見ては、うつり変わって常なきものをなげく心を起こし、

　欲を楽しむ人を見ては、幻の生活を離れてまことのさとりを得ようと願い、

　おいしい食物を得ては、節約を知り、欲を少なくして執着を離れようと願い、まずい食物を得ては、永く世間の欲を遠ざけようと願うがよい。

　また夏の暑さの激しいときには、煩悩の熱を離れて涼しいさとりの味わいを得たいと願い、冬の寒さの激しいときには、仏の大悲の温かさを願うがよい。

　経を誦むときには、すべての教えを保って忘れないようにと願い、

　仏を思っては、仏のようなすぐれた眼を得たいと願い、

　夜眠るときには、身と口と意のはたらきを休めて心を清めようと願い、朝目覚めては、すべてをさとって、何ごとにも気のつくようになろうと願うがよい。

clear to understand all things.

6.   Those who follow the teaching of Buddha, because they understand that everything is characterized by "non-substantiality," do not treat lightly the things that enter into a man's life, but they receive them for what they are and then try to make them fit tools for Enlightenment.

They must not think that this world is meaningless and filled with confusion, while the world of Enlightenment is full of meaning and peace. Rather, they should taste the way of Enlightenment in all the affairs of this world.

If a man looks upon the world with defiled eyes dimmed by ignorance, he will see it filled with error; but if he looks upon it with clear wisdom, he will see it as the world of Enlightenment, which it is.

The fact is there is only one world, not two worlds, one meaningless and the other full of meaning, or one good and the other bad. People only think there are two worlds, due to their discriminating faculty.

If they could rid themselves of these discriminations and keep their minds pure with the light of wisdom, then they would see only one world in which everything is

6. また仏教を信ずる者は、すべてのもののありのままの
姿、すなわち、「空_{くう}」の教えを知っているから、世の中の仕事、
人間の間のいろいろのことを軽視せず、そのまま受け入れ、
それをそのままさとりの道にかなうようにする。

人間の世界のことは迷いであって意味がなく、さとりの世
界のことは尊い、という二つに分けることなく、世間のすべ
てのできごとの中にさとりの道を味わうようにする。

無明_{むみょう}に覆われた眼で見れば、世間は意味のない間違ったも
のとなるであろうが、智慧をもって明らかにながめると、そ
のままがさとりの世界になる。

ものに、意味のないものと意味のあるものとの二つがある
のでなく、善いものと悪いものとの二つがあるのでもない。
二つに分けるのは人のはからいである。

はからいを離れた智慧をもって照らせば、すべてはみな尊
い意味を持つものとなる。

meaningful.

7.   Those who believe in Buddha taste this universal purity of oneness in everything, and in that mind they feel compassion for all and have a humble attitude to serve everyone.

Therefore, they should cleanse their minds of all pride and cherish humility, courtesy and service. Their minds should be like the fruitful earth that nourishes everything without partiality, that serves without complaint, that endures patiently, that is always zealous, that finds its highest joy in serving all poor people by planting in their minds the seeds of the Buddha's teaching.

Thus, the mind that has compassion for poor people, becomes a mother to all people, honors all people, looks upon all as personal friends, and respects them as parents.

Therefore, though thousands of people may have hard feelings and cherish ill-will toward Buddhist lay followers, they can do no harm, for such harm is like a drop of poison in the waters of a great ocean.

8.   A lay follower will enjoy his happiness by habits of recollection, reflection and thanksgiving. He will come to

7．仏教を信ずる者は、このようにして、仏を信じ、その信の心をもって世の中のことを尊く味わうが、またその心をもって、身をへり下らせて他人に仕える。

だから、仏教を信ずる者にはおごる心がなく、へり下る心、他人に仕える心、大地のようにすべてを載せる心、すべてに仕えていとわない心、すべての苦しみを忍ぶ心、怠りのない心、すべての貧しい人びとに善根を施す心が起こる。

このように、人びとの貧しい心を哀れみ、すべての人びとの慈母となってその心を育てようとする心は、そのまま、すべての人びとを父母のように敬い、自分の尊い善き師として崇める心である。

だから、仏教を信ずる者に対して、たとえ、百千の人びとが怨みを起こし、敵視し、害を加えようとしても、その心のままになしとげることはできない。例えば、どのような毒でも、大海の水を汚し損なうことができないようなものである。

8．仏教を信ずる者は、また、省みておのれの幸せを喜び、この仏を信ずる心はまったく仏の力によるものであり、仏の

realize that his faith is Buddha's compassion itself and that it has been bestowed upon him by Buddha.

There are no seeds of faith in the mud of worldly passion, but, because of Buddha's compassion, the seeds of faith may be sown there, and they will purify the mind until it has faith to believe in Buddha.

As has been said, the fragrant Candana tree can not grow in a forest of Eranda trees. In a like manner, the seeds of faith in Buddha can not be in the bosom of delusion.

But actually, the flower of joy is blooming there, so we must conclude that while its blossoms are in the bosom of delusion, its roots are elsewhere; namely, its roots are in the bosom of Buddha.

If a lay follower becomes carried away, he will become jealous, envious, hateful and harmful, because his mind has become defiled with greed, anger and foolishness. But if he returns to Buddha, he will accomplish even a greater service for Buddha as mentioned above. It is, indeed, beyond any expression.

たまものであると感謝する。

また煩悩の泥の中には、信仰心の種はないのであるが、この
泥の中に仏の慈悲が植えつけられて、仏を信ずる心となった
ことを、明らかに知る。

さきに説いたように、エーランダという毒樹の林に、チャ
ンダナ（栴檀）香木の芽が生えるはずはなく、煩悩の胸の中
に、仏を信ずる種が芽生えるはずはない。

しかも、いま現に芽生えて歓喜の花が煩悩の胸の中に開く
のは、その根はそこになく、別のところにあると知られるの
である。その根は仏の胸の中にある。

仏を信ずる者も、我の思いに立つときは、貪りと瞋りと愚
かさの心から、他人をそねみ、ねたみ、にくみ、損なったり
する。しかし仏に帰ると、いまいうような大きな仏の仕事を
するようになる。これはまことに、不可思議といわなければ
ならない。

CHAPTER TWO

PRACTICAL GUIDE TO TRUE
WAY OF LIVING

I
FAMILY LIFE

1.   It is wrong to think that misfortunes come from the east or from the west; they originate within one's own mind. Therefore, it is foolish to guard against misfortunes from the external world and leave the inner mind uncontrolled.

There is a custom that has come down from ancient times that common people still follow. When they get up in the morning, they first wash their face and rinse their mouth, and then they bow in the six directions — to the east, west, south, north, above and below — wishing that no misfortune may come to them from any direction and that they may have a peaceful day.

But it is different in the Buddha's teaching. Buddha teaches that we are to pay respect to the six directions of Truth and then that we are to behave wisely and virtuously and thus prevent all misfortunes.

To guard the gates in these six directions, people are

第2章　生活の指針

第1節　家庭のしあわせ

1．災いが内からわくことを知らず、東や西の方角から来るように思うのは愚かである。内を修めないで外を守ろうとするのは誤りである。

朝早く起き出て口をすすぎ、顔を洗い、東西南北、上下の六方を拝んで、災いの出口を守り、その日一日の安全を願うのは、世の人のするところである。

しかし、仏の教えにおいては、これと異なり、正しい真理の六方に向かって尊敬を払い、賢明に徳を行って、災いを防ぐ。

この六方を守るには、まず四つの行いの垢を去り、四つの

to remove the defilement of the "four deeds," control the "four evil minds," and plug the "six holes" which cause the loss of wealth.

By the "four deeds" it is meant killing, stealing, committing adultery and falsehood.

The "four evil minds" are greed, anger, foolishness and fear.

The "six holes" which cause the loss of wealth are desire for intoxicating drinks and behaving foolishly, staying up late at night and losing the mind in frivolity, indulging in musical and theatre entertainments, gambling, associating with evil companions, and neglecting one's duties.

After removing these four defilements, avoiding these four evil states of mind, and plugging these six holes of waste, the disciples of Buddha do reverence to the six directions of Truth.

Now, what are these six directions of Truth? They are east for the way of parents and child, south for the way of teacher and pupil, west for the way of husband and wife, north for the way of a man and his friend, below for the way of master and servant and above for the way of the disciples of Buddha.

悪い心をとどめ、家や財産を傾ける六つの口をふさがなけれ
ばならない。

この四つの行いの垢とは、殺生（せっしょう）と盗みとよこしまな愛欲と
偽りであり、

四つの悪い心とは、貪（むさぼ）りと瞋（いか）りと愚かさと恐れとである。

家や財産を傾ける六つの口とは、酒を飲んでふまじめにな
ること、夜ふかしして遊びまわること、音楽や芝居におぼれ
ること、賭博（とばく）にふけること、悪い友だちに交わること、それ
に業務を怠ることである。

この四つの行いの垢を去り、四つの悪い心をとどめ、家や
財産を傾ける六つの口をふさいで、それからまことの六方を
拝むのである。

このまことの六方とは何かというと、東は親子の道、南は
師弟の道、西は夫婦の道、北は友人の道、下は主従の道、そ
して、上は教えを信ずる者としての道である。

A child should honor his parents and do for them all that he is supposed to do. He should serve them, help them at their labor, cherish the family lineage, protect the family property, and hold memorial services after they have passed away.

The parents should do five things for their children: — avoid doing evil, set an example of good deeds, give them an education, arrange for their marriage, and let them inherit the family wealth at a proper time. If the parents and child follow these rules the family will always live in peace.

A pupil should always rise when his teacher enters, wait upon him, follow his instructions well, not neglect an offering for him, and listen respectfully to his teaching.

At the same time, a teacher should act rightly before a pupil and set a good example for him; he should correctly pass on to him the teaching he has learned; he should use good methods and try to prepare the pupil for honors; and he should not forget to protect the pupil from evil in every possible way. If a teacher and his pupil observe these rules, their association will move smoothly.

A husband should treat his wife with respect, courtesy and fidelity. He should leave the housekeeping

　まず、東の親子の道を守るというのは、子は父母に対して五つのことをする。父母に仕え、家業の手伝いをし、家系を尊重し、遺産を守り、父母の死後はねんごろに供養することである。

　これに対して、親は子に五つのことをする。悪をとどめ、善をすすめ、教育を施し、婚姻をさせ、よい時に家を相続させることである。互いにこの五つを守れば、家庭は平和であり、波風が立たない。

　次に南の師弟の道とは、弟子は師に対し、座を立って迎え、よく仕え、素直に命(めい)を守り、供養を怠らず、慎んで教えを受ける。

　それと同時に、師はまた弟子に対して、自ら身を正しくして弟子を正し、自ら学び得たところをすべて正しく授け、正しく説いて正しく教え、引き立てて名を表わすようにし、何ごとについても守護を忘れないようにする。こうして師弟の間が守られて平和になる。

　次に西方の夫婦の間は、夫は妻に対し、尊敬と、礼節と、貞操とをもって向かい、家政をまかせ、ときどきは飾りを与

to her and sometimes provide for her needs, such as accessories. At the same time, a wife should take pains with the housekeeping, manage the servants wisely, maintain her virtue as a good wife should. She should not waste her husband's income, and should manage the house properly and faithfully. If these rules are followed, a happy home will be maintained and there will arise no quarrelling.

The rules of friendship mean there should be mutual sympathy between friends, each supplying what the other lacks and trying to benefit the other, always using friendly and sincere words.

One should keep his friend from falling into evil ways, should protect his property and wealth, and should help him in his troubles. If his friend has some misfortune, he should give him a helping hand, even supporting his family, if necessary. In this way, their friendship will be maintained and they will be increasingly happy together.

A master in his dealings with a servant should observe five things: He should assign work that is suitable for the servant's abilities, give him proper compensation, care for him when he is in ill health, share pleasant things with him, and give him needed rest.

A servant should observe five things: He should

える。妻は夫に対し、家政をととのえ、使用人たちを適切に使い、貞操を守り、夫の収入を浪費せず、家政をうまく行うようにする。これによって夫婦の間はむつまじく、争いは起こらない。

次に北方の友人の道は、相手の足らないものを施し、優しいことばで語り、利益をはかってやり、常に相手を思いやる。

また友人が悪い方に流れ落ちないように守り、万一そのような場合にはその財産を守ってやり、また心配のあるときには相談相手になり、不幸のときは助けの手をのばし、必要の場合にはその妻子を養うこともする。このようにして友人の間は美しく守られ、互いに幸せが得られる。

次に下方の主従の道とは、主人は使用人に対して、次の五つを守る。その力に応じて仕事をさせる。よい給与を与える。病気のときは親切に看病する。珍しいものは分かち与える。ときどき休養させる。

これに対して使用人は、主人に向かって五つの心得をもって仕える。朝は主人よりも早く起き、夜は主人よりも遅く眠

get up in the morning before his master and go to bed after him, should always be honest, take pains to do his work well, and try not to bring discredit to his master's name. If these rules are observed, there will be peace and no controversy between master and servant.

A disciple of Buddha should see to it that his family observes the teachings of Buddha. They should cherish respect and consideration for their Buddhist teacher, should treat him with courtesy, attend to and observe his instructions, and always have an offering for him.

Then the teacher of Buddha's teaching should rightly understand the teaching, rejecting wrong interpretations, emphasizing the good, and should seek to lead believers along a smooth path. When a family follows this course, keeping the true teaching as its center, it will thrive happily.

A man who bows in the six directions does not do so in order to escape from external misfortunes. He does it in order to be on his guard to prevent evils from arising within his own mind.

2. A man should recognize among his acquaintances those with whom he should associate and those with whom he should not.

る。何ごとにも正直を守り、仕事にはよく熟練する。そして主人の名誉を傷つけないよう心がける。こうして主従の間にもつれがなくなり、常に平和が保たれてゆく。

教えを信ずる者としての道というのは、どんな家庭であっても、仏の教えが入っていなければならない。そしてこの教えを受ける人として、師に対し、身（からだ）も口も意（こころ）もともになさけに満ち、ていねいに師を迎え、その教えを聞いて守り、供養をしなければならない。

これに対して、仏の教えを説く師は、よく教えを理解し、悪を遠ざけ、善をすすめ、道を説き、人をして平安の境地に入らせるようにしなければならない。このようにして、家庭は中心となる教養を保って成長してゆく。

六方を拝むというのは、このように、六方の方角を拝んで災いを避けようとすることではない。人としての六方を守って、内からわいてくる災いを、自ら防ぎとめることである。

2、人は親しむべき友と、親しむべきでない友とを、見分けなければならない。

The ones with whom a man should not associate are those who are greedy, clever talkers, flatterers or wasters.

The ones with whom he should associate are those who are helpful, who are willing to share happinesses as well as sufferings, who give good advice and who have a sympathetic heart.

A true friend, the one with whom a man may safely associate, will always stick closely to the right way, will worry secretly about his friend's welfare, will console him in misfortune, will offer him a helping hand when he needs it, will keep his secrets, and will always give him good advice.

It is very difficult to find a friend like this, and, therefore, one should try very hard to be a friend like this. As the sun warms the fruitful earth, so a good friend shines in society because of his good deeds.

3. It would be impossible for a son to repay his parents for their gracious kindness, even if he could carry his father on his right shoulder and his mother on his left for one hundred long years.

And even if he could bathe the bodies of his parents in sweet-smelling ointments for a hundred years, serve as

　親しむべきでない友とは、貪りの深い人、ことばの巧みな
人、へつらう人、浪費する人である。

　親しむべき友とは、ほんとうに助けになる人、苦楽をとも
にする人、忠言を惜しまない人、同情心の深い人である。

　ふまじめにならないよう注意を与え、陰に回って心配をし、
災難にあったときには慰め、必要なときに助力を惜しまず、
秘密をあばかず、常に正しい方へ導いてくれる人は、親しみ
仕えるべき友である。

　自らこのような友を得ることは容易ではないが、また、自
分もこのような友になるように心がけなければならない。よ
い人は、その正しい行いゆえに、世間において、太陽のよう
に輝く。

　3、父母の大恩は、どのように努めても報いきれない。例
えば百年の間、右の肩に父をのせ、左の肩に母をのせて歩い
ても、報いることはできない。

　また、百年の間、日夜に香水で、父母の体を洗いさすり、

an ideal son, gain a throne for them, and give them all the luxuries of the world, still he would not be able to repay them sufficiently for the great indebtedness of gratitude he owes to them.

But if he leads his parents to Buddha and explains the Buddha's teachings to them, and persuades them to give up a wrong course and follow a right one, leading them to give up all greed and enjoy the practice of offering, then he will be more than repaying them.

Buddha's blessing abides in the home where parents are held in respect and esteem.

4.   A family is a place where minds come in contact with one another. If these minds love one another, the home will be as beautiful as a flower garden. But if these minds get out of harmony with one another, it is like a storm that plays havoc with the garden.

If discord arises within one's family, one should not blame others but should examine one's own mind and follow a right path.

5.   Once there was a man of deep faith. His father died when he was young; he lived happily with his mother, and then he took a wife.

あらゆる孝養を尽くしても、または父母を王者の位に昇らせるほどに、努め励んで、父母をして栄華を得させても、なおこの大恩に報いきることはできない。

しかし、もし父母を導いて仏の教えを信じさせ、誤った道を捨てて正しい道にかえらせ、貪りを捨てて施しを喜ぶようにすることができれば、はじめてその大恩に報いることができるのである。あるいはむしろ、それ以上であるとさえいえよう。

父母を喜び敬うものの家は、仏や神の宿る家である。

4、家庭は心と心がもっとも近く触れあって住むところであるから、むつみあえば花園のように美しいが、もし心と心の調和を失うと、激しい波風を起こして、破滅をもたらすものである。

この場合、他人のことは言わず、まず自ら自分の心を守ってふむべき道を正しくふんでいなければならない。

5、昔、ひとりの信仰厚い青年がいた。父親が死んで、母親とともに親ひとり子ひとりの親しい生活を送っていたが、新たに嫁を迎えて三人の暮らしとなった。

At first, they lived happily together and then, because of a small misunderstanding, the wife and her mother-in-law came to dislike each other. This dislike grew until finally the mother left the young couple to live by herself.

After the mother-in-law left, a son was born to the young couple. A rumor reached the mother-in-law that the young wife had said, "My mother-in-law was always annoying me and as long as she lived with us nothing pleasant ever happened; but as soon as she went we had this happy event."

This rumor angered the mother-in-law who exclaimed, "If the husband's mother is chased away from the house and a happy event takes place, then things have come to a pretty pass. Righteousness must have disappeared from the world."

Then the mother shouted, "Now, we must have a funeral of this 'righteousness'." Like a mad woman she went to the cemetery to hold a funeral service.

A god, hearing of this incident, appeared in front of the woman and tried to reason with her, but in vain.

The god then said to her, "If so, I must burn the

　初めは互いにむつみあい、平和な美しい家庭であったが、ふとしたことから姑と嫁との心持ちに行き違いが起こり、波風が立ち始めると、容易には納まらず、ついに母は、若い二人を後に、家を離れることとなった。

　母が別居すると、やがて若い嫁に男の子が生まれた。「姑と一緒にいる間は、口やかましいので、めでたいこともなかったが、別居をすると、こうしてめでたいことができた。」と、嫁が言ったという噂が、さびしいひとり暮らしの姑の耳に入った。

　姑は大変腹を立てて叫んだ。「世の中には正しいことがなくなった。母を追い出して、それでめでたいことがあるならば、世の中は逆さまだ。」

　姑は、「この上は、正しさという主張を葬り去らなければ。」とわめき立て、気違いのようになって、墓場へ出かけた。

　このことを知った神は、すぐに姑の前に現われて、ことの次第を尋ね、いろいろに諭したけれども、姑の心の角は折れない。

　神はついに、「それではおまえの気のすむように、これか

child and his mother to death. Will that satisfy you?"

Hearing this, the mother-in-law realized her mistake, apologized for her anger, and begged the god to save the lives of the child and his mother. At the same time, the young wife and her husband realized their injustice to the old woman and went to the cemetery to seek her. The god reconciled them and thereafter they lived together as a happy family.

Righteousness is never lost forever unless one casts it away oneself. Righteousness occasionally may seem to disappear but, in fact, it never disappears. When it seems to be disappearing, it is because one is losing the righteousness of one's own mind.

Discordant minds often bring disaster. A trifling misunderstanding may be followed by great misfortune. This is especially to be guarded against in family life.

6.   In family life, the question as to how the daily expenses are to be met always requires the utmost care. Every member must work hard like the diligent ants and the busy bees. No one must rely upon the industry of others, or expect their charity.

On the other hand, a man must not consider what he has earned as totally his own. Some of it must be

ら憎い嫁と孫を焼き殺してやろう。それでよいであろう。」
と言った。

　この神のことばに驚いた姑（しゅうとめ）は、自分の間違っていた心の罪
をわびて、嫁と孫の助命を願った。子も嫁もまたこのときに
は、いままでの心得違いを反省し、母を訪ねて、この墓場へ
来る途中であった。神は姑（しゅうとめ）と嫁とを和解させて、平和な家庭
にかえらせた。

　自ら正しさを捨てなければ、教えは永久に滅びるものでは
ない。教えがなくなるのは、教えそのものがなくなるのでは
なく、その人の心の正しさが失われるからである。

　心と心の食い違いは、まことに恐ろしい不幸をもたらすも
のである。わずかの誤解も、ついには大きな災いとなる。家
庭の生活において、このことは特に注意をしなければならな
い。

　6、人はだれでもその家計のことについては、専心に蟻（あり）の
ように励み、蜜蜂（みつばち）のように努めなければならない。いたずら
に他人の力をたのみ、その施しを待ってはならない。

　また努め励んで得た富は、自分ひとりのものと考えて自分
ひとりのために費してはならない。その幾分かは他人のため

shared with others, some of it must be saved for an emergency, some of it must be set aside for the needs of the community and the nation, and some of it must be devoted to the needs of the religious teachers.

One should always remember that nothing in the world can strictly be called "mine." What comes to a person comes to him because of a combination of causes and conditions; it can be kept by him only temporarily and, therefore, he must not use it selfishly or for unworthy purposes.

7.   When Syamavati, the queen-consort of King Udayana, offered Ananda five hundred garments, Ananda received them with great satisfaction.

The King, hearing of it, suspected Ananda of dishonesty, so he went to Ananda and asked what he was going to do with these five hundred garments.

Ananda replied: "Oh, King, many of the brothers are in rags; I am going to distribute the garments among the brothers."
    "What will you do with the old garments?"
    "We will make bed-covers out of them."
    "What will you do with the old bed-covers?"
    "We will make pillow-cases."
    "What will you do with the old pillow-cases?"
    "We will make floor-covers out of them."

にこれを分かち、その幾分かはたくわえて不時の用にそなえ、また国家のため、社会のため、教えのために用いられることを喜ばなければならない。

一つとして、「わがもの」というものはない。すべてはみな、ただ因縁によって、自分にきたものであり、しばらく預かっているだけのことである。だから、一つのものでも、大切にして粗末にしてはならない。

7、アーナンダ（阿難）が、ウダヤナ王の妃、シャマヴァティーから、五百着の衣を供養されたとき、アーナンダはこれを快く受け入れた。

王はこれを聞いて、あるいはアーナンダが貪りの心から受けたのではあるまいかと疑った。王はアーナンダを訪ねて聞いた。

「尊者は、五百着の衣を一度に受けてどうしますか。」

アーナンダは答えた。「大王よ、多くの比丘は破れた衣を着ているので、彼らにこの衣を分けてあげます。」「それでは破れた衣はどうしますか。」「破れた衣で敷布を作ります。」「古い敷布は。」「枕の袋に。」「古い枕の袋は。」「床の敷物に使います。」「古い敷物は。」「足ふきを作ります。」「古い足ふき

"What will you do with the old floor-covers?"

"We will use them for foot-towels."

"What will you do with the old foot-towels?"

"We will use them for floor-mops."

"What will you do with the old mops?"

"Your Highness, we will tear them into pieces, mix them with mud and use the mud to plaster the housewalls."

Every article entrusted to us must be used with good care in some useful way, because it is not "ours" but is only entrusted to us temporarily.

II
THE LIFE OF WOMEN

1.   There are four types of women. Of the first type there are those who become angry for slight causes, who have changeable minds, who are greedy and jealous of others' happiness, and who have no sympathy for the needs of others.

Of the second type there are those who grow angry over trifling affairs, who are fickle and greedy, but who do not feel envious of others' happiness and who are sympathetic for the needs of others.

Of the third type there are those who are more broad-minded and do not become angry very often, who know how to control a greedy mind but are not able to

はどうしますか。」「雑巾にします。」「古い雑巾は。」「大王
よ、わたしどもはその雑巾を細々に裂き、泥に合わせて、家
を造るとき、壁の中に入れます。」

　ものは大切に使わなければならない。生かして使わなけれ
ばならない。これが「わがもの」でない、預かりものの用い
方である。

第2節　女性の生き方

　1、世の中には四通りの婦人がある。第一種の婦人は、さ
さいなことにも腹立ちやすく、気まぐれで、欲深く、他人の
幸福を見てはそねみ、施すことを知らない。

　第二種の婦人は、腹立ちやすく、気まぐれで、欲深いが、
他人の幸福をうらやみねたむことがなく、また施すことを知
っている。

　第三種の婦人は、心広く、みだりに腹を立てない。また、
気まぐれでもなく、欲を抑えることを知ってはいるが、しか

avoid feelings of jealousy, and who are not sympathetic for the needs of others.

Of the fourth type there are those who are broad-minded, who can restrain feelings of greed and retain calmness of mind, who do not feel envious of others' happiness, and who are sympathetic for the needs of others.

2. When a young woman marries, she should make the following resolutions: "I must honor and serve the parents of my husband. They have given us all the advantages we have and are our wise protectors, so I must serve them with appreciation and be ready to help them whenever I can.

"I must be respectful to my husband's teacher because he has given my husband a sacred teaching and we could not live as human beings without the guidance of these sacred teachings.

"I must cultivate my mind so that I will be able to understand my husband and be able to help him in his work. I must never be indifferent to his interests, thinking they are only his affairs but not mine.

"I must study the nature, ability and taste of each of the servants of our family and look after them kindly. I will conserve the income of my husband and will not

し他人をうらやみ、ねたむ心が取れず、また施すことを知らない。

第四種の婦人は、心広く、腹を立てることがなく、欲を抑えて落着きがあり、そして他人をうらやまず、また施すことを知っている。

2、娘が嫁入るときには、次の心がけを忘れてはならない。夫の両親に敬い仕えなければならない。夫の両親は、わたしども二人の利益を計(はか)り、なさけ深く守って下さる方であるから、感謝して仕え、いつでもお役に立つようでありたい。

夫の師は夫に尊い教えを授けてくださるから、自分もまた大切に尊び敬ってゆこう。人として心の師を持たずには生きられないからである。

夫の仕事に理解を持ってそれを助けてゆくように、自分も教養に心がけよう。夫の仕事を他人の仕事のように考えてそれに無責任であってはならない。

夫の家の使用人や出入りの人たちについても、よくその気立てや能力や食べ物の好みなどを心得て、親切に面倒を見てゆこう。また夫の収入は大切にたくわえ、決して自分のため

waste it for any selfish purpose."

3.   The relation of husband and wife was not designed merely for their convenience. It has a deeper significance than the mere association of two physical bodies in one house. Husband and wife should take advantage of the intimacies of their association to help each other in training their minds in the holy teaching.

An old couple, an "ideal couple" as they were called, once came to Buddha and said, "Lord, we were married after we had been acquainted in childhood and there has never been a cloud in our happiness. Please tell us if we can be remarried in the next life."

The Buddha gave them this wise answer: — "If you both have exactly the same faith, if you both received the teaching in exactly the same way, if you perform charity in the same way and if you have the same wisdom, then you will have the same mind in the next birth."

4.   Sujata, the young wife of the eldest son of the rich merchant, Anathapindada, was arrogant, did not respect others and did not listen to the instruction of her husband and his parents and, consequently, some discord arose in the family.

One day the Blessed One came to visit Anathapinda-

にむだ遣いしないように心がけよう。

3、夫婦の道は、ただ都合によって一緒になったのではなく、また肉体が一つ所に住むだけで果たされるものでもない。夫婦はともに、一つの教えによって心を養うようにしなければならない。

かつて夫婦の鏡とほめたたえられたある老夫婦は、世尊のところに赴いて、こう言った。「世尊よ、わたしどもは幼少のときから互いに知りあい、夫婦になったが、いままで心のどのすみにも、貞操のくもりを宿したことはない。この世において、このように夫婦として一生を過ごしたように、後の世にも、夫婦として相まみえることができるように教えて頂きたい。」

世尊は答えられた。「二人ともに信仰を同じくするがよい。一つの教えを受けて、同じように心を養い、同じように施しをし、*智慧を同じくすれば、後の世にもまた、同じく一つの心で生きることができるであろう。」

4、アナータピンダダ（給孤独）長者の長子に嫁いだスジャーター（玉耶女）は、驕慢であって他を敬うことを知らず、父母や夫の命に従わず、いつも一家の波風を起こすもととなっていた。

da and noticed this state of affairs. He called the young wife, Sujata, to Him and spoke to her kindly, saying:

"Sujata, there are seven types of wives. There is a wife who is like a murderer. She has an impure mind, does not honor her husband and, consequently, turns her heart to another man.

"There is a wife who is like a thief. She never understands her husband's labor but thinks only of her desire for luxury. She wastes her husband's income to satisfy her own appetite and, by so doing, steals from him.

"There is a wife who is like a master. She rails at her husband, neglects the housekeeping and always scolds him with rough words.

"There is a wife who is like a mother. She cares for her husband as though he were a child, protects him as a mother does her son, and takes good care of his income.

"There is a wife who is like a sister. She is faithful to her husband and serves him like a sister with modesty and reserve.

"There is a wife who is like a friend. She tries to

　ある日、長者の家に入ってこの有様を見た釈尊は、その若い妻のスジャーターを呼んでこう教えた。

　スジャーターよ、世には七種の妻がある。

　第一は、人殺しのような妻で、汚れた心を持ち、夫に対して敬愛の思いがなく、はては他の男に心を移す妻である。

　第二は、盗人のような妻で、夫の仕事に理解を持たず、自分の虚栄を満たすことだけを考え、口腹（こうふく）の欲のために、夫の収入を浪費し、夫のものを盗む妻である。

　第三は、主人のような妻で、家政のことをかえりみず、自分は怠惰（たいだ）であって口腹の欲にだけ走り、常に荒々しいことばで、夫を叱咤（しった）している妻である。

　第四は、母のような妻で、夫に対して細やかな愛をいだき、母が子に対するように夫を守り、夫の収入を大切にする妻である。

　第五は、妹のような妻で、夫に仕えて誠を尽くし、姉妹に対するような情愛と、慚愧（ざんぎ）の心をもって夫に仕える妻である。

　第六は、友人のような妻で、常に夫を見て喜ぶことは、

please her husband as if he were a friend who had just returned from a long absence. She is modest, behaves correctly and treats him with great respect.

"Lastly, there is a wife who is like a maid-servant. She serves her husband well and with fidelity. She respects him, obeys his commands, has no wishes of her own, no ill-feeling, no resentment, and always tries to make him happy."

The Blessed One asked, "Sujata, which type of wife are you like, or would you wish to be like?"

Hearing these words of the Blessed One, she was ashamed of her past conduct and replied that she would wish to be like the one in the last example, the maid-servant. She changed her behavior and became her husband's helper, and together they sought Enlightenment.

5.   Amrapali was a wealthy and famous courtesan of Vaisali and kept many young and beautiful prostitutes with her. She called upon the Blessed One and asked Him to give her some good teaching.

The Blessed One said, "Amrapali, the mind of a woman is easily disturbed and misled. She yields to her desires and surrenders to jealousy more easily than a man.

ちょうど久しぶりに会った友に対するようであり、行いは正しくしとやかに、夫を敬う妻である。

第七は、女中のような妻で、よく夫に仕え、夫を敬い、夫のどんな行いをもよく忍び、怒りも恨みも抱かず、常に夫を大切に生かしてゆこうと努める妻である。

「スジャーターよ、おまえはこのうち、どの類の妻となろうとするのか。」

この教えを聞いたスジャーターは、大いにわが身を恥じて懺悔し、これから後は女中のような妻となって夫を助け、ともに道を修めてゆこうと誓った。

5、アンラパーリーは、ヴェーサーリーの名高い娼婦であり、自ら多勢の娼婦をかかえている主人であった。あるとき、この女がよい教えを聞こうとして仏を訪れた。*

釈尊はこの女にこう教えられた。

「アンラパーリーよ、女は心の乱れやすいもの、行いの間違いやすいものである。欲が深いから、惜しむ心ねたむ心が強い。男に比べて、障害の多いものといわなければならない。

"Therefore, it is more difficult for a woman to follow the Noble Path. This is especially true for a young and beautiful woman. You must step forth toward the Noble Path by overcoming lust and temptation.

"Amrapali, you must remember that youth and beauty do not last but are followed by sickness, old age and suffering. Desires for wealth and love are women's besetting temptations, but, Amrapali, they are not the eternal treasures. Enlightenment is the only treasure that maintains its value. Strength is followed by illness; youth must yield to old age; life gives way to death. One may have to go away from a loved one to live with a hated one; one may not obtain what one wishes for very long. This is the law of life.

"The only thing that protects and brings one to lasting peace is Enlightenment. Amrapali, you should seek Enlightenment at once."

She listened to Him, became His disciple and, as an offering, donated to the Brotherhood her beautiful garden park.

6.   There are no distinctions of sex on the path to Enlightenment. If a woman makes up her mind to seek Enlightenment, she will become a heroine of the True

　だから、女は男に比べて、道に進むことが困難である。まして年若くて容色の美しい者はなおさらである。財と色との誘惑にうち勝って、道に進まなければならない。

　アンラパーリーよ、女にとって強い誘惑である財と色は、決して永久の宝ではない。たださとりの道だけが、永久にこわれない宝である。強い者も病に犯され、若い者も老いに破れ、生は死に脅（おびや）かされる。また愛する者と離れて、恨みある人と一緒にいなければならないこともあり、そして求めることも、とかく思うようにならない。これが世のならわしである。

　だから、この中にあっておまえの守りとなるものには、たださとりの道がある。急いでこれを求めなければならない。」

　この教えを聞いた彼女は、仏弟子となり、教団に美しい庭園を寄進した。

　6、さとりの道においては、男と女の区別はない。女も道を求める心を起こせば、「さとりを求める者」といわれる。

Path.

Mallika, the daughter of King Prasenajit and the Queen of King Ayodhya, was such a heroine. She had great faith in the teaching of the Blessed One and made in His presence the ten following vows:

"My Lord, until I gain Enlightenment I will not violate the sacred precepts; I will not be arrogant before people who are older than myself; I will not become angry with anyone.

"I will not be jealous of others or envy their possessions; I will not be selfish either in mind or property; I will try to make poor people happy with the things I receive and will not hoard them for myself.

"I will receive all people courteously, give them what they need, and speak kindly to them; consider their circumstances and not my convenience; and try to benefit them without partiality.

"If I see others in solitude, in prison, or suffering from disease or other troubles, I will try to relieve them and make them happy, by explaining the reasons and laws to them.

"If I see others catching living animals and being

プラセーナジット（波斯匿）王の王女、アヨーディヤー国王の妃、マッリカー（勝鬘）夫人は、このさとりを求める者であって、深く世尊の教えに帰依し、世尊の前において、次の十の誓いを立てた。

「世尊よ、わたしは、今からさとりに至るまで、(1)受けた戒を犯しません。(2)目上の方々を悔りません。(3)あらゆる人びとに怒りを起こしません。(4)人の姿や形、持ち物に、ねたみ心を起こしません。(5)心の上にも、物の上にも、もの惜しみする心を起こしません。(6)自分のために財物をたくわえず、受けたものはみな貧しい人びとに与えて、幸せにしてあげます。(7)施しや、優しいことばや、他人に利益を与える行いや、他人の身になって考えてあげることをしても、それを自分のためにせず、汚れなく、あくことなく、さまたげのない心で、すべての人びとをおさめとります。(8)もし孤独のものや、牢獄につながれている者、または病に悩む者など、さまざまな苦しみにある人びとを見たならば、すぐに彼らを安らかにしてあげるために、道理を説き聞かせ、その苦しみを救ってあげます。(9)もし生きものを捕らえ、または飼い、あるいはさ

cruel to them or violating any such precept, I will punish them if they are to be punished, or teach them if they are to be taught, and then I will try to undo what they have done and correct their mistakes, to the best of my ability.

"I will not forget to hear the right teaching, for I know that when one neglects the right teaching one quickly falls away from the truth that abides everywhere, and will fail to reach the shore of Enlightenment."

Then she made the following three wishes to save poor people: "First, I will try to make everyone peaceful. This wish, I believe, in whatever life I may hereafter receive, will be the root of goodness that will grow into the wisdom of good teaching.

"Second, after I have received the wisdom of good teaching, I will untiringly teach all people.

"Third, I will protect the true teaching, even at the sacrifice of my own body, life or property."

The true significance of family life is the opportunity it gives for mutual encouragement and aid on the path to Enlightenment. Even an ordinary woman, if she has the same mind to seek Enlightenment, and makes the same vows and wishes, may become as great a disciple of Buddha as Mallika was.

まざまな戒を犯す人を見たならば、わたしの力の続く限り、懲らすべきは懲らし、諭すべきものは諭して、それらの悪い行いをやめさせます。⑽正しい教えを得ることを忘れません。正しい教えを忘れる者は、すべてにゆきわたるまことの教えから離れて、さとりの岸にゆくことができません。

わたしはまた、この不幸な人びとを哀れみ救うために、さらに三つの願いを立てます。⑴わたしはこのまことの願いをもって、あらゆる人びとを安らかにしてあげます。そして、その善根によって、どんな生を受けても、そこに正しい教えの智慧を得るでありましょう。

⑵正しい教えの智慧を得たうえは、あくことなく、人びとに説いて聞かせます。

⑶得たところの正しい教えは、体と命と財産を投げ捨てて、必ず守ります。

家庭の真の意義は、相たすさえて道に進むところにある。婦人といえども、この道に進む心を起こして、このマッリカー夫人のように大きな願いを持つならば、まことに、すぐれた仏の弟子となるであろう。

III
IN SERVICE

1.   There are seven teachings which lead a country to prosperity: First, people should assemble often to discuss political affairs, and to provide for national defense.

Second, the people of all social classes should meet together in unity to discuss their national affairs.

Third, people should respect old customs and not change them unreasonably, and they should also observe the rules of ceremony and maintain justice.

Fourth, they should recognize the differences of sex and seniority, and maintain the purity of families and communities.

Fifth, they should be filial to their parents and faithful to their teachers and elders.

Sixth, they should honor the ancestors' shrines and keep up the annual rites.

Seventh, they should esteem public morality, honor virtuous conduct, listen to honorable teachers and make offerings to them.

第3節　もろ人のために

1、ここに国家を栄えさせる七つの教えがある。

一つには、国民はしばしば会合をして政治を語り、国防を厳にして自ら守り、

二つには、上下心を一つにして相和し、ともに国事を議し、

三つには、国風を尊んでみだりにあらためず、礼を重んじ義を尊び、

四つには、男女の別を正し、長幼の序を守って、よく社会と家庭の純潔を保ち、

五つには、父母に孝し、師長に仕え、

六つには、祖先の祭壇をあがめて祭儀を行い、

七つには、道を尊び徳をあがめ、徳の高い師について教えを仰ぎ、厚く供養することである。

If a country follows these teachings well, it will surely prosper and will be held in respect by all other countries.

2. Once there was a King who was notably successful in ruling his kingdom. Because of his wisdom he was called King Great-Light. He explained the principles of his administration as follows:

The best way for a ruler to reign over his country is first of all to rule himself. A ruler should come before his people with a heart of compassion, and should teach and lead them to remove all impurities from their minds. The happiness that comes from good teachings far exceeds any enjoyment that the material things of the world can offer. Therefore, he could give his people good teaching and keep their minds and bodies tranquil.

When poor people come to him he should open his store-house and let them take what they want, and then he will take advantage of the opportunity to teach them the wisdom of ridding themselves of all greed and evil.

Each man has a different view of things according to the state of his mind. Some people see the city where they live as fine and beautiful, others see it as dirty and

　どんな国でも、この七つの教えをよく守って破ることがないならば、その国の栄えることは疑いがなく、外国の侮りを受けることはないであろう。

　2、昔、大光王は、自分の王道を次のように説いた。

「自分の国家を治める道は、まず自分を修めることである。自ら慈の心を養って、この心をもって国民に臨み、人びとを教え導いて心の垢を除き去り、身と心を和らげて、世の中の楽しみにまさる正しい教えの喜びを得させる。

　また、貧しいものが来たときには、蔵を開いて心のままに取らせる。そしてこれを手がかりとして、すべての悪から遠ざかるように戒める。

　人びとは各々その心をもととして、見るところを異にする。この城中の民にしても、この都を美しいと見るものもあれば、また汚いと見るものもある。

dilapidated. It all depends on the state of their minds.

Those who hold good teachings in respect, can see in common trees and stones all the beautiful lights and colors of lapis lazuli, while greedy people, who do not know enough to control their own minds, are blind even to the splendors of a golden palace.

Everything in the nation's daily life is like that. The mind is the source of everything, and, therefore, the ruler should first seek to have his people train their minds.

3.　　The first principle in wise administration is like the principle of King Great-Light: to lead the people to train their minds.

To train the mind means to seek Enlightenment, and, therefore, the wise ruler must give his first attention to the Buddha's teaching.

If a ruler has faith in Buddha, is devoted to His teachings, appreciates and pays tribute to virtuous and compassionate people, there will be no favoritism toward either friends or enemies and his country will always remain prosperous.

If a country is prosperous, it is not necessary for it

これは各々、その心、その環境がそうさせるのである。

教えを尊び、心の正しい素直な人は、木石にも瑠璃の光を
見るのであるが、欲が深くて自分を修めることを知らない者
は、どんな立派な御殿でもなお美しいと見ることはできない。

　国民の生活は、万事みなこのとおり、心がもとになってい
るから、わたしは国を治める大もとを、民にその心を修めさ
せることに置いている。」

　3、大光王のことばどおり、政道の大もとは、民にその心
を修めさせることにある。

　この心を修めることはさとりの道に進むことであるから、
政治の上に立つ人は、まず仏の教え*を信じなければならない。

　もし政治を行う人が、仏を信じ、教えを信じて、慈悲深く*
徳のある人を敬い、これに供養するならば、敵もなく、恨み
もなく、国家は必ず栄えるに違いない。

　そして、国が富み栄えるならば、他の国を貪り攻めること

to attack any other country and it does not need any weapons of attack.

When people are happy and satisfied, class differences disappear, good deeds are promoted, virtues are increased, and people come to respect one another. Then everyone becomes prosperous; the weather and temperature become normal; the sun and the moon and stars shine naturally; rains and winds come timely; and all natural calamities disappear.

4.   The duty of a ruler is to protect his people. He is the parent of his people and he protects them by his laws. He must raise his people like parents raise their children, giving a dry cloth to replace a wet one without waiting for the child to cry. In like manner, the ruler must remove suffering and bestow happiness without waiting for people to complain. Indeed, his ruling is not perfect until his people abide in peace. They are his country's treasure.

Therefore, a wise ruler is always thinking of his people and does not forget them even for a moment. He thinks of their hardships and plans for their prosperity. To rule wisely he must be advised about everything — about water, about draught, about storm and about rain; he must know about crops, the chances for a good harvest, people's comforts and their sorrows. To be in a

もなく、また他を攻める武器の必要もなくなるであろう。

したがって国民も満足して楽しみを受け、上下和らいでむつみあい、善を増し徳を積んで互いに敬愛し喜びあうから、いよいよ人は栄え、寒さ暑さもととのい、日も月も星も常の程度を失わず、風雨が時に従うようになり、こうしていろいろの災いも遠ざかるようになるであろう。

4、王たるものの勤めは、民を守ることにある。王は民の父母であり、教えによって民を守るからである。民を養うことは、父母が赤子を養うようなもので、父母が赤子のことばを待たず、湿ったものを取り替えて新らしい布を当てがうように、いつも民に幸いを与えて悩みを去るよう慈しみ養うのである。まことに王は、民をもって国の宝とする。これは、民が安らかでなければ政道が立たないからである。

だから、王たるものは、民を憂えてしばらくも心を離さない。民の苦楽を察し、民の繁栄をはかり、そのためには常に水を知り、風、雨を知り、実りの善悪を知り、日照りを知り、民の憂いと喜びを知り、罪の有無と軽重、功績の有無などを

position to rightly award, punish or praise, he must be thoroughly informed as to the guilt of bad men and the merits of good men.

A wise ruler gives to his people when they are in need, and collects from them when they are prosperous. He should exercise his correct judgment when collecting taxes and make the levy as light as possible, thus keeping his people consonant.

A wise ruler will protect his people by his power and dignity. One who thus rules one's people is worthy to be called a King.

5.   The King of Truth is the King of kings. His ancestry is of the purest and the highest. He not only rules the four quarters of the world, but he is also Lord of Wisdom and Protector of all Virtuous Teachings.

Wherever he goes, fighting ceases and ill-will vanishes. He rules with equity by the power of Truth, and by vanquishing all evil he brings peace to all people.

The King of Truth never slays or steals or commits adultery. He never cheats or abuses or lies or talks idly. His mind is free from all greed, anger and foolishness. He removes these ten evils and in their place establishes the ten virtues.

よく知って、賞罰の道を明らかにする。

このように民の心を知って、与えなければならないものは時をはかって与え、取るべきものはよく量って取り、民の利を奪わないよう、よく税を軽くして民を安らかにする。

王は力と権威によって民を守り、このようにして民の心になって民をよく見守るものが王と呼ばれる。

5、この世の中の王を転輪王というが、転輪王とはその家系が正しく、身分が尊くてよく四辺を統御し、また教えを守るところの王である。

この王のゆくところには、戦いもなく恨みもなく、よく教えによって徳をしき、民を安らかにして邪と悪を下す。

また転輪王は、殺さず、盗まず、よこしまな愛欲を犯さず、偽り、悪口、二枚舌、むだ口を言わず、貪らず、瞋らず、愚かでない。この十善を行って民の十悪を去らせる。

Because his rule is based upon Truth he is invincible. Wherever Truth appears violence ceases and ill-will vanishes. There is no dissension among his people, and, therefore, they dwell in quietness and safety; his mere presence brings peacefulness and happiness among them. That is why he is called the King of Truth.

Since the King of Truth is the King of kings, all other rulers praise his excellent name and rule their own kingdoms after his example.

Thus the King of Truth is the sovereign over all kings, and under his righteous way they bring safety to their people and fulfil their duties with Dharma.

6.   A wise ruler will temper his verdicts with compassion. He will try to consider each case with clear wisdom and then make his verdict in accord with the five principles.

The five principles are: First, he must examine the truthfulness of the facts presented.

Second, he must ascertain that they fall within his jurisdiction. If he renders a judgment with full authority, it is effective, but if he does so without authority, it only causes complications; he should await the correct conditions.

　また、教えによって政治を正すから、天下において思いのままになすことができ、そのゆくところには戦いがなく、恨みもなく、互いに相犯すこともない。したがって、民は和らぎ、国は安らいで、民にいよいよその生を楽しませることができる。だから教えを守る王といわれるのである。

　また転輪王は、王の中の王であるから、もろもろの王はみなその徳を喜び、その教えに従って各々その国を治める。

　このように転輪王は、もろもろの王をして各々その国に安んじさせ、正しい教えの下に王の任を果たさせる。

　6. また王は罪を裁決するにも、慈悲の心をもととしなければならない。明らかな*智慧をもってよく観察し、五つの原則をもってよく処置しなければならない。

　五つの原則というのは、

　一つには、実によって不実によらない。これは、事実を調べて、その事実によって処断することである。

　二つには、時によって非時によらない。これは、王に力のあるときが時であり、力のないときが非時である。力のあるときには罰しても効果があるが、力のないときには罰しても混乱があるだけであるから、時を待たなければならない。

Third, he must judge justly; that is, he must enter into the mind of the defendant. If he finds that the deed was done without criminal intent, he should discharge the man.

Fourth, he should pronounce his verdict with kindness but not harshness; that is, he should apply a proper punishment but should not go beyond that. A good ruler will instruct a criminal with kindness and give him time to reflect upon his mistakes.

Fifth, he should judge with sympathy but not in anger; that is, he should condemn the crime but not the criminal. He should let his judgment rest upon a foundation of sympathy, and he should use the occasion to try and make the criminal realize his mistakes.

7.   If an important minister of state neglects his duties, works for his own profit or accepts bribes, it will cause a rapid decay of public morals. People will cheat one another, a strong man will attack a weaker one, a noble will mistreat a commoner or a wealthy man will take advantage of the poor, and there will be no justice for anyone; mischief will abound and troubles will multiply.

Under such circumstances, faithful ministers will retire from public service, wise men will keep silent from

　三つには、動機によって結果によらない。これは、罪を犯すものの心に立ち入って、それが故意であるか故意でないかを見きわめ、故意のことでなければ許すのをいう。

　四つには、親切なことばによってあらいことばによらない。これは、罪が規則のどれに当たるかを明らかにして罪以上の罰を与えないようにし、また柔らかい優しいことばで諭してその罪を覚(さと)らせるのをいう。

　五つには、慈悲の心によって瞋(いか)りの心によらない。罪を憎んで人を憎まず、慈悲の心をもととして、罪を犯したものにその罪を悔いあらためさせるように仕向けるのである。

　7．もし王の重臣であって国家の大計を思わず、ただ自分の利ばかりを求め、賄賂(わいろ)を取って政道を曲げ、人民の気風を頽廃(たいはい)させるならば、人民は互いに相欺くようになり、強い者は弱い者をしいたげ、貴い者は卑しい者を軽んじ、富んだ者は貧しい者を欺き、曲がった道理をもって正しいものを曲げることになるから、災いがいよいよ増長するようになる。

　すると忠実な重臣は隠れ退き、心あるものも危害を恐れて

fear of complications, and only flatterers will hold government positions, and they will use their political power to enrich themselves with no thought for the sufferings of the people.

Under such conditions the power of the government becomes ineffective and its righteous policies fall into ruins.

Such unjust officials are the thieves of people's happiness, yet are worse than thieves because they defraud both ruler and people and are the cause of the nation's troubles. The king should root out such ministers and punish them.

But even in a country which is ruled by a good king and by just laws, there is another form of disloyalty. There are sons who give themselves up to the love of their wives and children and forget the grace of their parents who nursed and cared for them during many a year. They neglect their parents, rob them of their possessions and neglect their teaching. Such sons are to be counted among the most wicked of men.

And why? It is because they are unfilial to their parents whose long love has been very great, a love that could not be repaid even if the sons honored and treated them kindly throughout their lives. Those who are

沈黙し、ただへつらう者だけが政権をとって、みだりに公権を用いて私腹を肥やし、民の貧しさは少しも救われないようになる。

このようになると、政令は行われなくなり、政道はまったくゆるんでしまう。

このような悪人こそ、民の幸福を奪う盗賊であるから、国家のもっとも大きな悪賊といわなければならない。なぜなら、上を欺き下を乱して、一国の災いの源となるからである。王はこのような者を、もっとも厳しく処罰しなければならない。

また教えによって政治をしく王の国において、父母の生育の恩を思わず、妻子にだけ心を傾けて父母を養わず、あるいはまた、父母の所有を奪ってその教えに従わないものは、これをもっとも大きな悪の中に数えなければならない。

なぜなら、父母の恩はまことに重くて、一生心を尽くして孝養しても、し尽くせないものだからである。主君に対して

disloyal to their ruler and unfilial to their parents should be punished as the worst of criminals.

And also, in a country which is ruled by a good king and by just laws, there is still another form of disloyalty. There are people who are entirely forgetting the three treasures, the Buddha, the Dharma and the Samgha. Such people destroy their country's sanctuaries, burn the sacred scriptures, make the teachers of righteousness serve them, and thus violate the sacred teachings of Buddha. They are also among the worst of criminals.

And why? It is because they destroy the spiritual faith of their nation, which is its foundation and the source of its virtues. Such people, by burning the faith of others, are digging their own graves.

All other sins may be regarded as light in comparison with these disloyalties. Such disloyal criminals should be punished most severely.

8.   There may be a conspiracy against a good king who is ruling his country according to right teaching, or perhaps foreign enemies may raid the country. In such a case the king should make three decisions.

He should decide: "First, these conspirators or foreign enemies are threatening the good order and

忠でなく、親に対して孝でない者は、もっとも重い罪人として処罰しなければならない。

また教えによって政治をしく王の国の中においては、仏と教えと*教団の三宝に対して信ずる心がなく、寺を壊し経を焼き、僧侶(そうりょ)を捕らえて駆使するなど仏の教えを破る行いをする者は、もっとも重い罪の者である。

なぜなら、これはすべての善行のもとである民の信念を覆(くつがえ)すものだからである。これらの者は、みなすべての善根を焼き尽くして、自ら自分の穴を掘るものである。

この三種の罪がもっとも重く、したがってもっとも厳しく処罰しなければならない。その他の罪は、これらに比べると、なお軽いといわなければならない。

8. 正しい教えを守る王に対して逆らう賊が起こるか、あるいは外国から攻め侵すものがあるときは、正しい教えの王は三種の思いを持たなければならない。

それは、第一には、逆賊または外敵は、ただ人を損ない人

welfare of our country; I must protect the people and country even with armed force.

"Second, I will try to find some way of defeating them without resorting to the use of arms.

"Third, I will try to capture them alive, without killing them if possible, and disarm them."

By adopting these three decisions the king will proceed most wisely, after setting necessary posts and giving instructions.

By proceeding in this way, the country and its soldiers will be encouraged by the king's wisdom and dignity and will respect both his firmness and grace. When it is necessary to call upon the soldiers, they will fully understand the reason for war and its nature. Then they will go to the field of battle with courage and loyalty, respecting the king's wise and gracious sovereignty. Such a war will not only bring victory but also add virtue to the country.

民を虐げることばかりを考えている。自分は武力をもって民の苦しみを救おう。

第二には、もし方法があるなら、刃を動かさないで、逆賊や外敵を平らげよう。

第三には、敵をできるだけ生け捕りにして、殺さないようにし、そしてその武力をそごう。

王はこの三つの心を起こして、それから後に部署を定め訓令を与えて戦いにつかせる。

このようにするとき、兵はおのずから王の威徳をおそれ敬ってよくその恩になずき、また戦いの性質をさとって王を助け、そして王の慈悲が後顧の憂いをなくすことを喜びながら、王の恩に報いるために戦いに従うから、その戦いはついに勝利を得るだけでなく、戦いもかえって功徳となるであろう。

CHAPTER THREE
BUILDING A BUDDHA LAND

I
THE HARMONY OF BROTHERHOOD

1.   Let us imagine a desert country lying in absolute darkness with many living things swarming blindly about in it.

Naturally they will be frightened and as they run about without recognizing one another during the night, there will be frequent squirming and loneliness. This is indeed a pitiful sight.

Then let us imagine that suddenly a superior man with a torch appears and everything around becomes bright and clear.

The living beings in the dark solitude suddenly find a great relief as they look about to recognize one another and happily share their companionship.

By "a desert country" is meant a world of human life when it lies in the darkness of ignorance. Those who have no light of wisdom in their minds wander about in

第3章　仏国土の建設

第1節　むつみあうなかま

1. 広い暗黒の野原がある。何の光もささない。そこには無数の生物がうようよしている。

しかも暗黒のために互いに知ることがなく、めいめいひとりぼっちで、さびしさにおののきながらうごめいている。いかにも哀れな有様である。

そこへ急に光がさしてきた。すぐれた人が不意に現われ、手に大きなたいまつをふりかざしている。真暗闇の野原が一度に明るい野原となった。

すると、今まで闇を探ってうごめいていた生物が立ち上がってあたりを見渡し、まわりに自分と同じものが沢山いることに気がつき、驚いて喜びの声をあげながら、互いに走り寄って抱きあい、にぎやかに語りあい喜びあった。

いまこの野原というのは人生、暗黒というのは正しい智慧*の光のないことである。心に智慧の光のないものは、互いに

loneliness and fear. They were born alone and die alone; they do not know how to associate with their fellow men in peaceful harmony, and they are naturally despondent and fearful.

By "a superior man with torch" is meant Buddha assuming a human form, and by His wisdom and compassion He illumines the world.

In this light people find themselves as well as others and are glad to establish human fellowship and harmonious relations.

Thousands of people may live in a community but it is not one of real fellowship until they know each other and have sympathy for one another.

A true community has faith and wisdom that illuminate it. It is a place where the people know and trust one another and where there is social harmony.

In fact, harmony is the life and real meaning of a true community or an organization.

2.   Of organizations, there are three kinds. First, there are those that are organized on the basis of the power, wealth or authority of great leaders.

会っても知りあい和合することを知らないために、独り生まれ独り死ぬ。ひとりぼっちである。ただ意味もなく動き回り、さびしさにおののくことは当然である。

「すぐれた人がたいまつをかかげて現われた。」とは、仏が智慧の光をかざして、人生に向かったことである。

この光に照らされて、人びとは、はじめておのれを知ると同時に他人を見つけ、驚き喜んでここにはじめて和合の国が生まれる。

幾千万の人が住んでいても、互いに知りあうことがなければ、社会ではない。

社会とは、そこにまことの智慧が輝いて、互いに知りあい信じあって、和合する団体のことである。

まことに、和合が社会や団体の生命であり、また真の意味である。

2. しかし、世の中には三とおりの団体がある。

一つは、権力や財力のそなわった指導者がいるために集ま

Second, there are those that are organized because of its convenience to the members, which will continue to exist as long as the members satisfy their conveniences and do not quarrel.

Third, there are those that are organized with some good teaching as its center and harmony as its very life.

Of course, the third or last of these is the only true organization, for in it the members live in one spirit, from which the unity of spirit and various kinds of virtue will arise. In such an organization there will prevail harmony, satisfaction and happiness.

Enlightenment is like rain that falls on a mountain and gathers into rivulets that run into brooks, and then into rivers which finally flow into the ocean.

The rain of the sacred teaching falls on all people alike without regard to their conditions or circumstances. Those who accept it gather into small groups, then into organizations, then into communities and, finally, find themselves in the great Ocean of Enlightenment.

The minds of these people mix like milk and water and finally organize into a harmonious Brotherhood.

った団体、二つは、ただ都合のために集まって、自分たちに
都合よく争わなくてもよい間だけ続いている団体、

三つは、教えを中心として和合を生命とする団体である。

　もとよりこの三種の団体のうち、まことの団体は第三の団
体であって、この団体は、一つの心を心として生活し、その
中からいろいろの功徳を生んでくるから、そこには平和があ
り、喜びがあり、満足があり、幸福がある。

　そして、ちょうど山に降った雨が流れて、谷川となり、次
第に大河となって、ついに大海に入るように、

　いろいろの境遇の人びとも、同じ教えの雨に潤されて、次
第に小さな団体から社会へと流れあい、ついには同じ味のさ
とりの海へと流れこむのである。

　すべての心が水と乳とのように和合して、そこに美しい団
体が生まれる。

Thus, the true teaching is the fundamental requirement of a perfect organization and, as mentioned above, it is the light which enables people to recognize one another, to become adjusted to one another and to smooth out the rough places in their thinking.

Thus, the organization that is formed on the perfect teachings of Buddha can be called a Brotherhood.

They should observe these teachings and train their minds accordingly. Thus, the Buddha's Brotherhood will theoretically include everyone, but, in fact, only those who have the same religious faith are members.

3.   The Buddha's Brotherhood will have two types of members: — there will be those who are teaching the lay members, and those who are supporting the teachers by offering the needed food and clothing. They together will disseminate and perpetuate the teaching.

Then, to make the Brotherhood complete, there must be perfect harmony among the members. The teachers teach the members and the members honor the teachers so that there can be harmony between them.

だから正しい教えは、実にこの地上に、美しいまことの団体を作り出す根本の力であって、それは先に言ったように、互いに見いだす光であるとともに、人びとの心の凹凸を平らにして、和合させる力でもある。

このまことの団体は、このように教えを根本の力とするから、*教団といい得る。

そしてすべての人は、みなその心をこの教えによって養わなければならないから、教団は道理としては、地上のあらゆる人間を含むが、事実としては、同信の人たちの団体である。

3. この事実としての団体は、教えを説いて在家に施すものと、これに対して衣食を施すものと、両者相まって、教団を維持し拡張し、教えの久しく伝わるように努めなければならない。

それで、教団の人は和合を旨とし、その教団の使命を果たすように心がけなければならない。僧侶は在家を教え、在家は教えを受け教えを信じるのであり、したがって両者に和合があり得るのである。

-483-

Members of the Buddha's Brotherhood should associate together with affectionate sympathy, being happy to live together with fellow-followers, and seeking to become one in spirit.

4.   There are six things that will help to lead a Brotherhood to harmony. They are: first, sincerity of speech; second, sincerity and kindness of action; third, sincerity and sympathy of spirit; fourth, equal sharing of common property; fifth, following the same pure precepts; and sixth, all having right views.

Among these things, the sixth or "all having right views" forms the nucleus, with the other five serving as wrappings for it.

There are two sets of seven rules to be followed if the Brotherhood is to be a success. The first is, as a group:

(1) They should gather together frequently to listen to the teachings and to discuss them;

(2) they should mingle freely and respect one another;

(3) they should revere the teaching and respect the rules and not change them;

互いに和らぎむつみあって争うことなく、同信の人とともに住む幸せを喜び、慈しみ交わり、人びとの心と一つになるように努めなければならない。

4．ここに教団和合の六つの原則がある。第一に、慈悲の*ことばを語り、第二に、慈悲の行いをなし、第三に、慈悲の意を守り、第四に、得たものは互いに分かちあい、第五に、同じ清らかな戒を保ち、第六に、互いに正しい見方を持つ。

このうち、正しい見方が中心となって、他の五つを包むのである。

また次に、教団を栄えさせる二種の七原則がある。

(1)しばしば相集まって教えを語りあい、

(2)上下相和して互いに敬い、

(3)教えをあがめ尊んで、みだりにこれをあらためず、

(4) Elder and younger members are to treat each other with courtesy;

(5) they should let sincerity and reverence mark their bearing.

(6) they should purify their minds in a quiet place which they should, nevertheless, offer to others before taking it for themselves.

(7) they should love all people, treat visitors cordially, and console the sick with kindness.
A Brotherhood that follows these rules will never decline.

The second is, individually each should: (1) Maintain a pure spirit and not ask for too many things; (2) maintain integrity and remove all greed; (3) be patient and not argue; (4) keep silent and not talk idly; (5) Submit to the regulations and not be overbearing; (6) maintain an even mind and not follow different teachings; and (7) be thrifty and frugal in daily living.
If its members follow these rules, the Brotherhood will endure and never decline.

5. As mentioned above, a Brotherhood should maintain harmony in its very essence; therefore, one without harmony can not be called a brotherhood. Each member

⑷長幼相交わるとき礼をもってし、

⑸心を守って正直と敬いを旨とし、

⑹閑かなところにあって行いを清め、人を先にし、自分を後にして道に従い、

⑺人びとを愛し、来るものを厚くもてなして、病めるものは大事に看護する。この七つを守れば教団は衰えない。

次に、⑴清らかな心を守って雑事の多いのを願わず、⑵欲なきを守って貧らず、⑶忍辱を守って争わず、⑷沈黙を守って言わず、⑸教えを守っておごらず、⑹一つの教えを守って他の教えに従わず、⑺倹約を守って衣食に質素であること。この七つを守れば教団は衰えない。

5．前にも言ったように、教団は和合を生命とするものであり、和合のない教団は教団ではないから、不和の生じない

should be on guard not to be the cause of discord. If discord appears it should be removed as early as possible, for discord will soon ruin any organization.

Blood stains can not be removed by more blood; resentment can not be removed by more resentment; resentment can be removed only by forgetting it.

6.   Once there was a king named Calamity, whose country was conquered by a neighboring warlike king named Brahmadatta. King Calamity, after hiding with his wife and son for a time, was captured but fortunately his son, the prince, could escape.

The prince tried to find some way of saving his father but in vain. On the day of his father's execution, the prince in disguise made his way into the execution ground where he could do nothing but watch in mortification the death of his ill-fated father.

The father noticed his son in the crowd and muttered as if talking to himself, "Do not search for a long time; do not act hastily; resentment can be calmed only by forgetting it."

Afterward, the prince sought after some way of revenge for a long time. At last he was employed as an attendant in the Brahmadatta's palace and came to win

よう、生じた場合は、速やかにその不和を除き去るように努めなければならない。

血は血によって清められるものではなく、恨みは恨みによって報いられるものではない。ただ恨みを忘れることによってなくすことができる。

6. 昔、長災王という王があった。隣国の兵を好むブラフマダッタ王に国を奪われ、妃と王子とともに隠れているうちに、敵に捕らえられたが、王子だけは幸いにして逃れることができた。

王が刑場の露と消える日、王子は父の命を救う機会をねらったが、ついにその折もなく、無念に泣いて父の哀れな姿を見守っていた。

王は王子を見つけて、「長く見てはならない。短く急いではならない。恨みは恨みなきによってのみ静まるものである。」と、ひとり言のようにつぶやいた。

この後王子は、ただいちずに復讐の道をたどった。機会を得て王家にやとわれ、王に接近してその親任を得るに至った。

the king's favors.

On a day when the king went hunting, the prince sought some opportunity for revenge. The prince was able to lead his master into a lonely place, and the king, being very weary, fell asleep with his head on the lap of the prince, so fully had he come to trust the prince.

The prince drew his dagger and placed it at the king's throat but then hesitated. The words his father had expressed at the moment of his execution flashed into his mind and although he tried again he could not kill the king. Suddenly the king awoke and told the prince that he had had a bad dream in which the son of King Calamity was trying to kill him.

The prince, flourishing the dagger in his hand, hastily grasped the king and, identifying himself as the son of King Calamity, declared that the time had finally come for him to avenge his father. Yet he could not do so, and suddenly he cast his dagger down and fell on his knees in front of the king.

When the king heard the prince's story and the final words of his father, he was very impressed and apologized to the prince. Later, he restored the former kingdom to the prince and their two countries came to live in friendship for a long time.

　ある日、王は猟に出たが、王子は今日こそ目的を果たさなければならないと、ひそかにはかって王を軍勢から引き離し、ただひとり王について山中を駆け回った。王はまったく疲れはてて、親任しているこの青年のひざをまくらに、しばしまどろんだ。

　いまこそ時が来たと、王子は刀を抜いて王の首に当てたが、その刹那父の臨終のことばが思い出されて、いくたびか刺そうとしたが刺せずにいるうちに、突然王は目を覚まし、いま長災王の王子に首を刺されようとしている恐ろしい夢を見たと言う。

　王子は王を押さえて刀を振りあげ、今こそ長年の恨みを晴らす時が来たと言って名のりをあげたが、またすぐ刀を捨てて王の前にひざまずいた。

　王は長災王の臨終のことばを聞いて大いに感動し、ここに互いに罪をわびて許しあい、王子にはもとの国を返すことになり、その後長く両国は親睦を続けた。

The dying words of King Calamity, "Do not search for a long time," mean that resentment should not be cherished for long, and "Do not act hastily" mean that friendship should not be broken hastily.

Resentment can not be satisfied by resentment; it can only be removed by forgetting it.

In the fellowship of a Brotherhood that is based on the harmony of right teaching, every member should always appreciate the spirit of this story.

Not only the members of the Brotherhood but also people in general should appreciate and practise this spirit in their daily lives.

II
THE BUDDHA'S LAND

1. As has been explained, if a Brotherhood does not forget its duty of spreading Buddha's teaching and of living in harmony, it will steadily grow larger and its teaching will spread more widely.

This means that more and more people will be seeking Enlightenment, and it also means that the evil armies of greed, anger, and foolishness, which are led by the devil of ignorance and lust, will begin to retreat, and

　ここに「長く見てはならない。」というのは、恨みを長く
続かせるなということである。「短く急いではならない。」
というのは、友情を破るのに急ぐなということである。

　恨みはもとより恨みによって静まるものではなく、恨みを
忘れることによってのみ静まる。

　和合の教団においては、終始この物語の精神を味わうこと
が必要である。

　ひとり教団ばかりではない。世間の生活においても、この
ことはまた同様である。

第2節　仏　の　国

　1．前に説いてきたように、教団が和合を主として、その
教えの宣布という使命を忘れないときには、教団は次第にそ
の円周を大きくして、教えが広まってゆく。

　ここに教えが広まるというのは、心を養い修める人が多く
なってゆくことであり、いままでこの世の中を支配した無明
と愛欲の魔王が率いる貪りと瞋りと愚かさとの魔軍が退いて

that wisdom, light, faith and joy will dominate.

The devil's dominion is full of greed, darkness, struggling, fighting, swords and bloodshed, and is replete with jealousy, prejudice, hatred, cheating, flattering, fawning, secrecy and abuse.

Now suppose that the light of wisdom shines upon that dominion, and the rain of compassion falls upon it, and faith begins to take root, and the blossoms of joy begin to spread their fragrance. Then that devil's domain will turn into Buddha's Pure Land.

And just like a soft breeze and a few blossoms on a branch that tell the coming of spring, so when a man attains Enlightenment, grass, trees, mountains, rivers and all other things begin to throb with new life.

If a man's mind becomes pure, his surroundings will also become pure.

2.   In a land where the true teaching prevails, every dweller has a pure and tranquil mind. Indeed, Buddha's compassion untiringly benefits all people, and His shining spirit exorcizes all impurities from their minds.

A pure mind soon becomes a deep mind, a mind that is commensurate with the Noble Path, a mind that

ここに*智慧と光明と信仰と歓喜とが、その支配権を握ることになる。

悪魔の領土は欲であり、闇であり、争いであり、剣であり、血であり、戦いである。そねみ、ねたみ、憎しみ、欺き、へつらい、おもねり、隠し、そしることである。

いまそこに、智慧が輝き、*慈悲が潤い、信仰の根が張り、歓喜の花が開き、悪魔の領土は、一瞬にして*仏の国となる。

さわやかなそよ風や、一輪の花が春の来たことを告げるように、ひとりがさとりを開けば、草木国土、山河大地、ことごとくみな仏の国となる。

なぜならば、心が清ければ、そのいるところもまた清いからである。

2. 教えのしかれている世界では、人びとの心が素直になる。これはまことに、あくことのない大悲によって、常に人びとを照らし守るところの仏の心に触れて、汚れた心も清められるからである。

この素直な心は、同時に深い心、道にかなう心、施す心、

loves to give, a mind that loves to keep the precepts, an enduring mind, a zealous mind, a calm mind, a wise mind, a compassionate mind, a mind that leads people to Enlightenment by many and skillful means. Thus shall the Buddha's Land be built.

A home with one's wife and children is transformed into a home where Buddha is present; a country that suffers because of social distinctions is likewise transformed into a fellowship of kindred spirits.

A golden palace that is blood-stained can not be the abiding place for Buddha. A small hut where the moonlight leaks in through chinks in the roof can be transformed into a place where Buddha will abide, if the mind of its master is pure.

When a Buddha Land is founded upon the pure mind of a single man, that single pure mind draws other kindred minds to itself in the fellowship of a brotherhood. Faith in Buddha spreads from individual to family, from family to village, from village to towns, to cities, to countries, and finally to the whole world.

Indeed, earnestness and faithfulness in spreading the teaching of the Dharma are what build the Buddha Land.

戒を守る心、忍ぶ心、励む心、静かな心、智慧の心、慈悲の心となり、また方便をめぐらして、人びとに道を得させる心ともなるから、ここに仏の国が、立派にうち建てられる。

　妻子とともにある家庭も、立派に仏の宿る家庭となり、社会的差別の免れない国家でも、仏の治める心の王国となる。

　まことに、欲にまみれた人によって建てられた御殿が仏の住所ではない。月の光が漏れこむような粗末な小屋も、素直な心の人を主とすれば、仏の宿る場所となる。

　ひとりの心の上にうち建てられた仏の国は、同信の人を呼んでその数を加えてゆく。家庭に村に町に都市に国に、最後には世界に、次第に広がってゆく。

　まことに、教えを広めてゆくことは、この仏の国を広げてゆくことにほかならない。

3.   To be sure, when viewed from one angle, the world with all its greed and injustice and bloodshed appears as a devil's world; but, as people come to believe in Buddha's Enlightenment, blood will be turned into milk and greed into compassion, and then, the devil's land becomes a Buddha Land of Purity.

It seems an impossible task to empty an ocean with a single scoop, but the determination to do it, even if it takes many, many lives, is the mind with which one should receive Buddha's Enlightenment.

Buddha is waiting on the other shore; that is, His world of Enlightenment, wherein there is no greed, no anger, no ignorance, no suffering, no agony, but where there are only the light of wisdom and the rain of compassion.

It is a land of peace, a refuge for those who suffer and who are in sorrow and agony; a place of rest for those who take a break in their spreading of the teachings of the Dharma.

In this Pure Land there are boundless Light and everlasting Life. Those who reach this haven will never return to the world of delusion.

Indeed, this Pure Land, where the flowers perfume

3. まことにこの世界は、一方から見れば、悪魔の領土であり、欲の世界であり、血の戦いの場ではあるが、この世界において、仏のさとりを信じる者は、この世を汚す血を乳とし、欲を慈に代え、この世を悪魔の手から奪い取って、仏の国となそうとする。

一つの柄杓を取って、大海の水を汲み尽くそうとすることは、容易ではない。しかし、生まれ変わり死に変わり、必ずこの仕事を成しとげようとするのが、仏を信ずるものの心の願いである。

仏は彼岸に立って待っている。彼岸はさとりの世界であって、永久に、貪りと瞋りと愚かさと苦しみと悩みとのない国である。そこには智慧の光だけが輝き、慈悲の雨だけが、しとしとと潤している。

この世にあって、悩む者、苦しむ者、悲しむ者、または、教えの宣布に疲れた者が、ことごとく入って憩い休らうところの国である。

この国は、光の尽きることのない、命の終わることのない、ふたたび迷いに帰ることのない仏の国である。

まことにこの国は、さとりの楽しみが満ちみち、花の光は

the air with wisdom and the birds sing the holy Dharma, is the final destination for all mankind.

4. Though this Pure Land is the place for taking rest, it is not the place for idleness. Its beds of fragrant flowers are not for slothful indolence, but are the places for refreshment and rest, where one regains energy and zeal to continue the Buddha's mission of Enlightenment.

Buddha's mission is everlasting. As long as men live and creatures exist, and as long as selfish and defiled minds create their own worlds and circumstances, there will be no end to His mission.

The children of Buddha, who have crossed to the Pure Land by means of the great power of Amida, may be zealous to return to the land whence they came and where they still have ties. There they will take their part in the Buddha's mission.

As the light of a small candle will spread from one to another in succession, so the light of Buddha's compassion will pass on from one mind to another endlessly.

The children of Buddha, realizing His spirit of compassion, adopt His task of Enlightenment and Purification, and pass it on from one generation to another in

智慧をたたえ、鳥のさえずりも教えを説く国である。まことにすべての人びとが最後に帰ってゆくべきところである。

4．しかし、この国は休息のところではあるが、安逸のところではない。その花の台は、いたずらに安楽に眠る場所ではない。真に働く力を得て、それをたくわえておくところの場所である。

仏の仕事は、永遠に終わることを知らない。人のある限り、生物の続く限り、また、それぞれの生物の心がそれぞれの世界を作り出している限り、そのやむときはついにない。

いま仏の力によって彼岸の浄土に入った仏の子らは、再びそれぞれ縁ある世界に帰って、仏の仕事に参加する。

一つの燈がともると、次々に他の燈に火が移されて、尽きるところがないように、仏の心の燈も、人びとの燈に次から次へと火を点じて、永遠にその終わるところを知らないであろう。

仏の子らも、またこの仏の仕事を受け持って、人びとの心

order to make the Buddha's Land glorified eternally and forever.

III
THOSE WHO HAVE RECEIVED GLORY IN BUDDHA'S LAND

1.   Syamavati, the consort of King Udayana, was deeply devoted to Buddha.

She lived in the innermost courts of the palace and did not go out, but her maid, a hunchback, who had an excellent memory, used to go out and attend the Buddha's preachings.

On her return, the maid would repeat to the Queen the teachings of the Blessed One, and thus the Queen deepened her wisdom and faith.

The second wife of the King was jealous of the first wife and sought to kill her. She slandered her to the King until finally he believed her and sought to kill his first wife, Syamavati.

Queen Syamavati stood in front of the King so calmly that he had no heart to kill her. Regaining control of himself he apologized to her for his distrust.

The jealousy of the second wife increased and she

を成就し、仏の国を美しく飾るため、永遠に働いてやまない
のである。

第3節　仏の国をささえるもの

1．ウダヤナ王の妃シャマヴァティーは、あつく世尊に帰
依していた。

妃は王宮の奥深くにいて外出しなかった。侍女のせむしの
ウッタラーは、記憶力がよくて、いつも世尊の法座につらな
り、教えを受けて世尊のことばのとおりを妃に伝え、これに
よって、妃の信仰は、いよいよその深さを増したのであった。

第二の妃、マーガンディヤは、シャマヴァティーをねたん
でこれを殺そうと企て、ウダヤナ王にいろいろ中傷した。つ
いに心を動かした王は、シャマヴァティーを殺そうとした。

そのときシャマヴァティーは、従容として王の前に立った
が、王は妃の*慈悲に満ちた姿に打たれて矢を放つこともでき
ず、ついに心が解けて、妃にその粗暴なふるまいをわびた。

マーガンディヤは、いっそうの怒りを増して、ついに王の

sent wicked men to set fire to the innermost courts of the palace during the King's absence from home. Syamavati remained calm, quieted and encouraged the bewildered maids, and then, without fear, died peacefully in the spirit she had learned from the Blessed One. Uttara, the hunchback, died with her in the fire.

Among the many women disciples of Buddha, these two were most highly honored: Queen Syamavati as a compassionate spirit and her hunchback maid, Uttara, as a good listener.

2.   Prince Mahanama, of the Shakya clan and a cousin of Buddha, had great faith in the teachings of Buddha and was one of his most faithful followers.

At that time a violent king named Virudaka of Kosala conquered the Shakya clan. Prince Mahanama went to the King and sought the lives of his people, but the King would not listen to him. He then proposed that the King would let as many prisoners escape as could run away while he himself remained underwater in a near-by pond.

To this the King assented, thinking that the time would be very short for him to be able to stay underwater.

留守の間に、悪者と謀（はか）ってシャマヴァティーの奥殿に火を放った。妃はあわて騒ぐ侍女たちを教え励まして、驚きも恐れもせずに、世尊の教えに生きながら従容として道に殉じた。せむしのウッタラーもまた、火の中で死んだ。

シャマヴァティーは、在家の信女のうち慈心第一、ウッタラーは多聞（たもん）第一とたたえられた。

2．釈迦族の王、マハーナーマは世尊のいとこであるが、世尊の教えを信ずる心が至ってあつく、誠を尽くして帰依する信者であった。

コーサラ国の凶悪な王、バイルーダカ王が釈迦族を攻め滅ぼしたとき、マハーナーマは出ていって王に会い、城民を救いたいと願ったが、凶悪な王が容易に許さないのを知って、せめて自分が池の中に沈んでいる間だけ、門を開いて自由に城民を逃げさせてほしいと頼んだ。

王は、人間の水中に沈んでいる間だけのことなら、わずかな時間であるからと考えて、これを許した。

The gate of the castle was opened as Mahanama dived into the water and the people rushed for safety. But Mahanama did not come up, sacrificing his life for the lives of his people by tying his hair to the underwater root of a willow tree.

3.   Utpalavarna was a famous nun whose wisdom was compared with that of Maudgalyayana, a great disciple of Buddha. She was, indeed, the nun of all nuns and was always their leader, never tiring of teaching them.

Devadatta was a very wicked and cruel man who poisoned the mind of King Ajatasatru and persuaded him to turn against the teachings of Buddha. But later, King Ajatasatru repented, broke off his friendship with Devadatta, and became a humble disciple of Buddha.

At one time when Devadatta was repulsed from the castle gate in an attempt to see the King, he met Utpalavarna coming out. It made him very angry, so he struck and seriously wounded her.

She returned to her convent in great pain and when the other nuns tried to console her she said to them: "Sisters, human life is the unforeseen, everything is transient and egoless. Only the world of Enlightenment

　マハーナーマは池に沈み、城門は開かれ、人びとは喜んで逃げのびた。しかし、いつまでたってもマハーナーマは浮かび上がらなかった。彼は池に入って髪を解き、柳の根に結びつけ、自らを殺して人びとを救ったのであった。

　3. ウトパラバルナー（蓮華色）は神通第一の比丘尼であって、マウドガルヤーヤナ（目連）に比べられる人であり、多くの比丘尼を引き連れて常に教化し、比丘尼の中のすぐれた教導者のひとりであった。

　デーヴァダッタ（提婆達多）がアジャータサトル（阿闍世）王をそそのかして、世尊に対して反逆を企てたが、後、王が世尊に帰依してデーヴァダッタを顧みないようになり、城門に至ったがさえぎられて入ることができず、門前にたたずんでいたとき、おりから門を出てくるウトパラバルナーを見て、にわかに怒り出し、その大力にまかせてこぶしをあげて頭を打った。

　ウトパラバルナーは痛みを忍んで僧坊に帰ったが、弟子たちの驚き悲しむのを慰めて「姉妹よ、人の命ははかられない。ものみなすべて*無常であり、*無我である。さとりの世界ばかりが、

is tranquil and peaceful. You must keep on with your training." Then she passed away quietly.

4. Angulimalya, once a terrible bandit who had killed many people, was saved by the Blessed One, and he became one of the Brotherhood.

One day he went begging in a town and endured much hardship and suffering for his past evil deeds.

The villagers fell upon him and beat him severely, but he went back to the Blessed One with his body still bleeding, falling at His feet and thanking Him for the opportunity that had come to him to suffer for his former cruel deeds.

He said, "Blessed One, my name originally was 'No Harming,' but because of my ignorance, I took many precious lives, and from each I took a finger; because of that, I came to be called Angulimalya, the collector of fingers!

"Then, through your compassion, I learned wisdom and became devoted to the three treasures of the Buddha, the Dharma and the Samgha. When a man drives a horse or a cow he has to use a whip or a rope, but you, the Blessed One, purified my mind without the use of whip or rope or hook.

静かであって頼るべきところである。努め励んで道を修める
ように。」と教え、静かに死についた。

　4．かつて殺人鬼として、多くの人びとの命をあやめ、世
尊に救われて仏弟子となったアングリマールヤ（指鬘）は、
その出家以前の罪のために、托鉢の途上で、人びとの迫害を
受けた。

　ある日、町に入って托鉢し、恨みのある人びとに傷つけら
れて、全身血にまみれながら、やっと僧坊に帰って、世尊の
足を拝して喜びのことばをのべた。

「世尊、わたくしはもと、無害という名でありながら、愚か
さのために、多くの人の命を損ない、洗えども清まらない血
の指を集めたために、指鬘の名を得ましたが、

　いまでは三宝に帰依してさとりの智慧を得ました。馬や牛
を御するには、むちや綱を用いますが、世尊は、むちも綱も
かぎも用いずに、わたくしの心をととのえて下さいました。

"Today, Blessed One, I have suffered only what was my due. I do not wish to live, I do not wish to die. I only wait for my time to come."

5.   Maudgalyayana, together with the venerable Sariputra, was one of the Buddha's two greatest disciples. When the teachers of other religions saw that the pure water of the Buddha's teachings was spreading among the people and found the people eagerly drinking it, they became jealous and applied various hindrances to his preaching.

But none of the hindrances could stop or prevent his teaching from spreading widely. The followers of the other religions attempted to kill Maudgalyayana.

Twice he escaped but the third time he was surrounded by many heathens and fell under their blows.

Sustained by Enlightenment, he calmly received their blows, and though his flesh was torn and his bones crushed, he died peacefully.

　今日わたくしは、わたくしの受けるべき報いを受けました。生も願わず死も待たずに、静かに時の至るのを待ちます。」

　5．マウドガルヤーヤナ（目連）はシャーリプトラ（舎利弗）と並び称せられた世尊の二大弟子のひとりであった。世尊の教えが水のように人びとの心に浸みこむのを見て、異教の人びとがねたみを起こし、いろいろな妨げをした。

　しかし、どんな妨げも、まことの教えの広まってゆくのをとめることはできないで、異教の人びとは、世尊の手足をもぎ取ろうとして、目連をねらった。
　一度ならず二度までも、その人びとの襲撃を避け得た目連も、ついに三度めに大勢の異教者に取りまかれて、その迫害を受けることとなった。

　目連は、骨も砕け肉もただれ、暴逆の限りを静かに受け忍んで、さとりの心に何のたじろぎもなく、平和な心で死についた。

SOURCE REFERENCES FOR
"THE TEACHING OF BUDDHA"

各章節の典拠

Abbreviations: DN-Dīgha Nikāya
MN-Majjhima Nikāya
SN-Saṃyutta Nikāya
AN-Aṅguttara Nikāya

BUDDHA

「各章節の典拠」

「仏　陀」

「教　法」

「修　道」

「教　徒」

THE APPENDIXES

付　録

BRIEF HISTORY OF BUDDHISM

1. INDIA

One of the greatest epoch-making events in the spiritual history of mankind was marked when the "Light of Asia" was set out brightly in the central part of India, or, in other words, when the Spring of Great Wisdom and Compassion gushed up there, which, in the course of time has come to enrich the human mind over many centuries up to the present day.

Buddha Gautama, who came to be known by later Buddhist followers as Shakyamuni or the "Sage of the Shakya clan," abandoned His home, became a mendicant and turned His steps toward the south, to Magadha. It is believed to have been in the middle of the 5th century B.C., that He finally attained Enlightenment under a Bodhi-tree there. He continued His untiring efforts for forty-five long years, from this time on to His "Great Death" by which He entered Maha-pari-Nirvana, all the while preaching the teaching of Wisdom and Compassion. As a result, great Buddhist steadfastly continued to appear in the kingdoms and various tribes in mid-India.

During the time of King Asoka (reigning: 268—232 B.C.), the third ruler of the Maurya Kingdom, the teaching of Buddha Guatama spread throughout the whole of India and was also being propagated beyond the boundaries of the country.

Maurya had been the first of the consolidated kingdoms in India. This kingdom at the time of its first ruler, Chandragupta (reigning: 316—293 B.C. or thereabouts,) was already occupying a vast domain, extending from the Himalayan mountains in the north, to the Bay of Bengal in the east, to the Hindu Kush mountains in the west, and beyond the Vindhya mountains to the south. King Asoka further expanded this domain to the Deccan Plateau, by conquering Kalinga and others.

仏教通史

1. インド

　それは人類の精神史の上における最大のエポック・メイキングな世紀の１つであった。"アジアの光"はそのときあかあかと中インドに点ぜられたからであり、あるいは、別の言い方をするならば、そのときそこに滾々（こんこん）として湧きいでた智慧と慈悲の泉は、やがて多くの世紀にわたってアジアの人びとの心を潤すものとなって今日に及んでいるからである。

　ブッダ・ゴータマ、後の仏教者たちによって「シャーキャムニ」（釈迦牟尼）すなわち「シャーキャ（釈迦）族よりいでし聖者」とたたえられるその人が、家郷を立ちいでて出家し、南の方マガダに至って、ついにかの菩提樹のもとにおいて正覚を成就したのは、およそ西暦前第５世紀のなかばごろと推定される。それより、「大いなる死」（大般涅槃（だいはつねはん））に至るまでの45年、彼は智慧と慈悲の教えをひっさげて、たゆみない伝道説法（はうげ）の生涯を続けた。その結果、同じ世紀の終わりごろまでには、大いなる法城が、中インドの国々及び諸部族の間に不動に築かれていった。

　マウルヤ王朝の第３世アショーカ（阿育、在位西暦前２６８－２３２）王の時代に至って、ブッダ・ゴータマの教えは、インドの全域にゆきわたり、さらに、その領域を越えて、遠く国外にまで伝播される機会を持つことを得た。

　マウルヤ王朝は、インドにおける最初の統一王朝であった。その第１世チャンドラグプタ王（在位西暦前３１６－２９３ごろ）のころ、その領域はすでに、北はヒマラヤ山系、東はベンガル湾、西はヒンドゥ・クシュ山脈、そして南はヴィンディヤ山脈の南に及んでいたが、アショー

This King is said to have been very furious in nature, being called by his people Chandāsoka (the Furious Asoka); but his character showed a complete change when he witnessed the disastrous conditions caused by the war in which Kalinga had been conquered. He became an earnest devotee of the teaching of Wisdom and Compassion. After that, he did many things as a Buddhist believer, among which the following two undertakings are most noteworthy.

First was the "Asoka's carved edict," or the administrative concepts based on the Buddhist teaching carved onto stone pillars, or on polished cliff walls, which he ordered done at numerous places, thus spreading the teaching of Buddha. Secondly, he sent missions beyond his kingdom to countries in all directions conveying the teaching of Wisdom and Compassion. Especially remarkable is the fact that some of the missions were sent out to such places as Syria, Egypt, Kyrene, Macedonia and Epeiros, spreading Buddhism far and wide to the western world. Moreover, Mahendra (in the Pāli language Mahinda), the envoy sent to Tāmraparni or Ceylon, was successful in "Establishing the beautiful teaching on the beautiful Lankādvīpa (Pāli, Lankādīpa)", and thus founded the starting point of the Buddhist teaching for its successful propagation on the island.

2. THE RISE OF MAHAYANA BUDDHISM

The "Eastward Movement of Buddhism" has often been spoken of by the Buddhists of the later years. But during the B.C. centuries, the face of Buddhism was evidently turned toward the West. It was sometime around the beginning of the Christian Era that this "face" of Buddhism began to be turned toward the East. However, before we refer to this matter, we must speak of the great change that was occurring in Buddhism. This change was none other than the "New Wave" which is known as Mahayana Buddhism, or Greater Vehicle Buddhism, that was taking strong root and appearing as a conspicuous element in the teaching of the time.

カ王はさらに、その南方カリンガ等を討って、その領域をデカン高原にまで拡大した。

この王はもともと性格が狂暴で、人びとは彼を呼んでチャンダーショーカ（恐るべき阿育）と称したと伝えられるが、カリンガの征服にあたって、そこに展開された惨状を見てから性格が一変し、それが動機となって、智慧と慈悲の教えの熱心な信奉者となった。それ以来、この王が仏教者としてなした多くの事業の中で、次の2つのことがもっとも注目される。

その一つは、いわゆる「アショーカの刻文」、すなわち、仏教による施政方針を石柱もしくは磨崖に刻んだものを領内の各地に建立させたことである。第2は全インドにブッダの教法を弘布するとともに、さらに、王はその領域を越えて、使節を四方の国々に遣わし、智慧と慈悲の教えの旨を伝えさせた。なかでも、特に注目されることは、それらの使節のあるものは、遠くシリア、エジプト、キレネ、マケドニア、エピルスにまで派遣されたことであって、そのとき仏教は広く西方の世界に伝えられた。また、そのとき、タームラパルニすなわちセイロンに遣わされた使節マヘンドラは「うるわしきランカードヴィーパ（楞伽島）にうるわしき教えを樹立する」ことに成功して、いわゆる南方仏教の基点をかの島にうち立てた。

2. 大乗の興起

後代の仏教者はしばしば「仏教東漸」という表現を用いる。ところが、紀元前の諸世紀においては、仏教の顔は明らかに西に向けられていた。その顔が、やがて東に向けられ始めたのは、およそ紀元前後のころのことであった。だが、そのことに語り及ぶまえに、我々はまず、仏教の中

When, how and by whom was such a "New Wave" started? Nobody is as yet able to definitely answer these questions. All we know is: First, the trend must have been brought about in the so-called thought-genealogy constituent of the Mahāsaṁghika school by the progressive priests of the time; Second, the fact is that there had already existed some of the important elements of the Mahayana scriptures during the period from one or two centuries B.C. to the first century of the Christian Era. And when the superb thought of Nāgārjuna, backed by the Mahayana scriptures, developed, Mahayana Buddhism vividly presented itself in the foreground on the stage of the history of the religion.

The role that was played by Mahayana Buddhism was very great in the long history of Buddhism. Now, as to China and Japan, Buddhism in these countries through almost all their history has developed under the influence of the Mahayana teaching. This does not seem strange because there was already worked out a new ideal for the salvation of the masses, envisaging living saints in the form of Bodhisattvas to practise this ideal; moreover, to support them, the intellectual results in the metaphysical or psychological domains that were brought about by the Mahayana thinkers were really magnificent. In this way, althought it was linked with the teaching of Buddha Gautama on the one hand, many new phases of Wisdom and Compassion were added. With these new additions, Buddhism became full of ardor and energy and came to enrich the countries in the East like the rushing stream of a great river.

における大きな変化について語っておかなければならない。それはほか
でもない、「大乗」と称する「新しき波」が、いまや仏教の中に顕著な存
在として姿を現わしてきたことについてである。

　その「新しき波」が、いつごろ、いかにして、何びとによって生まれ
いでたか、その始動のいきさつは、だれも明確に語ることはできない。
それについて我々が指摘し得ることは、わずかに、第一には、それは明
らかに進歩主義の比丘たちによって、いわゆる大衆部の思想的系譜の中
に生まれたものに相違ないということであり、第二には、紀元前の1・
2世紀から紀元後の第1世紀ごろにかけて、いわゆる大乗経典なるもの
のうちの重要なもののいくつかがすでに存在していたということである。
そして、それらの大乗経典を背景として、ナーガールジュナ（龍樹）の
すぐれた思想的活動が展開されるに及んで、大乗仏教なるものの姿は、
いまやあざやかに仏教史の舞台の前景に現われいずるに至ったのである。

　長い仏教の歴史の中において、大乗仏教が果たした役割はまことに大
きい。やがて説き至ろうとする中国の仏教ならびに日本のそれのごとき
も、ほとんどその歴史のすべてを通して、まったく大乗仏教の影響のも
とにあった。それも決して不思議なことではあるまい。なんとなれば、
そこには大衆の救済という新しい理想がうち出されており、その理想を
実践するものとして、菩薩という新しい人間像が描き出されており、さ
らに、それらを支えるものとして、大乗の思想家たちが造り営んだ形而
上学あるいは心理学の領域における知的成果もまたすばらしいものであ
った。かくして、それは、明らかにブッダ・ゴータマの教法の系譜につら
なりながらも、他方、いくたの新しきものを智慧と慈悲の教えの流れに注
ぎ加えた。それによって、仏教は、いよいよ、熱情にあふれたものとな
り、エネルギーに富めるものとなり、滔々たる大河のさまをなして、東

3. CENTRAL ASIA

It was through the Central Asian countries that China came to learn of Buddhism for the first time. Therefore, to tell of the teaching spreading from India to China, it is necessary to speak of the Silk Road. This road passed through the boundless territories in Central Asia to connect the West and the East, and it was during the age of King Wu of the Han dynasty (reigning: 140–87 B.C.) that this trade route was opened. At that time, the domain of Han extended far westward, and in such adjoining countries as Ferghana, Sagdiana, Tukhara and even Parthia, the spirit of mercantilism which had formerly been inspired by Alexander the Great was still vigorously active. Along this ancient route that ran through these countries silk played the most important role, hence the name Silk Road. From the time a little before or after the beginning of the Christian Era, India and China started their cultural contacts first by means of the trade route. Thus, the road can be said to have been the route for Buddhism as well.

4. CHINA

The history of Chinese Buddhism starts from their acceptance of the Buddhist scriptures and translation thereof. The oldest work from the ancient times is said to be the "*Ssu-shih-êr-châng-ching* (Sutra in Forty-two Sections Spoken by Buddha)" a translation done by Kāśyapamātaṅga and others during the Ying-p'ing Era (58–76 A.D.) of King Ming of the Latter Eastern Han, but it is today regarded as a doubtful legendary story. The corroborated opinion now gives the credit to An-shih-kao who was engaged in translation at Lo-yang from about 148 to 171 A.D. From this time to the time of the Northern Sung Dynasty (960–1129 A.D.), the translation work continued for nearly one thousand years.

方の国々を潤すこととなるのである。

3. 西　域

　中国の人びとがはじめて仏教を知ったのは、西域を通してであった。したがって、インドから中国への仏教の道を語るものは、まずシルク・ロードのことから語り始めなければならない。その道が、アジアの中央部の荒涼たる地域をつらぬいて、西洋と東洋とをつらねる貿易路として開かれたのは、紀元前第２世紀の末ごろ、漢の武帝（西暦前１４０－８７）の時代であった。そのころ漢の領土は、はるか西の方にまで広げられ、それに接する西方の国々、大宛（Ferghana）康居（Sagdiana）大月氏（Tukhara）、さらに安息（Parthia）の諸国には、かつてアレクサンドロス大王によって吹きこまれた商業精神がまだ活発に生きていた。そして、それらの国々をつらねる古代貿易路においては、中国の絹がもっとも大きな役割を担う商品であった。それがシルク・ロードの名のいずるところであった。しかして紀元前後のころから、仏教を中心として始められたインドと中国の間の文化接触もまた、まずこの貿易路によって行われた。かくして、シルク・ロードはまた仏教の道であったということを得るのである。

4. 中　国

　中国人の仏教受容の歴史は、まず経典の招来とその翻訳の事業を主題としてつづられねばならない。その最初のものは、古来から、後漢の明帝の永平年間（A. D. 58－76）迦葉摩騰らによってもたらされ訳出された『四十二章経』であるとされているが、今日では、それは疑わしい伝説にすぎないとされている。その確証されるものは、紀元148年ごろから171年ごろにわたり、洛陽において訳業に従事した安世高の仕事で

During the earlier years, those who played pivotal roles in the introduction of the scriptures and in making translations thereof were mostly the priests from the Central Asian countries. For instance, An-shih-kao, mentioned above, came from Parthia; K'ang-sêng-k'ai, from the Samarkand region came to Lo-yang in about the 3rd century and translated "Sukhāvatīvyūha" (the Book of Limitless Life). Moreover, Chu-fa-hu or Dharmaraksha, who is known as the translator of the "Saddharmapundarīka," came from Tukhāra and stayed in Lo-yang from the latter part of the third century to the early part of the fourth century. When Kumārajīva, who came from Kucha, appeared in the early part of the fifth century, the translation work in China reached a high point.

From about that time priests began visiting India from China to learn Sanskrit. The pioneer of such priests was Fa-hsien (339—420? A.D.). He left Ch'ang-an in 399 for India and returned home fifteen years later. The most distinguished of these priests visiting India was Hsuan-chuang (600—664 A.D.) who left for India in 627 and returned home in 645, after nineteen long years. Further, I-ching (635—713 A.D.) (not to be confused with the book *I-ching*) left for India by sea in 671 and returned home by the same route twenty-five years later.

These priests visited India by themselves to learn Sanskrit and brought home those scriptures they had chosen, playing the leading role in the scriptures translation work. The linguistic ability that Hsuan-chuang showed was especially outstanding, and by his energetic work, the translation of the scriptures in China reached another peak. The works of the former days done by those represented by Kumārajīva are called the "Old Translations" and the works by Hsuan-chuang and the later translators are called the "New Translations" by Buddhist scholars in later periods.

ある。それ以来、北宋（960-1129）の時代に至るまで、中国の仏教経典翻訳の事業は、およそ千年にわたって営み続けられた。

その初期においては、経典をもたらし、かつ、その翻訳の中心的役割を演じた人びととは、たいてい西域からきた僧たちであった。例えば、いまの安世高は安息国すなわちパルティアからきた人であり、第3世紀のころ洛陽に来って『無量寿経』を訳した康僧鎧は康居すなわちサマルカンド地方の人であったし、あるいは、『正法華経』の訳者として知られる竺法護は月氏の出であって、第3世紀の後半から第4世紀のはじめまで、洛陽または長安にあった。そして、第5世紀のはじめ亀茲よりきたった鳩摩羅什に至って、中国の訳経は一つの頂点に達した。

そのころから、中国よりインドに至って梵語をまなび、法を求める人びと、すなわち、入竺求法僧の活動が始まった。その先駆者は法顕（339-420？）であって、彼は隆安3年（399）長安を出発し、15年を経て帰国した。そのもっとも有名なものは玄奘（600-664）であって、彼は貞観元年（627）に出発し、貞観19年（645）に帰国した。その間じつに19年に及んだ。さらに義浄（635-713）は、咸亨2年（671）海路によってインドに向かい、25年の後、同じく海路によって帰国した。

彼らは、自らインドに至って梵語をまなび、自ら経典を選んで持ち帰り、かつ、帰国の後には、たいてい訳経の中心的役割を演じた。ことに、玄奘がしめした語学力は、群を抜くものがあって、彼の精力的な訳業によって中国の経典翻訳の歴史はもう一つの頂点を迎えた。学者たちが、鳩摩羅什によって代表される旧来の翻訳を「旧訳」と称し、玄奘以後の新しいそれを「新訳」とよぶのは、その故をもってである。

そのようにして訳出されたぼう大な量にのぼる仏教経典をよりどころとして、彼らの営んだ思想的・宗教的営みもまた、しだいに中国化の傾

Based on this enormous number of volumes which they had translated from Sanskrit, the tendency of thought and religious activity of these learned men gradually but strongly turned toward Sinicism. There appeared plainly the racial nature, needs and confidences. That the priests in the early stages turned their minds metaphysically towards "Non-substantiality" especially, which is dealt with in the Prajñā of the Sutras, was a manifestation of this tendency. Later, they cast away the so-called "Hinayana", or the Lesser Vehicle, and turned their attention exclusively toward "Mahayana", the Greater Vehicle. Moreover, this tendency gradually became notable in the Tendai Sect and may be said to have reached its height when the Zen Sect appeared.

It was in the latter half of the sixth century that the Tendai Sect saw its completion in China, which was perfected by Tendai Daishi, Chih-i (538—597 A.D.), its third patriarch. He was one of the most outstanding figures in Buddhist thought, and the critical classification of Buddha's teaching into the Five Periods and Eight Doctrines worked out by this saint have long maintained a wide influence on the Buddhism of China as well as of Japan.

A review will show that in China the various sutras were brought in without regard to the order of the time of thier origins and were translated as they were taken in. In the face of the enormous number of these sutras, the problem was how to understand their origin and evaluations. It was necessary to appreciate Buddhism as a whole and to show how one should stand according to one's own understanding of it. As to the evaluation of the sutras, the trend of the Chinese thought, first of all, comes to the fore. Above all, that of Chih-i was most systematic and, therefore, splendidly persuasive. But, with the appearance of the Buddhist research work of modern times, even such a dominating influence was to come to an end.

向を強める。そこには、かの民族の資質や要求や自信が明らかに現われている。その初期のころ、彼らが特に般若部の経典が語る「空」の形而上学に心を傾けたのもその現われであった。やがて彼らが、いわゆる「小乗」を捨てて、もっぱら「大乗」に心を傾けるものとなったのもその現われであった。さらに、その傾向は、天台宗においてようやく顕著となり、禅宗の出現に至ってきわまったということを得るであろう。

　中国において天台宗が大成したのは、第6世紀の後半、その第3祖、天台大師こと智顗（538-597）によってであった。彼は、中国の生んだ仏教思想家の中の代表的な頭脳であって、彼の頭脳が生んだ「五時八教」の教判は、その後長きにわたって、中国ならびに日本の仏教に広い影響力をもった。

　思うに、中国においては、諸経はその成立の順序にかかわりなく招来され、招来されるにしたがって翻訳された。いまやそのぼう大な量にのぼる諸経を前にして、その成立と価値づけをいかに理解するか、その見解を示すことによって仏教全体の理解の仕方を語り、かつ、自己の依って立つところを示すことが必要であった。それがいわゆる教判もしくは教相判釈の課題であった。その意味において、教判とは、何よりもまず中国的な思想の営みであるが、その中でも、智顗の教判はもっとも整然たるものであり、したがってまた、見事な説得力をもっていたのである。だが、近代の仏教研究の出現とともに、その支配的影響はついに終わりをつげた。

　中国仏教の歴史の中において、その「最後に至れるもの」は禅宗であった。その初祖とされるものは、外国の沙門、菩提達磨（-528）であるが、彼によってまかれた種が、中国仏教の精華として大いなる花を開いたのは、第六祖、慧能（638-713）以後のことであって、第8世紀以後、

In the history of Buddhism in China "The one that came last" was the Zen Sect. Its founder is said to have been Sramana, of a foreign country, or Bodhidharma (—528 A.D.); but the seed sown by him had seen its glorious flower only after the time of Hui-nêng (638—713 A.D.), the sixth patriarch of the line. After the eighth century, the sect in China had sent out many priests of talent in succession, bringing about the prosperity of Zen for a period of several centuries.

It can be seen that there was a new way of thinking in Buddhism, which was deeply rooted in the nature of the Chinese people. It was nothing other than a Buddhism colored by the Chinese way of thinking. And yet the stream of the teaching of Buddha Gautama, with this fresh current added, had grown into a still larger river and came to enrich the countries to the east.

5. JAPAN

The history of Buddhism in Japan began in the sixth century. In 538 A.D., the King of Pochi (or Kudara, Korea) dispatched his envoy to present a Buddhist image and scroll of sutras to the Imperial Court of Emperor Kinmei. This marked the first introduction of Buddhism into this country. The history of the religion in Japan is therefore more than 1,400 years old now.

In this long history, we can think of Japanese Buddhism in connection with three foci. The first can be placed on the Buddhism of roughly the seventh and eighth centuries. To show this materially we can refer to the Horyuji Temple (607 A.D.) and the Todaiji Temple (752 A.D.), which were constructed during this period. In looking back to this time, the one thing that can not be overlooked is the fact that the tide of culture rose unusually high throughout the whole of Asia during this period, while the civilization of the

相ついで人材を輩出し、数世紀にわたる禅の隆盛を招来した。

彼らの所懐を問えば、「仏祖正伝」といい、また「教外別伝」と語る。しかるに、中国にあっては、「教」とは、さしあたり、経にほかならない。その故にこそ、中国人は、経の招来と翻訳に努力を傾けて、すでに幾世紀にも及ぶ。しかるに、いま彼らはそれらの功をほかにして、別伝ありとなし、ひたすらに対座して、仏祖の正伝するところとなす。その不思議な言説の機微を尋ね至ってみれば、そこには、中国人の資質に深く根を下ろした仏教の新しい考え方があって、それを支えていることが知られる。それはもはや中国人の仏教以外の何ものでもなかった。しかも、ブッダ・ゴータマの教えは、その新しき流れをとり加え、ますます滔々たる大河となって、東方の国々を潤し来ったのである。

5. 日 本

日本仏教の歴史は第6世紀に始まる。紀元538年、欽明天皇の朝廷に、百済の王が使臣をもって仏像・経巻を献じたのが、この国に仏教の伝来した始まりである。それ以来、この国の仏教の歴史は、すでに1400年を越える。

その長い歴史の中に、わたしどもは、3つの焦点を結んで考えてみることができる。

その第1の焦点は、第7・8世紀の仏教の上に結ばれる。それを物件をもっていえば、法隆寺の建立（607）より東大寺の建立（752）に至る時代である。その時代を回顧するにあたって、思い忘れてならないことは、かの時代のアジア全体にわたって、異常な高まりをしめしていた文化の潮のことである。西の方の文明が深い暗黒の中に閉じこめられていたそれらの世紀にあって、東の方の文明は、目を見張るような活発にして雄

West was shut up in deep darkness. The East was developing an astonishingly active and magnificent movement. In China, in Central Asia, in India and in the South-sea countries, the activities in the intellectual, religious and art fields were going on strongly. Joining these movements, Buddhism was washing the Eastern world with its vast tide of humanism. And this new movement of the Japanese culture as witnessed by the construction of the brilliant Horyuji and the magnificent Todaiji, and also in the colorful religious and art activities that came about in connection with these events, shows this absorption at the extreme eastern end of the general cultural tide that was covering all the vast area of Asia.

The people of this country, which had been in an uncivilized state for a long time, now bathed in the current of a great culture; the flower of civilization opened up all of a sudden. Such was the good turn of fortune that favored Japan in those centuries. And the chief champion responsible for the rise in this culture was none other than Buddhism, the Buddhist temples of the time became very important social centers, and the priests were the leaders of the new learning. There developed a wide and great culture rather than just a religion. This was the actual state of Buddhism that was first transplanted to this country.

In the ninth century, two great priests, Saicho (Dengyo Daishi, 767—822) and Kukai (Kobo Daishi, 774—835) appeared on the scene and founded two Buddhist denominations usually referred to together as Heian-Buddhism. This was the establishment of a purely Japanese Buddhism. They grasped Buddhism in its original standpoint and practice, and founded the central monasteries on Mt. Hiei and Mt. Koya respectively. During the three hundred years after their founding, until the Kamakura Period, these two esoteric denominations, the Tendai and the Shingon, prospered chiefly among the aristocrats and in the Imperial courts.

大な動きを繰り広げていた。中国でも、西域でも、インドでも、南海の国々でも、知的、宗教的、そして芸術的な活動が力強く営まれていた。仏教がそれらの動きを互に結びつけて、広大なヒューマニズムの潮が東方の世界を洗っていた。そして、あの絢爛たる法隆寺や雄大なる東大寺の建立と、それらをめぐる多彩な宗教的ならびに芸術的活動など、それらの世紀の新しい日本文化の動きは、すべて、かの荒漠たるアジア全域にわたる文化の潮の、最東端におけるいぶきであったと知られる。

　ぱっと一時に文化の花を開く、それがそれらの世紀におけるこの国の人びとのめぐりあわせであった。そして、その国際的な文化の主たる担い手が仏教にほかならなかったのである。したがって、その時代の寺院は国際的な明るい文化の中心であった。僧侶は新しい知識のリーダーであった。経典は優れた思想の乗物であった。そこには、一つの宗教というよりも、ずっと広汎な、大いなる文化そのものがあった。それがかの世紀における初伝の仏教の真相であった。

　やがて第9世紀に入ると、最澄（767-822）・空海（774-835）という二人の偉大なる仏教者が現われ、いわゆる平安仏教とよばれる、初めての日本仏教とでもいうべき宗派を創設するのである。ややもすると貴族たちのひまつぶしに流れがちになりつつあった仏教を、本来の修行という立場でとらえ、それまでの都会中心の仏教を、山の中に持ちこんで、そこに修行の根本道場を確立した。その後300年余、この二人の流れである天台と真言とが、主に朝廷や貴族を中心として栄えたのである。

　その第二の焦点は、第12・3世紀の仏教の上に結ばれる。そこには、法然（1133-1212）親鸞（1173-1262）道元（1200-1253）日蓮（1222-1282）など、この国の生んだすぐれた仏教者たちがあった。今日においても、わたしどもは、この国の仏教について語ろうとすれば、これら

The second of the foci can be placed on the Buddhism of the twelfth and thirteenth centuries. There appeared such great priests as Honen (1133–1212 A.D.), Shinran (1173–1262 A.D.), Dogen (1200–1253 A.D.) and Nichiren (1222–1282 A.D.). When we talk of the Buddhism of Japan we can not do so without mentioning the names of these great priests. Why then did only those centuries in question produce such outstanding men? It is because of the fact that a common problem was facing them all at that time. What was this common problem, then? Perhaps it was the fact that Buddhism was being accepted, but in a unique Japanese way.

This might lead to the question, "Why? Was it not true that Buddhism had been introduced to this country long before that time?" It is so historically. But it is also true that several hundred years were needed for the people of this country to sufficiently digest and remodel the imported religion so as to make it complately their own. In short, it was in the seventh and eighth centuries that the efforts in this country for the acceptance of Buddhism began, and as a result of these efforts, the religion bloomed through those Buddhists of the twelfth and thirteen centuries.

After this, Buddhism in Japan, based on the foundation built up by those prominent priests, has kept up its work to this day. Since the time those distinguished men appeared, no more of the brilliancy of those centuries has ever again appeared in the history of Japanese Buddhism. However, it seems to the present writer that there is another thing that attracts our attention and that is the fruit of the research into original Buddhism made in our modern times.

Since the time of its first acceptance, practically all of Buddhism in Japan, was Mahayana, under the influence of Chinese Buddhism. Especially after the appearance of the great teachers

の人びとの名をほかにしては語ることを得ない。では、何のゆえをもって、それらの世紀のみが、かくもすぐれた仏教者たちを輩出させたのであろうか。それは1つの大いなる共通の課題が彼らの前にあったからである。その共通の課題とは何か。それは仏教の日本的受容であったということをいい得るであろう。

かくいえば、あるいは問う者があるであろう。仏教はすでにそのときよりはるか以前に伝来していたのではないかと。歴史的事実はそのとおりである。だが、それをこの国の人びとが、じゅうぶんに消化し、変容して、まったく自己のものとする―そのような文化受容の仕事は、たいてい数百年の努力を必要とするのである。つまり、第7・第8世紀に始められた仏教受容の努力が、ようやく春来って、万花一時に咲ききそう―それが第12・3世紀における一群の仏教者たちの仕事であった。

それ以後の日本仏教は、それらの仏教者たちによって与えられた基盤の上に、その余栄を保って今日に至った。つまり、かの世紀に一群のすぐれた仏教者たちを輩出して以後は、日本仏教の歴史には、もはや輝かしい陽は輝かなかった。だが、それ以後の日本仏教の歴史にも、もう一つ注目されるべきことがあるように思われる。それは近代の仏教学における原始仏教の研究の成果である。

この国の仏教は、その初伝このかた、中国仏教の影響のもとに、ほとんどまったく大乗の仏教であった。ことに第12・3世紀のすぐれた仏教者たちの輩出以後は、宗祖たちを中心とする大乗の教えがその主流をなし今日に至る。そのようなこの国の仏教の歴史の中に、原始仏教の研究が起こってきたのは、およそ明治のなかば以後のことに属する。それによって、宗祖のほかに教祖のあることを忘れていた人びとの前に、ブッダ・ゴータマの姿があざやかに再現され、大乗の教えのほかは顧みなか

during the twelfth and thirteenth centuries, the Mahayana teaching formed the main current with the sect founders as its center; this view has continued to this date. In the history of Buddhism in Japan as such, the study of original Buddhism was started after the mid-Meiji Era. The figure of Buddha Gautama vividly reappeared before those who were apt to forget that there was also the founder of Buddhism besides the sect founders, and it was made plain to those who did not heed anything other than the Mahayana teaching that there was also the systematic creed of Buddhism. These new phases still remain within the sphere of scholastic learning and as yet are not strong enough to awake religious enthusiasm among the masses. But it seems that the knowledge of the people of this country in regard to Buddhism appears to be taking a turn. The writer would like to put a mark on this phase, to make it the third or the last of the three foci referred to above.

った人びとの前に、整然たるブッダの教法が明らかにされた。それはなお学問の領域にとどまり、新しい宗教的熱情をよび起こすものとはなっていないけれども、少なくとも、この国の人びとの持つ仏教の知識は、大きく変化しつつある。わたくしは、そっと、そこにスポットを当てて、第三の焦点とする。

TRANSMISSION OF BUDDHA'S TEACHING

Buddhism is a religion which is built up on the teaching Shakyamuni had preached for forty-five years of his life. The words he used in his teaching, therefore, have absolute authority in this religion, and in spite of the fact that there are 84,000 dharma gates and a large number of schools, all of them are related to the scriptures of Shakyamuni. Those books in which the Buddha's teaching is recorded are known as the *Issaikyo* or the *Daizokyo*, that is, a complete collection of the sacred scriptures.

Shakyamuni strongly advocated the quality of human beings and preached his teaching in the plain and simple words of everyday usage so that everyone could fully understand them. He continued his preaching for the benefit of multitudes of people up to the very minute of his death at the age of eighty.

After the demise of Shakyamuni, his disciples preached the gospel according to what they had heard. However, as the teaching was transmitted and retold, there might possibly have occurred some variations due to unconscious errors on the part of the disciples as to what they thought they had heard or understood. And, yet, the words of Shakyamuni must always be transmitted precisely and correctly, and opportunities of hearing the teaching must be afforded to every and all people without discrimination. Therefore, many of the senior priests got together for the purpose of adjusting and consolidating the words and teaching by mutually reciting what each thought he had heard, and they spent many a month on their discussions. The work that resulted in this way is known as the *Ketsuju* or regimentation. This shows how piously and deliberately they had tried to transmit the very words that had been spoken by the great teacher.

The teaching thus adjusted had come to be put into writing. To the teaching recorded in a written form were added the comments and interpretations made by the learned priests of the

仏教聖典流伝史

　仏教とは釈尊一代45年間の説法をもととする宗教である。だから、釈尊のことばは仏教においては絶対の権威を持つものであって、たとえ仏教に八万四千(はちまんしせん)の法門があり、多くの宗旨(しゅうし)、宗派を数えるとはいえ、いずれも釈尊の説法を離れたものではない。そしてこの説法を書き記したものが、一切経とか大蔵経などといわれる経典なのである。

　釈尊は人間の平等を強く主張された。どんな人にでも完全に理解できるような日常語で平易に教えを説かれたのである。そして80歳で亡くなられるまで1日も休まず、多くの人びとのために教えを説き続けられたのである。

　釈尊が亡くなられた後は、弟子たちはそれぞれ自分の耳で聞いた釈尊の教えを、人びとに伝えた。しかし、語り伝えられる間には聞き違いもあろうし、覚(おぼ)え違いも起こるであろう。しかも、釈尊のことばは常に正確に伝えられなければならない。

すべての人が平等にその教えに接する機会が与えられなければならない。そこでここに釈尊の教えを、間違いのない形で後世に伝えるために、長老たちが集まって、教えの整理を行うことになった。これを結集(けつじゅう)という。結集には大勢の長老比丘(びく)たちが集まり、各自の聞き伝えてきたことばや教えを誦(とな)えあって、間違っていないかどうか、何か月にもわたって討議した。このことからしても、いかに敬虔(けいけん)、かつ慎重に、釈尊のことばを伝えようとしたかがわかる。こうして整理された教えは、やがて文字によって記録されるようになる。文字に書き下された釈尊の教えは、後に

later ages, which came to be known as *Ron* or comments. The Buddha's teaching itself, the comments added in later ages and the Buddhist precepts all came to be called as the *Sanzokyo* (Three Sections of Buddhist Scriptures) or Tripitaka in Sanskrit.

Sanzokyo or Tripitaka includes *Kyozo, Ritsuzo* and *Ronzo*; the word *Zo* means a receptacle or container. *Kyo* refers to the Buddhist scriptures, *Ritsu* to the precepts for the Buddhist Brotherhood, and *Ron* to the comments written by the high priests.

According to tradition, Buddhism is said to have been introduced in China in 67 A.D. during the reign of King Ming of the Latter Eastern Han Dynasty (25—220 A.D.). But, actually, it was eighty-four years later that the Buddhist scriptures were introduced to and translated in China (in 151 A.D.) by King Huan of the same dynasty. For over a period of more than 1,700 years since then, efforts in the translation of the scriptures into the Chinese language continued. The number of books and volumes thus translated reached 1,440 scriptures in 5,586 volumes. Efforts toward the conservation of these translated scriptures were begun as early as the Wei Dynasty, but it was about the time of the Northern Sung Dynasty that their printing was started. However, from about this time the works of the high priests of China came to be added to the Buddhist scriptures and it was no longer appropriate to call these books Tripitaka. When the era of Suei came, the title of *Issaikyo* or a complete collection of all the sacred writings was given to the books, and in the era of Tang they came to be called by the new title of *Daizokyo* or the collection of all the Buddhist scriptures, laws and treatises.

Buddhism was introduced into Tibet around the seventh century A.D., and for about 150 years during the ninth through eleventh century, A.D., efforts in the translation of the Buddhist scriptures continued, and practically all of them had been translated by that time.

後世の高僧たちによって、注釈や解釈が加えられた。これを「論」という。仏陀の教えそのものと、後に加えられた論と、戒律の3つを「三蔵」という。三蔵とは経蔵、律蔵、論蔵、の3つであり、蔵とは「いれもの」の意味である。すなわち仏教の教えを収めてあるものという意味で、経とは仏陀の教えそのもの、律とは教団の戒律を説いたもの、論とは高僧たちによって書かれた注釈である。

　中国に初めて仏教が伝わったのは、伝説によると後漢の明帝の永平10年（67）だといわれているが、確実に聖典を伝えて翻訳したのは、それよりも84年の後、後漢桓帝の元嘉元年（151）であった。それより約1700年以上にわたって中国語に仏典を翻訳する努力が続けられた。訳出された経典の数は1440部5586巻に及んでいる。これらの翻訳経典をひとまとめにして保存しようとする努力は、早く魏の時代から始められた。しかしこれが印刷されるようになったのは北宋のころであった。このころから中国の高僧の著述も聖典の中に加えられるようになり、もはや三蔵と呼ぶには適当でなくなって、隋代になると「一切経」という名称が付され、唐代には「大蔵経」とよぶようになった。

　一方、チベットにおいても西暦7世紀ごろに仏教が伝わり、西暦9世紀から11世紀にかけて、約150年の間、経典を翻訳する努力が続けられ、仏典のほとんどが翻訳された。

　このほか、朝鮮、日本、セイロン、カンボジヤ、トルコ、その他、東洋のあらゆることばをはじめとして、ラテン語、フランス語、英語、ドイツ語、イタリヤ語等の各国語に翻訳されているところから見ても、今や釈尊の恩恵は、世界のすみずみにまで及んでいるといっても過言ではない。しかし、ひるがえってこれを内容から見ると、時代にして2000年

In view of the fact that the scriptures had been translated into not only the Korean, Japanese, Ceylonese, Cambodian, Turkish and almost all of the Oriental languages but also into the Latin, French, English, German and Italian tongues, it may safely be said that the blessing of the Buddha's teaching has now spread to every corner of the world.

But, on second thought, in reviewing from the standpoint of the quality of the translations, and the history of the religion's development and origin during more than two thousand years, with ten thousand or more translations of the books having been written, it still seems difficult to grasp the true meaning of the words spoken by Shakyamuni, even with the aid of *"Daizokyo"*. It is, therefore, indispensable to pick out those essential points from the *"Daizokyo"* and make them the criteria or foundation upon which one can base one's faith in the religion.

In Buddhism the supreme authority are the words uttered by Shakyamuni. Therefore, the teaching of Buddhism must be the teaching that is closely linked to and intimate with the realities of our everyday life; otherwise, it will but fail in inspiring the human mind from its very depths toward a belief in the teachings. In this sense, for the teaching to be one that we can make our own, it is desirable to be plain and simple, impartial in its quality, sufficient in representing the whole and yet accurate and familiar in the words that are used from our daily life.

This book has come into being under the above considerations, inheriting the "stream" of the *Daizokyo* with its history of more than two thousand and several hundred years. Of course, this publication can not be taken as perfect in its contents. The words of Buddha are infinitely deep in their meaning and His Virtues are so boundless that one can not easily appreciate them.

It is sincerely wished, therefore, that this book will be improved into a still more truthful and valuable one as the revised editions come out in the future, as is intended.

を越える発達と変遷があり、量は万巻を越えるため、たとえ大蔵経が完全に備わっていても、これによって釈尊の真意をつかむことは困難である。そこで大蔵経から重要なところをつかみ出して自己の信心の規範とし、よりどころとする必要がある。

　仏教では釈尊のことばが最大のよりどころである。だから釈尊の教えは、我々の現実生活に対して最も深いつながりをもった、親しみのあるものでなければならない。もしそうでなければ、万巻の聖典も、ついに我々の心をゆさぶることなく終わってしまうことになるからである。こういう意味で聖典は、少なくともいつも身につけている聖典は、量にして簡潔であること、質において一部に偏らず、よく全体を代表するに足るものであること、しかも正確であること、用語においてわれわれの日常語に親しいものであることが望まれるのである。

　この聖典は、こういう敬虔にしてかつ慎重な配慮のもとに作られた。この聖典は、過去二千数百年の大蔵の流れを承け継ぎ、釈尊の教えの海の中から生まれ出たものである。もとよりこれをもって完璧と信ずるものではない。釈尊のことばは無限に深く、その徳は無尽にして容易にうかがい難い。共に同じ道を行ずる同信の叱正を請いつつ、版を重ねて、常によりよきもの、より真実なもの、より尊きものにしてゆきたいと心から願うものである。　　　　　　　　　　　合　掌

HISTORY OF
"THE TEACHING OF BUDDHA"

This Buddhist text is based on a revised and compiled original Japanese edition of *Newly Translated Buddhist Text* published in July, 1925, by the Association for Spreading "Newly Translated Buddhist Text" headed by Rev. Muan Kizu. This first Japanese Edition was compiled by Dr. Shūgaku Yamabe and Dr. Chizen Akanuma, in cooperation with many Buddhist scholars in Japan, taking almost five years to publish.

In the Shōwa Era (1926—), the *Popular Edition of Buddhist Text* in Japanese was also published by the Association and distributed widely throughout Japan.

In July, 1934, when the Pan-Pacific Buddhist Youths' Meeting was held in Japan, *The Teaching of Buddha*, the English translation of the above *Popular Edition of Buddhist Text* was published by the All Japan Buddhist Youths' Federation, with the assistance of Mr. D. Goddard, as one of its works. In 1962, commemorating the 70th Anniversary of the Introduction of Buddhism to America, Mr. Yehan Numata, Founder of the Mitutoyo Company, published an English edition of *The Teaching of Buddha* himself.

In 1965, when Mr. Numata founded the Buddhist Promoting Foundation in Tokyo, the popularization of this English text all over the world was planned as one of activities of the Foundation.

In order to realize this plan, a committee to revise this *The Teaching of Buddha* was organized in 1966. Members of the committee were Professors Kazuyoshi Kino, Shūyū Kanaoka, Zennō Ishigami, Shinkō Sayeki, Kōdō Matsunami, Shōjun Bandō, and Takemi Takase. Prof. Fumio Masutani, Mr. N.A. Waddell

本聖典の由来

　この仏教聖典は、大正14年（1925年）7月に、木津無庵氏を代表とする新訳仏教聖典普及会から出版された『新訳仏教聖典』をもととして改訂・編集したものである。

　この初版本編集にあたっては、山辺習学、赤沼智善の両博士を中心に、広く仏教学界の諸師が監修、編集の労を寄せ、約5年の月日を経て出版された。

　ここに仏教伝道協会は、木津無庵氏をはじめとする、原『新訳仏教聖典』を編集された諸師に対して、甚深なる感謝と報恩の意を表するものである。

　昭和に入って『国民版仏教聖典』が同普及会で出版され広く全国に行き渡った。昭和9年（1934年）7月に汎太平洋仏教青年大会が日本で開催されたとき、その記念事業の1つとして、前掲の『国民版仏教聖典』より　英語版仏教聖典"The Teaching of Buddha"が、D・ゴダード氏の協力を得て全日本仏教青年連盟の手によって刊行された。

　昭和37年（1962年）、仏教東漸70周年を記念して、株式会社三豊製作所創立者沼田恵範氏が、同『英訳仏教聖典』を刊行した。昭和40年（1965年）同氏が浄財を投じて財団法人仏教伝道協会を設立するや、同協会の事業として、この聖典を全世界に普及することが企画された。

　この企画に従って、昭和41年（1966年）に、仏教聖典改訂、編集のための委員会が組織された。メンバーは紀野一義、金岡秀友、石上善応、佐伯真光、松濤弘道、坂東性純、高瀬武三、の7氏であり、増谷文雄氏、N・A・ワデル氏、清水俊輔氏などの協力も得て全面改訂し『日英対訳仏教聖典』が誕生した。

and Mr. Toshisuke Shimizu also worked on the revision. Thus, an English-Japanese edition of The Teaching of Buddha was published in a new style.

In 1972, Professors Shūyū Kanaoka, Zennō Ishigami, Shōyū Hanayama, Kwansei Tamura, and Takemi Takase corrected some typographical errors; and recompiled the text.

Again, in 1974, in order to correct inappropriate and inaccurate expressions in the English version which had been brought to the Foundation's attention by Mr. Richard K. Steiner, under his guidance, Professors Shōjun Bandō, Kōdō Matsunami, Shinkō Sayeki, Kwansei Tamura, Dōyū Tokunaga, and Shōyū Hanayama (Editor-in Chief) revised the text. In 1978 and 1980, in order to have a meeting on some topics suggested by Mr. Shinroku Inouye, the above editorial staff, plus Professors Shigeo Kamata and Yasuaki Nara, gathered together to review the book again. Thus the English-Japanese edition of *The Teaching of Buddha* was published in the present style as a result of their work.

In 1980, it was decided that the time had come to translate this book into even more languages than the four (English, French, Portuguese and Spanish) it already was in. So, once again the Foundation called upon Mr. Steiner to refurbish and refine the English, from which the German, Italian, Greek, Chinese, Dutch and Nepalese editions would be made.

Again in 1981, in order to make the book more readable, we asked several high school students, both Japanese and American, to read through it. After the editors had a meeting to discuss changes with these students, and as a result, the book was subsequently revised.

Oct., 1981

　昭和47年（1972年）、この聖典の不備を補うため、金岡秀友、石上善応（典拠）、花山勝友、田村完誓、高瀬武三、のスタッフをもって改訂作業を進め、まず『英文仏教聖典』を刊行した。

　昭和48年（1973年）、仮名遣い・表記法等において、適当ではないと思われる箇所が数多くみられることから、塩入亮達、高瀬武三、立川博、田村完誓、坂東性純、花山勝友（編集責任者）のスタッフが改訂作業を進め、全面的に手を加え、増補して、ここに『和文仏教聖典』を刊行した。

　更に昭和49年（1974年）、『英文仏教聖典』における不適当な訳語や表現を訂正するために、R・スタイナー氏の協力のもとに、松濤弘道、坂東性純、佐伯真光、徳永道雄、田村完誓、花山勝友（編集責任者）が集って全面的に手を加え、これを、先に刊行した『和文仏教聖典』と併せて刊行したものがこの『和英対照仏教聖典』である。昭和53年及び昭和55年、内容の一部に対する井上真六氏の提案を検討するために、新たに鎌田茂雄、奈良康明の両名を加えた編集スタッフが集って改訂作業を行い、さらに昭和56年、より読み易い聖典にするために、日本とアメリカの高校生数名に通読してもらい、指摘された難解な部分を編集委員会で検討した上で修正し、ここに改訂版『和英対照仏教聖典』を出版した。今後ともこのような改定作業は続けてゆく予定である。

　　　1981年10月

INDEX TO
"THE TEACHING OF BUDDHA"

生 活 索 引

Index

Index

修　養

Index

悩　み

Index

日 常 生 活

Index

政　治

Index

出 家 の 道

社 会

Index

SANSKRIT GLOSSARY (Alphabetical Order)

ANĀTMAN (Egolessness):

This is one of the most fundamental points in Buddhism. All existence and phenomena in this world do not, ultimately, have any substantial reality. It is very natural for Buddhism, which advocates an impermanence of all existence, to insist that such an impermanent existence could not therefore possess any perpetual substance in it. Anātman may also be translated as Non-Soul.

ANITYA (Transitoriness or Impermanency):

Another fundamental point in Buddhism. All existence and phenomena in this world are changing constantly and do not remain the same for even a single moment. Everything has to die or end someday in its future, and such a prospect is the very cause of suffering. This concept should not, however, be interpreted only from a pessimistic or nihilistic viewpoint, because both advancement and reproduction are also manifestations of this constant change.

BODHISATTVA (The One Striving for Enlightenment):

Originally, this name was used to indicate Gautama Siddhartha before he had attained the state of Enlightenment. After the rise of Mahāyāna Buddhism, all those who are striving for the Buddhahood have come to be called by this name. Finally, even those who are trying to lead others to the Buddhahood by means of their great compassion while striving themselves for the same goal, have been symbolically personified as Bodhisattvas; Avalokiteśvara (Kwannon), Kṣitigarbha (Jizō), Mañjuśrī (Mon-ju) are only a few of the better known ones.

BUDDHA (The Enlightened One):

Originally, Gautama Siddhartha (Shakyamuni), the founder of

Buddhism, was called by this name, as he was the one who had attained the state of Enlightenment at 35 about 2,500 years ago in India. The final goal for all Buddhists is, irrespective of their school or stream, to become a Buddha. Because of the difference of means as to how to reach this state, Buddhism has divided into various sects and schools. In Mahāyāna Buddhism, besides the historical Buddha Shakyamuni, many Buddhas such as Amitābha (Amida), Mahāvairocana (Dainichi), Vaisajyaguru (Yakushi), etc.,are generally accepted as symbols of Buddhist teachings. Being influenced by the concept of the Pure Land type of Buddhism in Japan, (one becomes a Buddha after rebirth in the Pure Land), all those who have passed away are usually called "Buddhas," or HOTOKE in Japanese.

DHARMA (True Teaching):

This is the Teaching taught by the Enlightened One, the Buddha. There are three types of canons in the teachings: Sūtras, (teachings taught by Buddha Himself), Vinayas, (disciplines provided by Buddha), and Abhidharmas, (commentaries and discussions on the Sūtras and Vinayas by scholars in later periods). These three are called the Tripitaka. Dharma is one of the Three Treasures of Buddhism.

KARMA (Deeds):

Although the original meaning of this term simply meant "Deeds", it has, in relation with the theory of causation, come to be regarded as a kind of potential power gained as a result of each deed done in one's past. That is, each of our acts results in either good or bad, suffering or pleasure, depending upon the act, and it has an influencing power upon our future and this is regarded as one's Karma. It is believed that if a good deed is repeated, good will be accumulated, and its potential power will function upon the future as a beneficial influence. There are three kinds of deeds; physical, oral, and mental, in this concept.

MAHĀYĀNA (Great Vehicle):

In the course of Buddhist history, there appeared two main streams of thought, Mahāyāna and Theravāda (or Hīnayāna). The Mahāyāna type of Buddhism spread to Tibet, China, Korea, Japan, etc., while Theravāda to Burma, Śrī Lanka (Ceylon), Thailand, etc. The term means a "Great Vehicle" which can accept all beings suffering in this world of birth and death, and can lead all of them, without any discrimination, to the state of Enlightenment.

NIRVĀṆA (Perfect Tranquility):

Literally, it means "to blow off." This is the state where all human defilement and passion have been completely extinguished through certain practices and meditation based upon Right Wisdom. Those who had attained this state are called Buddhas. Gautama Siddhartha had attained this state and became a Buddha at 35. However, it is now believed that it was only after he had passed away that he reached such a state of perfect tranquility, because some residue of human defilement would continue to exist as long as his physical body existed.

PĀLI (Language):

This is the language used in Theravāda Buddhism. The oldest type of Buddhist canons are believed to have been written in this language. As this is a kind of Prakrit, a dialect of Sanskrit, there is not a big difference between Pāli and Sanskrit; Dharma in Sanskrit, Dhamma in Pāli; Nirvāna in Sanskrit, Nibbāna in Pāli. See—Sanskrit.

PĀRAMITĀ (To cross over to the Other Shore):

"To cross over to the Other Shore" means to reach the Buddha Land by means of practising various Buddhist disciplines. Usually the following six practical disciplines are regarded as those which enable one to cross from this world of birth and death to the world of Enlightenment: Offerings, Morality, Patience, Endeavoring, Concentration, and Right Judgment (or Wisdom). The traditional Japanese HIGAN weeks in spring and autumn are derived from this Buddhist concept.

PRAJÑĀ (Wisdom):

One of the Six Pāramitās. The mental function which enables one to perceive life without error and to distinguish between what is true and what is false. One who had acquired this perfectly is called a Buddha. Therefore, this is the most refined and enlightened wisdom, distinct from ordinary human intelligence.

SAṀGHA (Buddhist Brotherhood):

It consists of monks, nuns, laymen and laywomen. In early times, it consisted of homeless monks and nuns. Later, when the Mahāyāna movement arose, those who aimed at the state of Bodhisattva, regardless of being layman or monk, joined together in a Brotherhood. One of the Three Treasures of Buddhism.

SANSKRIT (Language):

The classical literary language of ancient India; one of the Indo-European family of languages. It is divided into Vedic and Classicial Sanskrit. The scriptures of the Mahāyāna tradition had been written in this language which style is called Buddhist Hybrid Sanskrit.

SAṂSĀRA (Reincarnation):

Perpetual repetition of birth and death from the past through the present to the future through these six illusory realms: Hell, Hungry Spirits, Animals, Aśura or Fighting Spirits, Men, and Heaven. Unless enlightened, one cannot be freed from this wheel of transmigration. Those who are free from this can be called Buddhas.

ŚŪNYATĀ (Non-Substantiality):

This is the concept that everything has neither substance nor permanence and is one of the fundamental points in Buddhism. Since everything is dependent upon causation, there can be no permanent ego as a substance. But, one should neither adhere to the concept that everything has substance nor that it does not. Every being, human or non-human, is in relativity. Therefore, it is foolish to hold to a certain idea or concept or ideology as the only absolute. This is the fundamental undercurrent in the Prajñā Scriptures of Mahāyāna Buddhism.

SŪTRA (Scriptures):

The records of the Buddha's teachings. The term means originally "string", which signifies compendium threading through the vast quantity of studies in religion or science. One of the Tripitaka.

THERAVĀDA (or Hīnayāna: Elders' Advocators):

The southern tradition of Buddhism is represented generally by this appolation. "Thera" means elders. This is the school of elders which was historically a group of conservative senior monks who advocated a strict adherence to the precepts as opposed to another group of rather freer progressive monks (whose beliefs were to develope later into Mahāyāna, that is the northern tradition). This kind of opposing trends in Buddhist Orders is said to have started in an early period, a few centuries after the decease of the Buddha, when Mahādeva, a progressive monk, insisted upon the freer interpretation under the five categories of the Buddhist precepts. This provoked the split into Theravāda and Mahāsaṁghika which was the fountainhead of later Mahāyāna.

TRIPIṬAKA (Three Baskets):

The three branches of the Buddhist scriptures, Dharma, are meant by this. They are Sūtras, which contain the Buddha's teachings; Vinayas, which contain his disciplines; and Abhidharmas, which contain various commentaries and essays on Buddhist doctrines and precepts. Later, Buddhist writings by Chinese and Japanese high-priests were also included in the Buddhist canons. See—Dharma

用 語 解 説 （五十音順）

この解説に含まれている言葉には、本文では、
各節の最初に出てくるものに＊印が付してある。

因縁 (hetu-pratyaya)

　　因と縁とのことである。因とは結果を生じさせる直接的原因、縁とはそれを助ける外的条件である。あらゆるものは因縁によって生滅するので、このことを因縁所生などという。この道理をすなおに受け入れることが、仏教に入る大切な条件とされている。世間では転用して、悪い意味に用いられることもあるが、本来の意味を逸脱したものであるから、注意を要する。なお縁起という場合も、同様である。

廻向 (pariṇāma)

　　自分のなしたよい行為をふり向けることで、これに、自分自身の未来のさとりにふり向ける場合と、他の人びとにふり向ける場合とがある。現在一般に世間で使われているものは、「死んだ人が、この世でなした悪行の罪を消して、来世での良い結果を得るように」という願いをもって、葬式や法事の際の読経の功徳によって死者の冥福を祈念する、という形の廻向である。

縁起 (pratītyasamutpāda)

　　因縁生起の略である。あらゆる存在が互いに関係しあって生起することである。

仏教の教えの基本となる思想である。あらゆる存在のもちつもたれつの関係を認めるから、「お蔭さまで」という感謝となり、報恩という奉仕も生まれてくる。この縁起思想は、さらに哲学的な展開を遂げ、煩瑣な組織をもつに至る。転じて寺院や仏像の由来や伝説を指したり、吉凶をかつぐのに用いられるようになったりするが、本来の意味を忘れてはならない。

教団 (saṃgha)

　同じ教えを奉じて集まった人びとの集団をいう。一般に、教義を説き教える聖職者層と、教えを受け入れる信者から構成される。仏教では古来、これをサンガと称した。しかし厳密には初期においては出家者教団を指したと思われる。後に大乗が興起すると、菩薩という人間像を目指して実践する人びとの集まりは、在家、出家の区別を超えて連帯した教団となったといわれる。組織としての教団は、現在では一宗一派についていわれている。

空 (śūnyatā)

　存在するものには、実体・我がないと考える思想である。すべてのものは相縁り、相起こって存在するにすぎないから、実体として不変な自我がその中に存在する筈がない。

　したがって実体ありととらわれてはならないし、存在しないととらわれてもならないわけである。すべてのものは、人もその他の存在も相対的な関係にあり、1つの存在や主義にとらわれたり、絶対視したりしてはならない。般若経系統の思想の根本とされる。

解脱 (vimukti・vimokṣa)

　文字どおりに、この輪廻転生する迷いの世界という縛から解き離れて、涅槃とよばれるさとりの境地へと脱出することである。そして、この迷いの世界から脱出して、永遠にさとりの状態にとどまるものが、〝仏陀〟であり、そこでは一切の縛、すなわち煩悩から離れているので、自由自在なのである。

業（karman）

本来の意味は行為ということであるが、因果関係と結合して、行為のもたらす結果としての潜在的な力とみなされている。つまり1つの行為は必ず善悪・苦楽の果報をもたらすから、その影響力が業と考えられ、例えば前世の行為の果報としての宿業などが説かれるに至っている。善い行為を繰り返し、積み重ねれば、その影響力が未来に及んで作用すると考えられている。なお業には、身・口・意の3種の行為があるとされる。

慈悲（maitrī・karuṇā）

仏教におけるもっとも基本的な倫理項目で、〝慈〟とは相手に楽しみを与えること、〝悲〟とは相手から苦しみを抜き去ることである。これを体得して、対象を差別せずに慈悲をかけるものが〝覚者〟すなわち仏であり、それを象徴的に表現したものが、観音・地蔵の両菩薩である。やさしくいうと、慈悲とは〝相手と共に喜び、共に悲しんであげる〟ということになる。

出家（pravrajana）

家庭生活を捨離して、専ら道の修行を行うこと。またその実践者をいう。インドでは修道のために家庭を出て、宗教的実践の生活に入ることが、ごく普通のこととされていて、釈尊もそれに従って出家し、沙門（バラモン以外の修行者）となり、遂に悟りを開いて仏陀となり、仏教の開祖となった。在家信者に対して、出家修行者をはっきり区別する仏教教団の伝統は、日本では厳格とはいい難い。

智慧（般若・prajñā）

　普通に使われている〝知恵〟とは区別して、わざわざ仏教では〝般若〟の漢訳としてこの言葉を用いているが、正邪を区別する正しい判断力のことで、これを完全に備えたものが〝仏陀〟である。単なる知識ではなく、あらゆる現象の背後に存在する真実の姿を見ぬくことのできるもので、これを得てさとりの境地に達するための実践を〝般若波羅蜜〟という。

中道（madhyamā pratipad）

　偏見を離れた中正の道をいう。仏教の立場を指していう。したがって仏教のそれぞれの流れでは、中道の思想は尊重され、高揚されてきた。中間の道という意味ではなく、とらわれを離れ、公平に現実を徹見する立場を形容していうわけだが、その内容は両極端を否定し、止揚する思想として表われてくる。例えば有・無の両極端、断・常の二見を否定する立場となる。一種の弁証法哲学といえないこともない。

涅槃（nirvāṇa）

　梵語の〝吹き消す〟という意味の、ニルバーナという単語の漢音写で、〝滅〟・〝滅度〟・〝寂滅〟などと訳される。丁度ローソクの火を吹き消すように、欲望の火を吹き消したものが到達する境地で、これに到達することを〝入涅槃〟といい、達したものを〝仏陀〟とよぶ。釈迦牟尼仏が亡くなった瞬間を〝入涅槃〟ということもあるが、肉体が滅びたときに完全に煩悩の火が消える、という考え方からで、普通は、35才で仏になったときに〝涅槃〟の状態に達したと考えられている。

波羅蜜（pāramitā）

　　パーラミターという梵語の漢音写で、"度"とか"到彼岸"と訳される。此の迷いの岸である現実の世界から彼のさとりの岸である仏の世界へと渡してくれる実践行のことで、普通六波羅蜜といって、六種類があげられる。六とは、布施・持戒・忍辱・精進・禅定・智慧のことで、日本では、春秋の"彼岸"とよばれる行事は、これらを実践するということから名づけられたのである。

仏（仏陀・Buddha）

　　梵語の"さとれるもの"という意味の単語を漢字に音写したものが"仏陀"で、その省略が"仏"であり、"ほとけ"とも読ませる。普通"覚者"・"正覚者"と漢訳され、もともとは、仏教の創始者である"釈迦牟尼仏（ゴータマ・シッダルタ）"を指した。仏教の目的は、各人がこの"仏"の状態に到達することで、その手段や期間等の違いによって宗派が分かれている。

　　大乗仏教の場合、歴史上の仏である釈迦牟尼仏の背後に、種々な永遠の仏の存在が説かれるようになる。例えば、阿弥陀仏・大日如来・毘盧舎那仏・薬師如来・久遠実成の釈迦牟尼仏といった仏が、各宗派の崇拝の対象とか教主として説かれている。

　　なお日本では、死者のことを"ほとけ"とよぶが、これは浄土教の"往生成仏"思想の影響で、死者が浄土に生まれ、そこで"仏"になるという信仰に由来する。

仏性（buddhatā・buddhatva）

　　"仏になる種子"といったもので、あらゆる存在にこれを認めるところに仏教の特徴がある。"覚りに達する潜在力・可能性"といってもよい。又、"仏心"といってもよいが、"一切衆生悉有仏性"という句

にも表われているように、すべての存在に、差別しないでこの仏性を認めたところに、仏教の平等説の立場が見られる。この内在する仏性を外に現わしたものを〝仏〟とよぶ。

法（達磨・dharma）

さとれるものである〝仏陀〟によって説かれた〝真実の教え〟ということで、その具体的な内容は、三蔵とよばれる、経（仏の説かれた教え）・律（仏の定めた日常規則）・論（経と律とに対する解釈や註釈）の三種の聖典である。これは、覚者である〝仏陀〟・仏教徒の集まりである〝僧伽〟と共に、仏教の基本的なよりどころである三宝をなしている。

菩薩（bodhisattva）

元来、釈尊の成道以前の修行時代を指す。悟りを求める人という意味である。大乗仏教が興起してからは、拡大解釈されて、大乗仏教徒を指すことになる。向上的には仏の悟りを目指しつつ、向下的にはすべての人びとを同様に仏の悟りへと導こうと努力する人間像を菩薩とよぶようになる。さらに仏の慈悲や智慧の働きの一部をにない、仏の補佐役として人びとの悩みに応じて現われる、観音とか地蔵のような威神力のある救い手もそうよばれる。

煩悩（kleśa）

悟りの実現を妨げる人間の精神作用のすべてを指していう。人間の生存に直結する多くの欲望は身体や心を悩まし、かき乱し、煩わせる。その根元は我欲・我執であり、生命力そのものに根ざしているともいえる。貪り、瞋り、愚かさがその根本であり、派生して多くの煩悩が数えられる。これらは悟りの実現に障害となるから、修道の過程で滅ぼさなければならないとする。しかし生命力に直結しているものを否定できないとして、悟りへの跳躍台として肯定する思想もある。

無我（anātman）

　仏教の最も基本的な教義の1つで、「この世界のすべての存在や現象には、とらえられるべき実体はない」ということである。それまでのインドの宗教が、個々の存在の実体としての "我" を説いてきたのに対し、諸行無常を主張した仏教が、"永遠の存在ではあり得ないこの世の存在や現象に実体があるわけはない" と説いたのは当然である。なお "我" は他宗教でいう霊魂にあたるといえる。

無常（anitya）

　あらゆる存在が生滅変化してうつり変わり、同じ状態には止まっていないことをいう。仏教の他宗教と異なる思想的立場を明示する1つである。あらゆるものは、生まれ、持続し、変化し、やがて滅びるという4つの段階を示すから、それを観察して「苦」であると宗教的反省の契機とすることが大切である。これもいろいろな学派の立場から、形而上学的な分析がなされてきたが、単なるペシミズム、ニヒリズムの暗い面のみを強調してはならない。生成発展も無常の一面だからである。

無明（avidyā）

　正しい智慧のない状態をいう。迷いの根本である無知を指す。その心理作用が愚痴であるという。学派によって分析、解釈はさまざまであるが、いずれも根源的な、煩悩を煩悩たらしめる原動力のようなものと把えられている。したがって、例えばあらゆる存在の因果を12段階に説明する十二因縁説では、最初に無明があると設定しているくらいである。生存の欲望の盲目的な意志と把えてもよいであろう。

唯識（vijñaptimātratā）

　この世のあらゆる存在と現象とは、人間の〝こころ〟から生まれたもので、実際にあるのは、この〝こころ〟だけなのだ、という説で、大乗仏教の中に表われたもの。即ち、眼耳鼻舌身意という6つの感覚器官がそれぞれの対象を認識する6つの識のほかに、第7、第8（阿頼耶識）の2識をたて、これら8つの識の動きが、この世に存在や現象を生じさせているとするのである。

輪廻（saṃsāra）

　過去世から現在世へ、更に未来世へと、生まれ変わり死に変わることを、輪がまわるのにたとえたもので、輪廻転生という言葉もある。人間が、この迷いの世界からさとりの世界へと脱出しない限り、地獄・餓鬼・畜生の三悪道や、それに阿修羅・人間・天上を加えた六道の世界への転生を永遠に繰り返すのである。この輪廻の輪から抜け出たものが、〝仏陀〟とよばれる。

DHAMMAPADA

Victory breeds hatred; the defeated live in pain. The peaceful live happily, giving up victory and defeat. (*Dhammapada* 201)

Hunger is the greatest disease, the body the greatest ill; knowing this as it really is, the wise realize the bliss supreme. (*Dhammapada* 203)

Cut off your cravings as if they were autumn lotuses. Cultivate that very path of Peace. The bliss supreme is preached by the Blessed One. (*Dhammapada* 285)

Hard is it to be born as man, hard is it to live as a mortal, hard is it to hear the Sublime Truth, hard is it to see Buddha. (*Dhammapada* 182)

Hard is it to find an authentic man. He is not born everywhere. Where such a wise man is born that family thrives happily. (*Dhammapada* 193)

Happy is the birth of a Buddha, happy is the teaching of the Noble Doctrine, happy is the unity of the Sangha, happy are the efforts of the united. (*Dhammapada* 194)

法 句 経

勝つものは恨みを招き、敗れるもの苦しみに臥す。勝ち負けの2つを捨てたる、心平和なるものは、幸せに住す。

（法句経201）

飢えはこの上なき病、この身はこの上なき苦しみ、このことわりをあるがままに知らば、涅槃こそこよなき楽しみとさとれり。

（法句経203）

自らの手にて秋の蓮を断つごとく、己れの欲望を断つべし。寂静への道を養うべし。涅槃は、尊きみ仏によりて説かれたり。

（法句経285）

人の生を受くるは難く、死すべきものの今生命あるは難く、み法を耳にするは難く、み仏の世にいづること難し。

（法句経182）

尊き人の世にいづるを見るは難く、その人いづくにも生まるるにはあらず。かかる賢き人の生まるる、その種族は、幸せにして栄えん。

（法句経193）

み仏の生まれ給うは幸せなり、み仏の尊き教えを説くは幸せなり、もろ人の心一つなるは幸せなり、心一つなるものの励むは幸せなり。

（法句経194）

Monks, there is one person whose birth into the world is for the welfare of many, for the happiness of many: who is born out of compassion for the world, for the profit, welfare and happiness of heavenly beings and mankind. Who is that person? It is a Tathagata who is an Arahàt, a fully Enlightened One. This, monks, is that one person.

Monks, the manifestation of one person is hard to find in the world. Of what person? Of a Tathagata who is an Arahat, a fully Enlightened One. He is the one person.

Monks, hard to be found in the world is that one extraordinary person. What person? A Tathagata who is an Arahat, a fully Enlightened One. He is the one person.

Monks, the death of one person is to be regretted by all. Of what person? Of a Tathagata who is an Arahat, a fully Enlightened One. He is the one person.

Monks, there is one person born into the world who is incomparable and unequalled. Who is that person? It is a Tathagata who is an Arahat, a fully Enlightened One. He is the one person.

Monks, the manifestation of one person is the manifestation of a mighty eye, a mighty light, a mighty radiance. Of what person? Of a Tathagata who is an Arahat, a fully Enlightened One. He is the one person. (*Aṅguttara Nikāya I-13*)

比丘たちよ、1人の人のこの世に生まるるは、多くの人の利益のため、多くの人の幸せのため、又、世間をあわれむがため、人と天との利益と幸せのために生まるるなり。その1人の人とはたれぞ。これ如来、応供、正等覚なり。比丘たちよ、これこそその1人の人なり。

比丘たちよ、1人の人のこの世に現わるるは、難きことなり。その1人の人とはたれぞ。これ如来、応供、正等覚なり。これこそその1人の人なり。

比丘たちよ、この世に見ること難きは、1人の希有の人のこの世に生まるることなり。その1人の人とはたれぞ。如来、応供、正等覚なり。これこそその1人の人なり。

比丘たちよ、1人の人のこの世を去りて、多くの人の愁い嘆くことあり。その1人の人とはたれぞ。如来、応供、正等覚なり。これこそその1人の人なり。比丘たちよ、1人の人のこの世に生まるるとは、比ぶべきものなき人の生まるるなり。その1人の人とはたれぞ。これ如来、応供、正等覚なり。これこそその1人の人なり。比丘たちよ、1人の人のこの世にいづるは、大いなる眼、大いなる明り、大いなる光の現わるるなり。その1人の人とはたれぞ。如来、応供、正等覚なり。これこそその1人の人なり。

（増支部Ⅰ－13）

BUDDHIST PROMOTING FOUNDATION
AND DISTRIBUTION OF

"THE TEACHING OF BUDDHA"

In describing the Buddhist Promoting Foundation it is necessary to speak of a businessman, and this gentleman is Mr. Yehan Numata, the Founder of Mitutoyo Manufacturing Company.

He established a company to manufacture precision measuring instruments more than forty years ago. His solid conviction is that the success of an enterprise depends on the harmonious association of Heaven, Earth and Man and that the perfection of the human mind is attainable only by a well-balanced coordination of wisdom, compassion and courage. He is doing everything he can under this conviction towards the technical improvement of measuring instruments manufacture, and the development of the human mind.

It is his belief that the attainment of world peace is possible only upon the perfection of the human mind, for the purpose of which there is the teaching of Buddha. Therefore, along with managing his enterprise, he has been exerting his efforts for more than forty years in the spreading and modernization of Buddhist music and the spreading of Buddha's pictures and teaching.

In December, 1966, he had a foundation incorporated with his private funds to engage in the propagation of Buddhism, and at the same time, to be an aid towards world peace. Thus, the Buddhist Promoting Foundation was initiated as a public organization.

What is being done to diffuse the Teaching of Buddha far and wide so that every human being can benefit by it and enjoy the Light of His Great Wisdom and Compassion? It is the work of this Buddhist Promoting Foundation to seek the solution to this problem, keeping up the will of its founder.

仏教伝道協会について

仏教伝道協会のことを語るには、先ず一人の実業家沼田恵範氏（株式会社三豊製作所創立者）のことを語らなければならない。

彼は、今から40余年前に現在の事業を始めたとき以来、事業の繁栄は天・地・人により、人間の完成は智慧と慈悲と勇気の三つが整ってのみできるものであるとして、技術の開発と心の開発をめざして会社を設立した。世界の平和は人間の完成によってのみ得られる。人間の完成をめざす宗教に仏教がある。

彼は40余年にわたる会社経営のかたわら、仏教伝道のために仏教音楽の普及と近代化を志し、仏教聖画や仏教聖典の普及に努めてきたが、1966年12月にこれら一切の仏教伝道事業を組織化し、これを世界平和の一助とするために私財を寄進した。

かくて仏教伝道協会は、仏教伝道の公の機関として発足した。仏陀の教えを遍く一切に及ぼして、すべての同胞と共にこの大智と大悲の光に浴するにはどうしたらよいか。

仏教伝道協会は創設者の意志を引き継ぎ、この問題を永遠に問い続けてゆこうとするものである。

In short, every possible effort toward the propagation of the Buddha's teaching is the very heart and soul that this Buddhist Promoting Foundation is undertaking.

This book, "The Teaching of Buddha," is a result of our reflecting on the history in this country of the religion, that there has hardly been anything written that we can call a book of Buddhist teaching as interpreted in the Japanese way, in its real sense, in spite of the fact that we have always regarded our Buddhist culture with great pride.

This book will serve as spiritual "food" for each and everyone who reads it. It is so prepared that anyone can keep it on one's desk or carry it with him and come in contact, at will, with the Light alive spiritually.

Though still not as perfect as we would like, the present edition of "The Teaching of Buddha" has come a long way, through the work and efforts of many people, to meeting the need by contemporary people for an accurate, easy to read and authoritive introduction to Buddhism that is, at the same time, a practical guide and daily source of inspiration and truth.

It is the wish of the Buddhist Promoting Foundation to see a day come soon when as many homes as possible will have this book and as many as possible of our fellow-men will enjoy and bathe in the Light of the Great Teacher.

Readers' comments are always welcome. Please feel free to write to the Buddhist Promoting Foundation any time.

約言すれば、仏教普及のためのあらゆる努力が仏教伝道協会の事業の
すべてである。

　この聖典は日本の長い歴史をふり返ったとき、我々が仏教文化をその
誇りとしながら、真に日本人の経典といえるものを持たなかったことを
反省して生まれたものである。

　したがってこの聖典は、だれでも読める、読んで心の糧となる、どん
な人でも、その机上に置いて、また外出時に携え、生きた釈尊の大人格
に触れることができるように作られている。

　仏教伝道協会は、この聖典が一つでも多くの家庭に入り、一人でも多
くの同胞の手に渡り、すべての人がひとしく教えの光に浴することので
きる日のくることを願ってやまない。

合掌

和 文 仏 教 聖 典	第62版	Japanese, 62nd edition, 1982	
英 文 仏 教 聖 典	第64版	English, 64th edition, 1981	
フ ラ ン ス 語 仏 教 聖 典	第 2 版	French, 2nd edition, 1977	
ポルトガル語仏教聖典	第 2 版	Portuguese, 2nd edition, 1977	
ス ペ イ ン 語 仏 教 聖 典	第 2 版	Spanish, 2nd edition, 1978	
ネ パ ー ル 語 仏 教 聖 典	初 版	Nepali, 1st edition, 1980	
インドネシア語仏教聖典	初 版	Indonesian, 1st edition, 1979	
ド イ ツ 語 仏 教 聖 典	初 版	German, 1st edition, 1982	
イ タ リ ア 語 仏 教 聖 典	初 版	Italian, 1st edition, 1982	
和 葡 対 照 仏 教 聖 典	第 2 版	Japanese-Portuguese, 2nd edition, 1978	
英 葡 対 照 仏 教 聖 典	第 2 版	English-Portuguese, 2nd edition, 1981	
仏 英 対 照 仏 教 聖 典	第16版	English-French, 16th edition, 1981	
中 英 対 照 仏 教 聖 典	第12版	English-Chinese, 12th edition, 1981	
英 西 対 照 仏 教 聖 典	第 4 版	English-Spanish, 4th edition, 1981	
和 西 対 照 仏 教 聖 典	第 4 版	Spanish-Japanese, 4th edition, 1981	
和英西対照仏教聖典	第 4 版	English-Spanish-Japanese, 4th edition, 1981	

和英対照仏教聖典

昭和57年10月1日　第257版発行

発行所　財団法人　仏教伝道協会
東京都港区芝 4 丁目 3 番14号
電話 03（455）5851
郵便番号108　振替東京 6 −19249
印刷・製本　廣済堂印刷

ISBN4-89237-251-X